*The Many Lives of
Elton John*

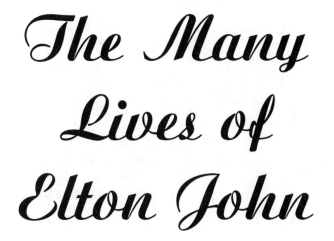

The Many Lives of Elton John

by Susan Crimp
and Patricia Burstein

A BIRCH LANE PRESS BOOK
Published by Carol Publishing Group

A Birch Lane Press Book
Published by Carol Publishing Group
Birch Lane Press is a registered trademark of Carol Communications, Inc.
Editorial Offices: 600 Madison Avenue, New York, N.Y. 10022
Sales & Distribution Offices: 120 Enterprise Avenue, Secaucus, N.J. 07094
In Canada: Canadian Manda Group, P.O. Box 920, Station U, Toronto, Ontario M82 5P9.

Queries regarding rights and permission should be addressed to Carol Publishing Group, 600 Madison Avenue, New York, N.Y. 10022

Carol Publishing Group books are available at special discounts for bulk purchases, for sales promotions, fund raising, or educational purposes. Special editions can be created to specificatons. For details, contact: Special Sales Department, Carol Publishing Group, 120 Enterprise Avenue, Secaucus, N.J. 07094
Manufactured in the United States of America
10 9 8 7 6 5 4 3 2 1

Library of Congress Cataloging-in-Publication Data

Crimp, Susan.
    The many lives of Elton John / Susan Crimp and Patricia Burstein.
        p. cm.
    "A Birch Lane Press book."
    Includes bibliographical references.
    ISBN 1–55972–111–1
    1. John, Elton.   2. Rock musicians—England—Biography.
I. Burstein, Patricia.   II. Title.
ML410.J64C7   1992
782.42166'092—dc20
    [B]   91-46624
                                                                    CIP
                                                                    MN

To Nanna, whom I love and miss, and Igloo.
—Susan Crimp

For my twin sister, Ellen, who inspired me to
reach the finish line.
—Patricia Burstein

Contents

Authors' Note

The object in writing this book was to piece together the many lives of Elton John. We had hoped to interview Elton, but his manager, John Reid, denied us access to him. However, through extensive reporting and research, we believe that we have paid tribute to Elton's prolific talent while telling how his life has informed his work. We thank the many people who have helped in this endeavor. They include Michael Alcock, Long John Baldry, Margaret Baldry, Jack Barrie, Eric Beaumont, Jr., Joanne Blackwell, John Blakely, Paul Buckmaster, Melanie Busch, Ed Caraeff, Bill Carnie, Winnie Cluer, Lionel Conway, Roger Cook, John Craig, Steve Crighton, Wayne Darwen, Elton Dean, Elayne DeLaurian, Lesley Duncan, Roy Dwight, Guy Farrow, Doc Field, Ken Filar, Paul Francis, Steven Gaines, Steve Geller, Bill Graham, Roger Greenaway, Stuart Hardman, Belinda Harvey, Richie Havens, Dave Herman, Robert Hilburn, Andrew Hill, George and Anne Hill, A. F. Hitchens, Nan and Bill Howe, Jimmy Horowitz, Stephen James, Ronald Johnson, Hilary Kay, Patti LaBelle, Brad Letsinger, Joan Lewis, Tony and Ellen Lyons, Mike McGrath, Scott Muni, Dee Murray, Karen Newman, Tommy Nutter, Nigel Olsson, Helen Piena, Audrey Purcell, Caleb Quaye, Phil Ramone, Mick Randall, Heather Redwood, Tim Rice, Tom Robinson, John Rockwell, Jonathan Ruffle, Elena Salvoni, Ethel Seaford, Neil Sedaka, Emily Smith, R. W. Thomson, Steve Todoroff,

Larry Uttal, Molly Weir, Doug Weston, Ray Williams, Norman Winter, Ron Wong, Steve Wright and Richard Young.

We also want to thank our editor, Hillel Black, president of Birch Lane Press, for his patience and endurance; his assistants, Susan Hayes and Denise O'Sullivan, for their courtesies; and our publisher, Steve Schragis, for his rapid-fire decision to go ahead with this book.

Prologue

New York City, August 1976

> "The gentleman you've all been waiting for. . . .The biggest, most colossal, gigantic, fantastic ELTON JOHN!"

Dressed like the Statue of Liberty, Elton John croons, belts and roars his way through twenty-four songs at New York's Madison Square Garden. The stage set is a mock-up of an old Wurlitzer juke-box and its centerpiece is a saucer-shaped, silver-painted fiberglass piano that changes colors to fit the mood of each tune. Using his emotive baritone while pounding the keys of his piano, he fills the huge arena with rock 'n' roll, alternating between ballads, tender and mawkish, and buoyantly melodic pop-gospel tunes. Hit follows hit, ranging over the maudlin "Funeral for a Friend," the melancholic "Don't Let the Sun Go Down on Me," the winsome "Your Song" and one of the most evocative ballads of the decade, "Goodbye Yellow Brick Road."

During the course of this three-hour, nonstop performance, Elton, known for his plumage as much as his pipes, dons an oversized gold lamé banana, a velvet carrot and a sequined strawberry. For encores, he returns as Uncle Sam, complete with a red, white and blue top hat.

The self-styled incarnations of Elton John are matched only by his strangely diverse audience, in a way typified by the eight-year-old

1

girl in the front row and the middle-aged couple beside her. Among the crowd on this summer night are the usual legion of teenagers and college students, and the more unlikely blue-rinsed ladies who have dragged their muttering husbands to witness what they believe to be the Second Coming of Liberace.

Elton John's arrival at center stage, here or elsewhere, is a miracle in itself. The unlikeliest of pop heroes—bisexual, bald, lumpy and frequently overweight—he is the antithesis of the sexy rock star.

Over the next six evenings he will break the record for consecutive sellouts at Madison Square Garden. The tour is appropriately titled Elton John: Louder Than Concorde, but Not Quite as Pretty, borrowed in part from still another fan, Britain's Princess Margaret, who described to Elton the decibel level of his own music.

Yet offstage, when this chameleon-like superstar sheds his "Captain Fantastic" or his "Rocket Man" persona, he is more like a "Candle in the Wind," another of his songs, about the loneliness of fame. As he sings this ballad, a Milky Way of lights punctuates the darkened arena, from candles held aloft by fans creating a shrine to the superstar.

Indeed, Elton John has battled many demons—alcoholism, obesity, homosexuality and a desperately unhappy childhood never fully resolved—throughout his life. How this pudgy pianist, born Reginald Kenneth Dwight forty-five years ago in the London suburb of Pinner, made it to the top of popular music is a story as bizarre and magical as any of Elton's performances.

Growing Pains

1

His Mother's Son

"He's got to get all this pop nonsense out of his head," Stanley Dwight cabled his wife Sheila from an overseas post. "Otherwise he is going to turn into a wild boy. He should get a sensible job with British European Airways or Barclays Bank." As with every command he gave his son, directly or indirectly, Stanley expected total obedience.

But this was one order that sixteen-year-old Reg, whose childhood had been burdened by his father's belittling judgments, would never accept. Reg had always dreamed of a career in pop music, and whether his Royal Air Force squadron leader father liked it or not, he was determined to have one.

The relationship between father and son had always been awkward and humiliating for the boy, leaving him with feelings of worthlessness and abandonment. "It was pure hatred on his part," Elton says. "Maybe I was a mistake." The music was a way for Reg to believe in himself as much as hide from a father who tried to rule his life.

Even to this day the two cannot agree on whether Stanley was present at Reg's birth. "There were long spells when my father was posted overseas to Aden and Australia," Elton recalls. "And he didn't see me for the first two years of my life." Stanley meanwhile claims, "It's quite ridiculous for him to say this, because I didn't go into the air force until he was eighteen months old."

Whichever version of Reg's earliest days is true, it is a fact that, owing to Stanley's frequent overseas assignments, the boy lived during his first five years with his mother, Sheila, at her family home at 55 Pinner Hill Road in Pinner, a suburb twelve miles northwest of London. When twenty-two-year-old Sheila gave birth to her first child on March 25, 1947, it was her own family, the Harrises, who helped her through what had been a difficult pregnancy. As Sheila's younger sister, Winnie, remembers, "His birth was traumatic. She was three days in having him." A midwife assisted in the delivery of the five-and-three-quarter-pound baby, with hazel eyes and beautiful eyelashes, in Winnie's bedroom.

Twenty-two-year-old Stanley, meanwhile, unaware of his wife's ordeal, apparently remained in Persia, where he was stationed at the time. Yet baby Reg did not lack for affection. Sheila and her family doted on him. Though their two-story semi-detached gray mortar house, a government-subsidized dwelling called in England a "council house," looked cheerless, it was the opposite inside.

It was a happy and affectionate atmosphere in which Reg spent his early years. There was Grandfather Fred, a groundskeeper at the local tennis club; Grandmother Ivy, an indomitable woman; Aunt Winnie, the youngest of the Harris children; and Sheila, all living under the same roof. Reg was the center of their lives. By then Sheila's older brother had already moved out of the house, but she named her only son, Reginald Kenneth, after him.

Elton remembers those years with affection. "The radio was always on," he says. "My mother collected records and I grew up really with a background of Nat King Cole, Dean Martin, Guy Mitchell, Rosemary Clooney, all those sort of people. It was really a good environment."

But the world outside was less secure and comforting. Britain was trying to repair the damage inflicted by the German bombs during World War II. Over 41,000 civilians had lost their lives and another 137,000 were injured. Homes and offices throughout England, especially in the London area, had to be rebuilt. The war had been costly, and the nation was heavily in debt. The British, trying to rebuild their lives, had to watch every shilling.

The Harris family was no exception. With little money to spare, they amused themselves at home around the upright piano on which Winnie had taken lessons. Before long, Reg joined in the fun, playing his first notes by the age of three. "We used to put him on the piano stool to keep him quiet," Winnie recalls, "and he started picking out chords, and that was it. He took off where I left off." Reg's mother, quick to spot her son's natural ability at the age of four, encouraged him to bang away at the ivory keys until he could pick up melodies. One day, while vacuuming, she heard him play "The Skater's Waltz" and declared, "I'll bet a million pounds you're going to be famous." At six, Reg started private piano lessons with a teacher in Pinner.

From that moment on, Sheila became a caretaker of her son's talent, believing in him at times when even Reg seemed to lose faith. "She was always protective of me," says Elton. "When my parents rowed, she would stick up for me. Usually the rows were about me, so I always felt allied to my mother more than my father." By the time Reg reached the age of eleven, a deep and enduring bond between mother and son had formed. In later years it would be Sheila to whom Elton confided about his first homosexual experience. "She was the first person I phoned and told," Elton says. "She was understanding and still is." But when discipline was needed, according to her sister Winnie, "Sheila was quite strict with Reg and didn't put up with his tantrums."

Early on, Reg also found a consoling companion in the piano. The instrument helped stave off the isolation he felt as an only child who longed desperately for a brother or a sister. Reg was not entirely friendless, however. By the time he was four, he had already found a girlfriend, Carol Fish, a neighbor who was the same age. She remembers him with fondness. "We played mothers and fathers and went to Saturday morning cinema together," she says. "And he played the piano so that I could sing 'On Mother Kelly's Doorstep.' "

Even at her young age Carol sensed that Reg was different from other kids. "I used to feel sorry for him," she says, "because the other boys teased him and took his cap." At home the situation was just as hurtful. There were problems in his parents' marriage, and his father took his unhappiness out on Reg by constantly criticizing him.

Right from the start, it seemed, the Dwights were doomed as a couple, and managed to avoid facing their incompatibility only by virtue of Stanley's frequent absences. They had polar personalities:

Sheila's ebullient nature clashed with Stanley's arch manner. As a result, Reg, embarrassed by his parents' battles, rarely invited anyone home after school.

Sadly, when Stanley returned permanently from his overseas post and moved his wife and son into a house in nearby Northwood Hills, Reg longed for his father's earlier absences. "I was suppressed and petrified by my father," Elton says. "I was always being told not to do things. My father wasn't the slightest bit interested in me, and he was such a snob. I dreaded it when he came home."

Yet despite Reg's grievances, Stanley at least provided his son with a first-class education, enrolling him, at five, in Reddiford, a private school. "Stan was always a good provider," his sister-in-law Winnie says. "And as Reg was particularly bright, he wanted him to have the best possible education." It's not hard to understand why Stanley wanted so much for his only child, and why he was so strict with him in many ways. Stanley had dropped out of school at fifteen and worked as a milkman to help support his family.

Poverty had ruled Stanley's early life as the youngest of five children growing up as Hitler was advancing across Europe. The son of a factory worker and housewife, he lived in Erith, about twelve miles south of London, in the direct line of Nazi bombers. Every other house in the area was destroyed by German air attacks. Home for Stanley was a two-room cottage with no indoor plumbing, and what little the family managed to put on the table was bought with government food stamps.

Music, the sole diversion from their hard life, was apparently in the Dwight genes. Stanley learned the trumpet from his father, Edwin. But any dreams of pursuing a music career were snuffed out by economic necessity. A desire for security prompted Stanley to enlist in the Royal Air Force and relegate his trumpet playing to a hobby. He rose to be a flight lieutenant in the class-ridden British armed forces, a rank that surpassed his and Sheila's backgrounds.

It was music, too, that had brought Sheila and Stanley together. In late 1943 they met at the now-defunct Headstone Hotel in North Harrow, where Stanley was playing trumpet in the Eric Beaumont Band, a local amateur group. The short, stocky, round-faced trumpet player glimpsed the trim, lively brunette with an obvious flair for dancing, and he insisted she go out with him. Soon they were courting, and a year and a half later, early in the winter of 1945, on a day thick with snow, Sheila Harris became Mrs. Stanley Dwight at the Pinner Parish Church. Two years later the couple had their first and only child together, and they were determined to give him every possible opportunity.

Reddiford, with its emphasis on individuality and the arts, proved the ideal place for a boy like Reg. Teachers there tried to instill a love of reading in their pupils. Reg particularly liked adventure stories. Latin was also a requirement for pupils, beginning at the age of nine. Most important for a boy who had already begun a love affair with the piano, daily lessons were available at the school.

"I must have got my musical ability from my father," Elton admits. "And when I was seven my dad gave me a copy of Frank Sinatra's album *Songs for Swinging Lovers*, which really wasn't the ideal present for a seven-year-old. I really wanted a bicycle. He also bought me a record of the Nat King Cole Trio (with King Cole playing the piano, not singing), and George Shearing. So I grew up with a wide selection of the music of the time."

Before long Reg was making his mark at Reddiford as the school pianist, and one year he was selected to play on Speech Day, the prize-giving ceremony at the end of the summer term. By the age of ten he was performing popular tunes like "English Country Gardens" for his classmates during school assembly. Sheila, proud of her son's progress, did everything possible to motivate him in his music. "He was forced to play classics when he wanted to play popular tunes," she remembers. "It wasn't until he was eleven or twelve that I found him a teacher who let him play pop, and from that time on this was all he was interested in."

She also bought Reg his first rock-'n'-roll records, Bill Haley's "A.B.C. Boogie" and Elvis Presley's "Heartbreak Hotel." A few days earlier, while getting his hair cut, he had picked up *Life* magazine and seen a picture of Elvis Presley in it. Reg believed this was a good omen. As he remembers, "I said, 'Oh, mum, I just saw the bloke [Elvis] in a magazine.' It was just weird how it happened the same week. It changed my life."

Indeed it did, and that moment was also the start of Elton's record collection, which today is one of the world's largest in private hands. Stanley Dwight, however, was not keen on his son's new passion for pop music. He demanded Reg stick with the classics. Though Sheila gave Reg more lattitude, even *she* drew the line at Little Richard. "I remember buying 'She's Got It' and 'The Girl Can't Help It' but my mother wouldn't let me play them," Elton says. "I was really annoyed because it was my favorite record. I was star-struck. Pop was my whole life."

Fortuitously, at Pinner County Grammar School, which Reg attended after Reddiford, music was also a valued part of the curriculum. The school housed a Steinway grand piano, and the teachers were particularly encouraging of musically gifted pupils. Both headmaster J. Westgate Smith, a pianist himself, and Reg's music teacher saw enormous promise in the boy and recommended him for a scholarship to the Royal Academy of Music's junior program.

Founded in 1822, the academy is Britain's senior conservatory and is one of the oldest institutions for advanced musical education in the world. The school has spawned thousands of classical musicians and, in more recent times, rock stars David Palmer of Jethro Tull and Annie Lennox of the Eurythmics.

Joining an elite group of one hundred musically gifted children in 1957 was a grueling experience for Reg. He had to endure a rigorous audition, at which he played Mozart sonatas and Chopin études in front of the admissions board. But the ten-year-old boy gave an impressive recital, and before long he was riding the "tube," as London's subway system is called, every Saturday for the twenty-minute trip from Pinner to central London for five hours of musical study. The curriculum included a forty-five-minute piano lesson, an "orals" class, in which he learned to take rhythm from dictation, and chorus rehearsal.

In Reg's day there were no popular music classes, so, grudgingly, he had to concentrate on Beethoven and Bach. From the beginning, his piano professor, Helen Piena, saw unusual talent in him. "When he came in here he could not read music," Piena recalls. "But he had a marvelous ear. I played him a Handel sonata four pages long. And he played it back to me like a gramophone. I had never had a pupil who could do that. He was a model student at that age."

Even squadron leader and amateur trumpeter Stanley Dwight conceded that his son had done very well indeed by winning a scholarship to one of the world's most prestigious musical training academies. "If Reg was going to play the piano," he instructed at the time, "he was going to learn how to do it properly."

But Stanley could not be placated for long. "Stan was a snob who only smiled when Elton played Chopin," Sheila says. "He wanted his son to be a concert pianist, but Elton wanted to play pop. To keep him attending the academy, I encouraged the pop music."

While both parents were constantly bickering over whether to allow their son to play pop music, they each, according to Elton's cousin, Roy Dwight, contributed to his future success. "Elton had two opposites in Stanley and Sheila," Roy explains. "He obviously got the talent from his father, who was a very good musician, and the will to do well from his mother, who was enthusiastic about everything she did. And I'm sure the enthusiasm rubbed off on him."

Whatever ambitions Stanley had for his son as a classical pianist, Reg fell short of achieving them. "He was above average," Piena says of her pupil. "I knew he had a lot of talent, but you have to be really brilliant to succeed as a concert pianist. Reg would not have made it." His orals professor, Elizabeth Cooper, who taught him rhythm, harmony, dictation and form, echoes her opinion: "He wasn't outstandingly good or bad."

While just average at the academy, back at Pinner Grammar School Reg's musical ability rescued him from obscurity and made him feel special. Former senior mistress Joan Lewis remembers, "Until you actually saw him sit down at the Steinway and play, he would have passed through here as ordinary." At twelve, he was an instant hit with his fellow pupils when he played Jerry Lee Lewis's "Great Balls of Fire" at the year-end concert.

Seated at the Steinway grand, Reg earned the admiration of his peers, yet in the playground he was a figure of ridicule. The pupils referred to him as a "tubby weed," and his walk was, according to one Pinner student, "halfway between a lope and a waddle." A pudgy boy whose clothes had to be specially ordered, he was forbidden by his father to wear the popular fashions, mohair sweaters and Hush Puppy shoes. Says former pupil Gay Search, today a journalist and teleplay writer, "My memory of him is in short trousers with his protruding little bottom and his blazer tightly buttoned over it."

It seemed that no matter how hard he tried, Reg just did not fit in. Ungainly and unathletic, he failed to qualify for any of the school sports teams. "All you needed to play for one of them was a pair of legs, really," Search says, "but I don't think Reg ever got the call."

This was a great disappointment for Reg. Second only to his music was his passion for soccer. "I was really quite large, and inside myself

I was very competitive," he explains. "I could never see the point in playing games for pleasure. I wanted to win, but I wasn't good enough. I had a huge inferiority complex."

So on weekends he resigned himself to a spectator role, attending local soccer games with his father. It was humiliating to Reg that it was his cousin who had won the admiration of his father for excelling at the game. Stanley's nephew, Roy Dwight, played professionally and earned something of a name for himself in Britain as the first player ever to break a leg while scoring a goal; this was in the 1959 Soccer Cup Final. Alone with his father in the car on the six-mile drive from home to the stadium, Reg felt uneasy. "It's a child's wish to have a relationship with his father," he says, "and I never really did. And he never had one with me."

By the time Reg reached his teens, his parents' marriage had seriously deteriorated, and all too often he became the target of his father's rage. "Once he even ordered me to leave the table," Elton recalls, "because he said I made too much noise eating celery." Eventually, after intermittent separations, his parents got divorced and his father moved out. The divorce caused fifteen-year-old Reg enormous pain, and like most children caught in the middle of a marital rift, he blamed himself at first. He hid his parents' separation by telling people that his father was away on air force business. Secretly, Elton admits, he was relieved that his father was gone. "I lived in fear of the fights," he says. "Finally we had peace at home."

"I was very bitter at the time because of the way my mom was treated," Elton says. "When they got divorced, she had to bear all the costs. She more or less gave up everything and had to admit adultery while he was doing the same thing behind her back and making her pay for it. He was such a sneak. Then he went away and five months later got married to this woman and had four kids in four years. My pride was really snipped 'cause he was supposed to hate kids."

Stanley Dwight disputes Elton's story. "I paid the divorce costs," he insists, "and I just don't understand why he is saying all these awful things. I love my son. I'm very proud of him. I can only think someone is putting all these ideas in his head. I didn't meet Edna [his current wife] until after the divorce."

Soon after the divorce, another man, Fred Farebrother, arrived in Reg's life. A handyman-decorator, Farebrother was named as a co-respondent in the divorce action Stanley brought against Sheila. He later became Reg's stepfather. "He helped us when we were faced with hard times," Elton recalls. "My mother had to work in a grocery shop to make ends meet and then take a clerical job at the Northwood Air Base."

The three of them moved into a small flat in Croxley Green, Hertfordshire, near London, and for the first time, Reg felt part of a family unit. Whereas Reg's father was a bookworm, his stepfather liked a beer and a chat at the pub. Easygoing and nonjudgmental, Fred did not hover about Reg's life and tell him what to do. At the same time he was always available when Reg needed him: "I'm very fond of my stepfather," Elton says. "He gave me more care and attention than my own father." Actually, Sheila and Fred did not marry for another decade, though she changed her name legally to Farebrother before then.

Still, it was difficult for Reg to accept his father's rejection. His academy piano professor remembers Reg's confusion and desire, at fifteen, to win his father's respect. "I spent the whole of one lesson trying to encourage him to continue with his studies and go on to university, but he only wanted to follow in his father's footsteps. He said his father was in the Royal Air Force and that was what he was going to do."

Professor Piena tried to get him back on track. "I gave him some Mozart sonatas to play, but musically he had begun to drift away. What I sensed was that there was so much in this boy, and I couldn't bring it out. There was a barrier. I suppose it was the wrong kind of music."

Only in the privacy of his bedroom, it seemed, could Reg find any escape from the suffocating values of middle-class respectability that Stanley had tried to hammer into him. There, surrounded by photographs of his favorite star, Dusty Springfield, fifteen-year-old Reg dreamed about becoming a superstar. It would be a way out of suburbia with its customary main street and repetition of brick timber-framed houses. These were referred to as the "late thirties Middlesex style," reflecting the suburban blandness of the area and the conservative cast of its residents.

Unknown to the academy, Reg had already formed his own band a year earlier with a guitar player named Stuart Brown, who was the boyfriend of a friend of Reg's cousin. They called themselves the

Corvettes after a popular shaving cream of the day. "I was fourteen when I met him," Elton recalls. "I was extremely fat at the time, and when I told him I could play piano, he just laughed. He was a very moody sort of fellow, so I showed him and went through my Jerry Lee Lewis bit. So we got this band together that played at Boy Scout gatherings, but we never had any amplifiers or anything, and it all faded away. It was just a pastime."

Inspired by the Beatles' "Love Me Do," Reg believed that pop music offered him an enormous future. But he was unable to convince everyone that rock 'n' roll was here to stay. Another Pinner student, Mike Noble, whom they tried to recruit as a drummer, rejected the offer. He told Reg, "Sorry, pop won't last." That may be one reason why the recalcitrant Noble ended up working for a carpet-cleaning firm while the enterprising Reg Dwight became international superstar Elton John.

By the age of sixteen Reg had got himself a regular gig as a pub pianist at the Northwood Hills Hotel, a mock-Tudor building about three times the size of a standard pub, with a circular driveway out front, a garden out back and guest rooms upstairs.

Inside, it was like any other British pub, with its stale air, wooden tables and chairs and its shaggy gold carpet. Proprietor George Hill remembers feeling uneasy about giving Reg his first break after the boy, accompanied by his new stepfather, turned up asking for work. At the time Hill was looking for a replacement for a brilliant albino pianist named Bob who could perform sing-along tunes from the latest chart hits on demand. Even to this day, Hill believes, "Bob is the one who should have become the star."

Initially, Hill's instinct about Reg proved correct. Fat Reg had now started wearing eyeglasses to emulate his hero Buddy Holly. "I only needed specs for reading," Elton admits, "but as a result of wearing them all the time to try to look like Buddy I became genuinely near-sighted." And in his gray trousers and ginger-colored Harris tweed jacket, he was something of a laughingstock with the rowdy patrons.

Says Hill, "People used to pull the leads out of Reg's microphone and put beer inside the piano to try to stop him." (That same piano is today inscribed: "This is to certify that this piano has played many a wrong note due to me," and signed *Elton John*.) Reg's only fans, it seemed, were his mother and stepfather, who came along for every performance and sat at the table next to the piano to bolster Reg's spirits.

Despite the boozy objections of Hill's patrons, an undaunted and determined Reg played on, soon winning over the crowd with a repertoire that included witty songs he made up about some of the regulars. One of the characters he parodied was a cockney, Toby Barry, who had an Irish tenor voice and a somewhat unrealistic belief in himself as a singer. Toby's job was to pass around the collection plate for tips, sometimes garnering as much as five pounds (then worth about fourteen dollars), to supplement Reg's nightly salary of one pound, five shillings (a little over four dollars) for over three hours' work.

Northwood Hills was the first place where Reg learned how to manipulate a crowd: When his favorite rock-'n'-roll tunes by Chuck Berry and Jerry Lee Lewis and soul music by Ray Charles were not going over well, he would pull out some old music-hall songs like "My Old Man Says Follow the Van" or standard saloon numbers like "When Irish Eyes Are Smiling."

Around this time, Reg ran into Stuart Brown again. "He suggested we put another band together," Elton recalls, "so we did. That was Bluesology." The band's name came from a Django Reinhardt record, and inspired by the Tamla/Motown and Stax sounds they concentrated on soul music. Together, Reg and Stuart, who played guitar and sang lead vocals, assembled a quartet of four musicians from the Pinner-North Harrow area. Brown, six feet tall and trim, with gypsy looks and shoulder-length black hair, was better suited than fat Reg to be the band's main attraction.

With the money Reg saved from the pub he managed to buy an electric organ keyboard. It was an exhausting existence. In addition to his pub job and his schoolwork, Reg practiced with the band every Sunday morning when the pub was shut. "We were ambitious and dedicated to the point of adding a trumpet and saxophone," Elton remembers. Bluesology, a cut above other groups, started to obtain bookings around the suburban areas of London.

Increasingly frustrated by Stuart Brown's refusal to relinquish the spotlight as the band's vocalist, and still convinced that he, Reg Dwight, had a big future as a solo artist, he started looking for other opportunities in the music business while continuing to play keyboard.

"When I was at school I knew what I wanted to do," Elton says. "I was academically bright, but I had to be involved in music."

Reg was not alone in keeping his eye on success. His soccer-playing cousin, Roy Dwight, also had faith in him. At six, Reg had served as a page at Roy's wedding, and while the two hundred guests waited for the hired band to arrive, Reg decided to entertain the crowd himself. Cousin Roy, remembering how the boy jumped on the piano stool and started banging out a few Winnie Atwell tunes, says, "From that moment on I knew he was a showman!"

All these years later Roy, still believing in him, wanted to help. He arranged a full-time job for him with a music publishing firm, Mills Music. Though the position of office boy at a weekly salary of four pounds (eleven dollars) was not in itself inspiring, at least it placed Reg in Denmark Street, Britain's Tin Pan Alley, the heart of the music industry.

The down side was that Reg, a particularly bright student, would have to quit school at seventeen before taking his A levels, national qualifying examinations in Britain—a necessity for entering a university or obtaining a good white-collar job in later life. Reg's last date of school attendance was March 5, 1965. His Pinner music teacher, for one, failed to understand why a boy with so much promise would throw it all away. He warned, "You'll still be filing at thirty."

Whatever the risk, at least it was the professional foothold Reg had been seeking in the music industry. Reg had made up his mind and with the full backing of his mother accepted the job at Mills. Because he was underage, being a few weeks shy of his eighteenth birthday, Sheila had to cosign his job contract.

But Reg knew from this moment on that it was all up to him. And so, equipped with his Buddy Holly glasses, the former class nerd with an abundance of talent was about to leave Reg Dwight behind in the small suburb of Pinner once and for all.

2

Breaking Out

In the mid-sixties the British were changing the face of rock 'n' roll. The Beatles and the Rolling Stones were conquering America and defining the twin poles of the British invasion: sweet and light versus dark and nasty. In the middle came groups of all descriptions, from the silly Herman's Hermits with their "I'm Into Something Good" to the bluesy, hard-bitten Animals and their version of "House of the Rising Sun." One by one they swarmed up the charts in America where Simon & Garfunkel, Bob Dylan and the Mamas and the Papas had already taken the nation by storm.

Fat, bespectacled Reg was inspired by this music explosion. He wanted to be involved in the recording industry on any level. Even if it meant serving tea and packing sheet music, it was at least a foot in the door. On the first day of his job at Mills Music, as he walked down Denmark Street Reg had high hopes. Determined to stretch his talents, he juggled his day job with piano playing on weekends in a pub, while appearing at night with Bluesology, which had by this time turned professional.

Reg knew, contrary to his music teacher's prediction, that he would not end up as a file clerk. Even at his low-level office-boy job, the enterprising eighteen-year-old began seizing every opportunity to get ahead. He cleverly managed to ingratiate himself around the office: On one hand he was a dutiful office boy making the mail rounds with quiet efficiency; on the other he was a renegade tacking outrageous tabloid headlines to the bulletin board or playing rowdy pub piano at company parties. Because of his shy manner and girth—the latter earning him the nickname Fat Reg—his fierce ambition had to masquerade as a cross between naïveté and desperation.

But Mills managing director Cyril Gee knew what Reg wanted and sized him up immediately. "This was not an innocent little lad," Gee remembers, "but a very determined boy." Within weeks of starting his job, Reg demonstrated that he was certainly no ordinary office boy, but a young man with a mission: "Suddenly I found I was employing this teaboy by the name of Reg Dwight who came to see me for permission to use one of the pianos during the lunch hour when everyone was out," Gee recalls. "And I told him, 'Yes, that is permissible, provided that it does not interfere with the work you were hired to do.' And he said, 'Yes, sir, I promise it won't.' "

Within a few months Reg approached Gee again for another favor. "Next thing I knew," Gee relates, "I came home one evening and said to my wife, 'Even little office boys are writing songs these days. Little Reg Dwight has come up with a song called 'Come Back Baby' and he wants to know will I publish it.' "

"Come Back Baby," an unsophisticated, amateurishly produced, sugary up-tempo teen ballad about getting your girl back, was the first of a trio of singles recorded by Bluesology. In July of 1965 it was released on the Fontana label. Because the vocals were beyond the range of lead singer Stuart Brown, Reg, usually relegated to playing keyboard, was allowed to stand in for him. However, it was never incorporated into the band's live stage act.

Even to this day, Gee is mystified why he published this commercial dud as sheet music—but at least he had spotted Reg's potential. "I suppose I did it out of kindness," he says, adding, "In my opinion Reg Dwight had created a sound before its time. And there was obviously this tremendous talent that had to come out."

Though his publishing debut earned Reg exactly one shilling (fourteen cents), it did mean that he was at least beginning to be taken seriously. Although "Come Back Baby" never got airplay, during

Reg's final days as a pub pianist he included the song in his act and proudly announced that he had written it.

In addition to his new publishing career, Reg was busy with his band. Unfortunately, from time to time, when a gig ran late into the night, he found himself skipping work the next day. His truancies caused a conflict of interest, and his immediate supervisor would ask if Reg wanted to remain at his job. Reg would apologize profusely and promise to show up.

Still, Reg was clever enough to realize the value of an association with Mills. The London office of the music publisher, a subsidiary of a prestigious and gentlemanly American firm, was a virtual hit factory. Situated in the heart of Tin Pan Alley, the cozy two-story offices of Mills buzzed with excitement and, from Reg's point of view, opportunity.

While there he made some useful contacts. Among them were hot young songwriters Roger Cook and Roger Greenaway. In the near future they would create some important sixties hits, among them "I'd Like to Teach the World to Sing in Perfect Harmony" and "Here Comes That Rainy Day Feeling." Both would later figure in Reg's career.

Back then Cook and Greenaway were just two men Reg believed it was good to know, and on his daily mail rounds the office boy made it known to both of them that he loved playing music and was working up some ideas of his own. Strangely, neither was aware of Reg's Royal Academy music training. "In those days, Reg, like many people in pop music, was almost ashamed of his classical background," Greenaway explains. "I only found out about it years later when my daughter started studying the piano and he gave her some sheet music from his Royal Academy days."

Although Mills had provided a good foot in the door of the music business, it did not take long for Reg to tire of his job. Convinced that he belonged behind a piano instead of a filing cabinet, he was unwilling to postpone his ambitions any longer. He quit Mills after eighteen months on the job. As he later admitted, "I never started out wanting to be a songwriter—only an artist."

While the British were climbing the charts in the United States, American artists were also arriving on the British scene. Reg's band, Bluesology, became a beneficiary of this migration. At an audition in the North Kilburn section of London, the band attracted the attention of Roy Tempest, an agent who brought American stars to tour the United Kingdom. To Reg's thinking, the timing could not have been better: British artists were just becoming hooked on the type of black rhythm and blues and soul that were his band's hallmarks.

Naturally, Reg was ecstatic when, in March of 1966, Bluesology was hired to back Wilson Pickett. A fiery American black performer whose song "In the Midnight Hour" became a soul classic, Pickett, in Reg's bespectacled eyes, was a hero of the highest order. "You can imagine how we felt," Elton explains. "He was such an important figure in the music we were playing—and here we were about to tour as his band." Pickett, riding high with his first Number One R&B hit, "634–5789," had started out singing in gospel groups, and this black American church music would inflect many of Reg's melodies throughout his career.

His elation about the Pickett tour was short-lived, however. Bluesology was fired before the start of the tour. As Reg recalls, "We went to rehearse with his guitarist, but he didn't like our drummer, and he didn't particularly like the rest of us either. So that tour was blown out and we were brought down." But it provided an invaluable lesson: not to rely on enthusiasm alone to get by. And the next time a similar opportunity presented itself, they were fully prepared.

It came a few weeks later when they were hired to back another American soul star, Major Lance, whose song "The Monkey Time" was a hit on both sides of the Atlantic, and who had started a dance craze with another tune, "The Bird." "We learnt every song he'd ever made," Elton recalls, "to the point where he didn't even feel the need to go through the songs more than one time."

Soon, with their more meticulous approach, Bluesology was backing countless American stars, including Billy Stewart, the Ink Spots, Doris Troy and Patti LaBelle and the Blue Belles. Patti was eighteen years old and Reg's favorite performer. After the performance with LaBelle, Reg and the band would meet up in her dressing room to play tunk, a card game. She remembers, "I wore Reg and his little band members out and took all their pounds. Afterward I felt really awful and took them all back to my flat and cooked for them because they had no money to eat." At the time Reg earned only thirty dollars a week, and he believed he was unfairly compensated for the work.

Even more annoying to Reg was the way the band's agent, Roy Tempest, embellished descriptions of their gigs. On one occasion,

Reg remembers, the band was hired to tour with a group Tempest billed as "the fabulous Temptations." He believed the agent meant the Temptations, Motown's first male group to have a Number One hit, "My Girl," in 1965. "When I'd ask Tempest what was going on," Reg remembers, "he'd say things like 'Oh, I meant, the *Fabulous* Temptations, not *the* Temptations.'"

Fed up with these exaggerations and excuses, Reg and his band left Tempest after a year to sign with Marquee Artists, a top agency already familiar with their performances and the operator of the popular Marquee Club in London's Soho. They were booked into the Top Ten Club in Hamburg as well, and a club in St. Tropez for a month-long gig. "The money was good," Elton says, "and I was growing up and finding out what life was about."

Back in the London area they played trendy rhythm-and-blues clubs with catchy and eccentric names like the Bag O' Nails and the Cromwellian. But it was still tedious to Reg, who felt stuck in the same old groove behind a Continental Vox Box, a plastic keyboard finished in orange glitter with tapered legs. Instead of the customary eighty-eight keys, it only had fourty-four. The Vox Box was dwarfed by the five-foot-six Reg, who had ballooned to over two hundred pounds. "I was really fat," he says. "All I wanted to do was sing, but that was not possible."

The band's repertoire was beginning to bore him silly too. "We'd got into the rut of playing 'Knock on Wood' and 'Shake,'" Elton recalls, "every night for about four years." Archetypal sixties soul, both songs were hits recorded by artists like Otis Redding and Eddie Floyd on the Stax label.

Unfortunately, Reg had nowhere else to go, for this was hardly a propitious time for him to try to launch a solo career. Nor did he have the experience for it.

In the mid-sixties, bands—and not teen idols like Elvis—were in the forefront of British rock 'n' roll. Though fans might have had a favorite Beatle or Rolling Stone, the group was always a larger presence. Bluesology, really a semiprofessional band, was not in the same league and had yet to emerge as an important fixture on the music scene. Today the group is barely a footnote in the annals of British music. Its only claim to fame, in fact, is the Elton John connection.

In November 1966, British blues singer Long John Baldry, a charismatic six-foot-seven-inch entertainer, was at least able to offer a solution to Reg. Baldry's group, Steampacket, in which he had shared vocals with Rod Stewart, had recently broken up, and he was looking for a backup band. After hearing Bluesology at the Cromwellian, a three-story Victorian building with a gambling parlor and dance club which often featured live bands, Baldry was so impressed that he hired them as a backing band on the spot.

This pleased Reg. With Baldry headlining the band, he figured, Bluesology would attract more attention. But most important, as Long John planned to expand the group, there might be a spot for Reg as a singer. However, as with his other attempts at moving over to vocals, this plan did not work out. An understandably deflated Reg was horribly disappointed when Baldry instead asked Stuart Brown to give up guitar to sing full time. Adding an additional humiliating insult, Baldry hired a third singer, Alan Walker, five feet eleven inches tall, stocky and blond. While Long John recognized Reg as "an extremely accomplished musician who brought a symphonic flourish to his piano playing," he rejected him outright as a singer— frontline or backup. Thick-waisted Reg, with his short hair and little round spectacles, just did not project the image of a rock-'n'-roll singer.

Reg, meanwhile, relegated to the keyboards, was the victim of a further embarrassment with the assignment of a new nickname, Little Bunter, after a fat, clownish comic strip character named Billy Bunter. Bluesology's saxophone player Elton Dean remembers, "The singers were all good-lookers and snappy dressers, with Little Bunter in his blazer sulking in the background because Baldry wouldn't let him sing." Worse still, Long John even turned Reg's mike off during sound checks. Baldry's sister Margaret recalls, "We'd all fall about laughing when Reg sang, because he had a dreadful voice."

Reg's weight, still over two hundred pounds, caused him a lot of pain. It bothered him that female fans doted on other band members and completely ignored him. But his annoyance at this circumstance had more to do with his vanity and image as a musician than any particular longing for women. Even at twenty, Reg's attraction for the same sex manifested itself in the way he was in awe of the twenty-six-year-old Baldry, who was at that time appearing on practically every television music special.

The attention Reg lavished on the lead singer verged on a crush. Saxophone player Elton Dean says, "Reg just liked the way he acted, and he started acting that way too. If they'd see a bunch of Boy Scouts, Baldry would say, 'Look at that trade,' and Reg would mimic him." Jimmy Horowitz, who later replaced Elton as Bluesology's keyboardist, disputes this description of both Baldry and Reg. "I never found Baldry campy," he says. "And he is terribly straight acting. Reg was unbelievably straight—he didn't even look like a *musician!*"

Whether or not he camped it up with the boys in the band, during solitary moments Reg was miserable. Convinced that his weight was all that stood in the way of a singing career, Reg consulted a doctor who prescribed Predalin, an amphetamine. Aimed at curtailing his appetite, it also produced sharp mood swings. Margaret Baldry remembers her first encounter with Reg at a West End club. "He was having a comedown from the pills," she says. "He was always going on strange diets like a half cup of yogurt. It was the in thing to be thin as a stick, and it was a quite an obsession with Reg."

On other occasions, as a result of the medication, Reg became verbally abusive, screaming and shrieking at band members, except for Baldry, who was never a target of these outbursts. At other times Reg went back to his shy, introverted self, often going a whole day in the musicians' van without uttering a word. "Reg was always a watcher, a listener, an observer," Baldry says. "He would absorb everything happening around him and then make a particularly accurate comment that summed up everything."

The one constant in Reg's life on the road, it seemed, was a desire to make perfect music. He was unwavering in his expectations of himself and his fellow band members. "A great show would make him joyous," Baldry explains, "but if anyone flubbed up or played out of tune, he would blow up. Music was the most precious thing to him."

Indeed, from Reg's point of view, the relationship between the singer and Bluesology's keyboardist was as much a shared labor of love as a romantic stirring, albeit unrequited. Baldry, a great blues shouter, introduced Reg to the gospel playing of Mildred Falls, the pianist for Mahalia Jackson. Both men also enjoyed listening to jazz greats like Bill Evans and Billy "Fat Boy" Stuart. (The latter became so big that his heart eventually gave out, killing him.)

Reg, of course, empathized with Stuart's obesity problem. His own excess weight affected not only his personality, but also the look of the group. Reg was mortified at his first MIDEM* Festival in the south of France, where Baldry took him as both keyboardist and musical director. "I dressed the band in German suits that were quite elegant," Baldry relates. "When Reg sat down on the piano stool the back seat of his pants split—so that rather threw him for the rest of the festival."

Often Reg and Long John Baldry met at the latter's house in North London to wait for the van to pick them up for an engagement. Reg would drive over in his second-hand Hillman IMP, bought with a twenty-five-pound (seventy-dollar) loan from his mother, and park it outside until they returned from winding down at a club after a late gig. Wherever Long John turned up, Reg followed close behind. "It was really a matter of 'monkey see, monkey do,'" Baldry recalls of his protégé. "It was actually quite flattering."

Though yet to come to terms with his own sexuality, Reg, in the company of Baldry, began to mingle in quasi-homosexual circles. The setting was the apartment of Mike McGrath, then a reporter-photographer for the now-defunct entertainment magazine *Rave*, and today publisher and editor of a male pornographic publication, *Mike Arlen's Guys*, in Earls Court, an area of London with a large homosexual community.

During the course of any week, music industry people, including Baldry, the future Elton John and his manager-to-be John Reid might turn up at McGrath's place. Back in the sixties, McGrath, a bearded man with a lifestyle that belied his monkish robes, ran a kind of after-hours music salon of sorts in his apartment, which was dark and resembled a cross between an Arab bazaar and a brothel. McGrath's overtly homosexual personality seemed to set the tenor of these gatherings.

A flamboyant, campy McGrath recalls, "Reg had this enormous inferiority complex and he weighed two stones [twenty-eight pounds] heavier than he was when he came to fame. He just sat there around Baldry with his horn-rimmed glasses and a duffel coat, and said nothing. The room would be scattered with eight to ten people. Reg looked at the floor. I would try to talk generally instead of at anyone in particular, and just let him sit there, once I sensed he was self-

*Marché Internationale du Disques et de l'Edition Musicale.

conscious. I can't honestly remember one line that Elton ever came up with in this room because he was just so inhibited."

Bluesology's pianist was, in fact, so nondescript that when, four years later, Elton released "Your Song" and Baldry commented to McGrath, "Isn't it wonderful that Reg Dwight has a hit record!" a bewildered McGrath replied, "Who is Reg Dwight?" Baldry reminded him: "Oh, that chubby little pianist of mine—he's been to your place dozens and dozens of times."

Apparently, however, these gatherings made a far greater impression on Reg than on the host. "When I went with Baldry to the record reception," McGrath recalls, "Elton came up and put his arms around me and said, 'I'll never forget those nights,' and Baldry told me how Elton would ask him every week, 'When are we going up to see Mike in Earls Court?' "

Quite possibly, McGrath's apartment offered Reg the homosexual sanctuary he so desperately longed for. It was not difficult to understand why young Reg was so loath to "come out" in the Britain of the 1960s, a country that had often been so cruel to homosexuals. And so Reg was more inclined to struggle privately with his sexual identity. Any personal declarations or overt behavior in this area, he realized, could put his musical future in jeopardy in an industry where male and female roles were clearly defined.

Ironically, marriage and fatherhood were also off limits in those days: Heroes in the music business could only be popular if they were eligible. In 1963, for example, Beatles manager Brian Epstein, tortured by his own homosexuality, had tried to negate any evidence that Paul McCartney had a "steady" girlfriend. Iris Caldwell, for whom McCartney had written "Love Me Do," recalls, "I wasn't allowed to go anywhere with the group in case their fans saw me."

From Epstein's point of view, it was bad enough that John Lennon's first wife, Cynthia, was pregnant with their son, Julian, and he was determined to keep the other three band members eligible Beatle bachelors whom any of their fans could dream about marrying. Back then no one could have foreseen the acceptance of the fey trappings and bisexual intonations of the "glam rock" started by David Bowie at the beginning of the seventies and amplified by Elton John (billed initially as a post-Vietnam Liberace).

The sixties in Britain, albeit rebellious—but nonviolently so and without the bitterness that attended the Vietnam War in America—

was also a time of brightness and boundless possibility. This was deeply felt by Reg and his contemporaries. "It was a kind of Golden Age of Music," says Jimmy Horowitz, who later replaced Reg as Bluesology's keyboardist and whose first wife wrote "Love Song," which Elton recorded. "It was like a small village where everyone knew everyone, and we'd all kind of meet up."

A particularly important showcase for bands was the Marquee Club, located in Reg's day in Wardour Street in London's Soho. Agents and managers used the Marquee to promote their bands, and over the years both British and American groups played there, among them the Rolling Stones, Rod Stewart, Jethro Tull, Vanilla Fudge and Joe Cocker. The club, converted from a warehouse, attracted several hundred patrons nightly.

On Friday, April 21, 1967, the Marquee booked Long John Baldry with Bluesology and Alan Walker—the latter occupying the singing role that Reg so desperately wanted for himself. For their debut performance they split fifty percent of the club's gross receipts. Because no alcohol was allowed on the premises, Reg and the band frequently repaired to other clubs in the area after an appearance. Their first stop was usually La Chasse, which they called "the green room of the Marquee." Many a night they ended up drinking and gossiping until closing time at the Speakeasy, which resembled an American undertaker's parlor.

Reg started to feel more comfortable with himself, breaking out of the confines of his shyness. Traces of the outrageous began to appear in his manner of dress, presaging his flamboyance as Elton John. "Hanging out with me," Baldry explains, "Reg became more extroverted and a very amusing mimic. Had Elton not been a musician, he would have made a very good stand-up comic, like Tony Hancock or the actress Beryl Reed."

Margaret Baldry remembers, "Reg would always come up with the latest Carnaby Street fashions—he was the first person I knew to wear a caftan." And her brother adds, "Because Reg was quite porky he looked like a myopic nun in it." He was also sporting capes and hats. One nosy neighbor of the Baldrys', spying Reg getting into his car at three o'clock in the morning, mistook him for a London bobby.

Even Sheila was embarrassed to be seen with her son in the conservative suburb of Pinner: "I used to tell him to walk down the street on his own. I didn't want to be associated with him when he looked like that. I used to be a bit shocked by his clothes—his huge hairy fur coat, big wide-brimmed hat and the dark glasses."

Sheila, nevertheless, was always turning up at club dates Reg played in the London area to cheer him and the band on. She was also considered something of a showwoman herself: On one occasion she wore a miniskirt to a party given by Baldry's parents. "We were all amazed at what she was wearing," Margaret Baldry says. "It was quite surprising because Sheila was well into her forties then, and in those days the dividing line was more pronounced than now."

In contrast to his wardrobe, Reg's nascent recording career, however, was far less dramatic. In October of 1967, Bluesology released another single, "Since I Found You Baby" with "Just a Little Bit" on the B side, this time on the Polydor label. It had the same lack of commercial success as "Mr. Frantic," another Reg Dwight composition, and his first, "Come Back Baby," a year before.

The band members soon became disheartened. Singer Alan Walker quit, and he was replaced by Marsha Hunt, who Baldry believed would solve the problem. "A good-looking bird" was how Baldry described Hunt, a black American singer-actress with exotic features and an exquisite model's figure. She would later gain notoriety as the unwed mother of Mick Jagger's first child, Karis, and the star of *Hair*. Baldry believed that she would draw more attention to their act. But the tactic didn't work.

By November 1967, Reg had grown disenchanted with Baldry, and this disenchantment extended to a contempt for their now-stale act. Instead of trendy clubs, the group played the cabaret circuit. And while Baldry was in great demand by virtue of his one and only Number One hit on the British charts, "Let the Heartaches Begin" (a maudlin ballad he recorded independently of the band), still nobody paid any attention at all to Reg. "The high spot of our act," Elton remarks disdainfully, "was when Baldry used to sing his hit to a backing tape we had to mime to."

Ironically, Baldry, the man who had inspired Reg to be more adventurous, now catered to middle-aged, suburban audiences. In Reg's eyes, he was a fallen idol as a personal and professional mentor. And so for Reg—forever wedded and faithful to his own musical vision—it was time to move on.

He began to disengage from Long John the artist and also to shed any romantic aspirations in his direction, though the two men remained friends. With Baldry no longer the object of Reg's fascination, it was time to find someone else—not to guide him professionally, but to fill the void in his emotional life. During the Christmas season of 1967, he met Linda Woodrow at the Sheffield Cavendish Ballroom in Sheffield, two hundred miles north of London, where Reg was playing keyboard with Bluesology.

On a break between sets, Reg, standing at the bar, spotted Linda—ash blond and skinny, and, at five feet ten, four inches taller than Reg. He asked Baldry to introduce them. Minutes after their meeting a smitten Reg invited her out for the following evening after the band finished working. "It was the oddest thing," Baldry remembers, "because she was quite tall and was at the time the girlfriend of the dwarf disc jockey named the Mighty Atom. Over the week that we were up there, the relationship between her and Reg solidified, and all of a sudden the dwarf was out of the picture."

Linda's family owned Epicure, an old British pickles, preserves and canned foods manufacturer. She had been privately educated, and her vaguely arch manner made her appear sophisticated to Reg. And she, in turn, was quite taken with Reg. In fact, later, when she introduced him to her father, Al Woodrow, a sometime stand-up comic and amateur magician, she described Reg as a star in the making.

Not only did the twenty-four-year-old Linda instill confidence in fat, shy Reg, but she also enabled him to lose his virginity—a milestone in any young man's sexual career. Reg was by now twenty, and all along his reticence with women was attributed to shyness. In truth, he had already been struggling with his sexual identity, but hoped and believed that the right girl could resolve his confusion in this area.

Initially, though, Reg behaved like a gentleman, taking a separate room for Linda at the bed-and-breakfast hotel on the outskirts of Sheffield where he was staying with the band. They had their first tryst after Linda migrated, with her two small dogs, to London. This was within two months of their meeting. The setting was a Victorian-style hotel in the Bloomsbury quarter of the city. "When Reg finally rolled into bed," she says, "he was clumsy, and, frankly, he didn't have a clue."

Still, she was willing to put up with his naïveté and ineptitude because of his wonderful disposition. "Reg is a gentle person by nature and he was that way in bed," Linda explains. "I was so keen on him that I didn't mind the fact that he was a lousy lover. I realized that I would have to be patient with him."

She seemed the perfect woman for Reg, strong and dominant, like his mother. She soothed his feelings of homesickness when Reg was on the road. "He was a right mummy's boy," Linda says. "He was always ringing home. In many ways I mothered him the whole time." Sheila remembers his devotion to her as well. "He'd always ring home to say he'd arrived safely and when he was home he'd tiptoe into my room to say he was back and how it had all gone."

Reg was so taken initially with Linda that he even proposed marriage, albeit somewhat less than passionately. Ultimately, though, as saxophonist Elton Dean relates, "He got the horrors and did a runner. He was toying with homosexuality in those days even though he would say he was thinking of getting married to her."

As always, it seemed, his musical future was uppermost in Reg's mind. But his career at this stage was nearly in tatters. Singers Stuart Brown and Marsha Hunt, as fed up as Reg with the band's schmaltzy ballads, left the group. Reg knew that he could not hold out much longer.

Though yet to devise any particular strategy, Reg felt that if he did not get out quickly his whole future was in jeopardy. "Well, that was it," Elton remembers thinking. "I had to do something and I didn't want to join another band because, quite honestly, I wasn't that good an organist, and I didn't look that good either. Really, I wanted to be a singer—but who would consider employing me in that capacity?"

Based on his experience with Baldry, it seemed that Reg was the only one who believed he had a future as a vocalist. But always resourceful, he considered other options. "Although I didn't really want to write, I continued to toy with the idea because I thought that was the only way I'd get anywhere."

And so off went the future "Captain Fantastic" in search of greater horizons and his "brown dirt cowboy," namely, lyricist Bernie Taupin. Meanwhile, he would continue with Bluesology, a band he felt was going nowhere.

3

Two Heads Are Better Than One

While Reg was still traveling across Britain with Bluesology, he found a possible escape route—away from the band gigs he had now begun to loathe. As he thumbed through the June 17, 1967, issue of the *New Musical Express*, the bible of the British industry, an advertisement caught his attention. Two words in it, "Talent Wanted," were enough to lift his spirits. As he remembers, "I thought 'Hello—they've put an advert in and I shall answer it immediately!' And I answered it and someone telephoned me and said, 'Come in.'"

That someone was Ray Williams, a talent scout for the newly created Liberty Records, who had just launched a media blitz to attract young artists and songwriters. From Reg's point of view it was a wonderful outlet, since Liberty had just become a licensed label of EMI, then Britain's largest record distributor. But a few weeks later, when Reg walked into Liberty's offices on Albemarle Street in London's West End, the piano player from Pinner did not inspire Williams immediately.

Then aged twenty, Williams, trim and blond, looked more the part of a pop artist than Reg, whose image was the exact opposite of what Williams wanted for his new label. "This dumpy little figure came in and sat down and started to explain that his name was Reg Dwight, but he was thinking about changing it," Williams relates. "He also said he felt lost, and I felt sorry for him, because I was a kid, too. So I said, 'Well, play me some songs,' which he did on the upright piano."

Reg chose five Jim Reeves numbers from his days as a pub pianist at Northwood Hills, and then promptly despaired over his choice of material. "The audition was just dreadful," Elton recalls. " 'You must be joking,' they said, and I thought that my one golden chance of getting anywhere had gone down the drain."

But he was mistaken. One of the songs, "He'll Have to Go," sparked the talent scout's interest. "I loved something about his voice," Williams says, "and I asked him to make some demos." Williams suggested Regent Sound Studios, then a popular and inexpensive place for musicians to make tapes of their work. It was in Denmark Street, and when Reg approached the studio, he felt he was making some progress in his career. After all, only a short time earlier he had traveled that same street to make tea for the employees at Mills Music.

In the course of his conversation with the talent scout, Reg expounded on his misery, complaining about his job with Bluesology. "Reg said he was confused and frustrated and did not know what to do," Williams recalls. "He was very keen to be allowed to sing in his own right, and he also wanted to write, but needed help with the lyrics."

Meanwhile, a couple of hundred miles to the north, a farm boy from Lincolnshire had responded to the same advertisement. Elfin-like Bernie Taupin, seventeen, from Market Rasen, was a fanciful character, a poet and a dreamer, imagining himself as a hero from one of Jack Kerouac's novels. And much like the Beat author, Bernie was also something of an itinerant worker, scribbling verse as a kind of vocation. The son of a farmer who later became a Ministry of Agriculture meat inspector, Bernie had only recently been fired from a job chasing and crating chickens.

Though proud of his farming roots, Bernie was drawn to a life of poetry and music. He felt hemmed in by the flat brown land of Lincolnshire and desperately longed to stretch his boundaries. The radio had been his contact with the outside world, and his ambitions grew with his exposure to the music of the Beatles in Britain and Bob Dylan in America. Although he had never written a song before, he felt it was worth a try. "I was immediately interested—here was at least a chance, no matter how slight," Taupin recalls.

Bernie Taupin's childhood, in the north of England, was totally different from Reg's. While Reg had grown up in the suburbs of London, reared on music, Bernie was brought up on adventure stories. Bernie believed in literary heroes and secret places and was very much the product of a warm, compassionate family who introduced him to books at an early age.

A. A. Milne's *Winnie the Pooh* was the first literary character to enter Taupin's life, and Pooh Bear, along with his friends Piglet and Tigger, became a familiar friend to young Bernie. Within a short time the tales of C. S. Lewis also took Taupin's fancy. And daily his mind would travel to the riverbank world of Kenneth Grahame's *Wind in the Willows*.

Though Lincolnshire, with its cruel wind and black terrain, hardly evokes the grace and beauty of the English countryside, Bernie survived the physical hardships by living inside his imagination. The farmhouse in which Bernie spent his earliest years had no electricity, and the family had to rely on candles and kerosene for light and heat. The concentrated orange juice and powdered milk they kept in the kitchen were bought with ration coupons. Though World War II had ended, in the Taupin home the deprivations it had created were still obviously very much felt.

Like Reg, who lived at his grandparents' home for the first five years of his life, Bernie spent a great deal of time with *his* grandparents. His grandfather, Leonard Patchett Cott, affectionately known as Poppy, was a teacher of classics. Though he died when Bernie was only nine, he managed to instill in his grandson a passion for words and verse. "Wise, distinguished and kind" is how Bernie remembers him. And spending time in Poppy's study, with its mounted butterflies and moths hanging on the walls, was an adventure in itself for the young boy and would influence his poetry and lyrics in later years. Grandfather and grandson would also take long walks, hand in hand, in the countryside. During these strolls Bernie would be given Latin instruction. Whenever the pair found an insect, the grandfather would give him the Latin name for the creature, and the young boy would be expected to memorize it.

Poppy also regularly visited London, and on his return to Lincolnshire he would tell Bernie tales of the big city hundreds of miles away. While Bernie learned about the life of the mind from his grandfather, from his own father he learned the value of physical labor as he watched Taupin Senior farm the land.

Bernie, with a brother to keep him company, did not suffer the loneliness felt by Reg Dwight. Nor was there any marital tension in the Taupin home. On the rare occasions that his parents became annoyed with him, he got "the silent treatment," in contrast to the verbal abuse Reg suffered at his father's hands.

Bernie's first exposure to music came at seven, when he went to London to visit an uncle who had a record player. Apparently, the first time he heard the sound of a record player, Bernie was mesmerized. The song was Lonnie Donegan's *Rock Island Line*. Donegan used to cover Leadbelly and Woody Guthrie songs with strong narratives that later influenced Bernie's writing. Over the next few days Bernie sat glued to the machine.

Later, back in Lincolnshire, he awaited news of other musical releases of the day in the industry papers which he began reading with enthusiasm. By the age of fourteen Bernie was listening to bands like the Animals on the blue-colored radio he borrowed from his father. Bernie thought the band's "House of the Rising Sun" was the best thing he'd ever heard. Every night he would take his dad's radio to bed with him and tune in to Radio Luxembourg, which, despite poor reception, allowed him to find out what was happening on the music scene in America.

Bernie was inspired by the way the Beatles had captivated America and loved their music as well as the songs of Jerry and the Pacemakers and the Rolling Stones. One night, while listening to his transistor, Bernie heard a sound foreign to him, but which made him euphoric. The music belonged to Bob Dylan, and from that moment on, Bernie was an eager fan of the folksinger, saving his every shilling to purchase Dylan's records.

Within a few years, however, Taupin's early enthusiasm for living evaporated. At seventeen, he was unemployed. He believed his life was in ruins, and each day became a struggle as he walked the streets or sat at home sipping tea with his parents. Then, suddenly, hope appeared in the form of the Liberty Records advertisement in the *New Musical Express*. Once he had composed his letter, Bernie was again burdened by feelings of tremendous self-doubt.

But fortunately, like Sheila Dwight, Bernie's mother had also encouraged her son. When he got nervous about sending his letter to Ray Williams and hid it, thinking the exercise would lead to nothing more than a rejection letter, Mrs. Taupin decided to mail it herself. Even to this day, Taupin credits his mother with saving him from another short-lived menial job and with changing his life.

In the end, enthusiasm about a chance, however slight, to become part of the Liberty roster won the day. "Without melodic accompaniment," Taupin later mused in his 1988 autobiography, *A Cradle of Heroes: Sketches of a Childhood*, "how could I be classed as a songwriter? Still, it was worth a shot. . . . Somewhere there might be a melody missing words or some Tin Pan Alley tunesmith struggling for correct phrases to turn his tune to gold." His letter was accompanied by several sheets of abstract poetry that he had been writing all these years, including lyrics to "Velvet Fountain" and "Hymn on the Funeral of a Scarecrow."

When Ray Williams received Bernie's letter and lyrics, he liked what he read. "They appeared to have something different and be better than average," Ray recalls. He responded immediately, suggesting Bernie come in to Liberty Records on his next trip to London. Flattered that anyone might think that he could just "pop in to" the big city, Bernie made a special visit. His mother arranged for him to stay with an aunt in Putney, south of the River Thames, for a small weekly fee.

Reg, in the meantime, had already been given the lyrics Bernie had sent Williams. As Ray remembers, "Reg had a problem writing lyrics, and when Bernie told me he did not write music, I suggested that he give me some of the lyrics, and I gave them to Reg, who worked on them." Among the lyrics were those for "Scarecrow," a composition that would inspire other songs on their *Captain Fantastic* album. The record, an autobiographical work, told the story of their childhoods and early years together.

At the outset of their collaboration, Bernie sent Reg the lyrics through the mail. "I sat down and tried to write music to them," Elton says, "and it seemed to work, even though the lines wandered a lot. [In the early days, Bernie did not write in verse form.] And I thought, 'Well, this is quite easy.' "

Ray Williams, believing he had found the perfect team, was eager to get Reg and Bernie a contract. But his enthusiasm was not matched by others in the industry. Even inside Liberty there were no takers. "I wanted to sign Reg to Liberty as a recording artist," Williams relates, "and Bernie as a writer to its sister company, Metric Music."

Williams refused to give up and began looking elsewhere. Next he went to his friend Graham Nash, of the Hollies, a British band with whom he planned to form a company called Niraki. Two years later, in 1969, the Hollies' "He Ain't Heavy, He's My Brother" became a huge hit on both sides of the Atlantic. And in 1970, Elton would play with them on the successful U.K. single "I Can't Tell the Bottom From the Top," made at Abbey Road Studios, once the recording home of the Beatles. Niraki was administered by Gralto Music, which also published the Hollies' music. Gralto, in turn, was fifty percent owned by Dick James Music (DJM), publisher to the Beatles.

Elton and Bernie did not meet until Reg had written music to ten of Bernie's lyrics. In late summer 1967, Bernie turned up at the DJM offices where Reg was doing a piano overdub in the studio. Bernie, who hid his shyness behind dark sunglasses, waited in the control room. Once Elton emerged, they went off to the Lancaster Grill on Tottenham Court Road in the heart of London for coffee and talked nonstop about music.

Shortly thereafter Bernie moved in with Reg, who was still living at his mother's home in Northwood Hills. They shared a room with bunk beds. "So I would sit on the bunk bed writing lyrics," Bernie remembers, "and I'd walk down the corridor to the living room to his piano and then go back and write some more." Thus was born the John-Taupin music machine or, as Bernie calls it, "the factory syndrome," with the two of them churning out a whole album's worth of songs in a week. Their achievement was and still is remarkable for another reason. Elton explains: "It's usually the melody that comes first and then the lyrics. But we work the other way round, with the lyrics coming first."

By Reg's own reckoning, theirs was a blissful arrangement, despite the difficulty Reg had in deciphering Bernie's handwriting and its "many spelling mistakes" as well as their living in cramped quarters:

"his bed, my bed; his records, my records; his clothes, my clothes—what we didn't have in that room was nobody's business."

Elton, who was twenty, remembers this interlude with Bernie, seventeen, fondly. "All my life I always wanted a brother and a real close friend, and when Bernie and I started writing we became very close. It was a magic thing. I was in love with him at the time, not a physical love relationship, but an incredible bond between two people. We understood each other and each other's needs."

Elton and Bernie bought a stereo system by staggering the payments of six shillings ($1.70) a week. This "hire-purchase" plan enabled them to afford the stereo, which was a great boon to them. Without it they could not have listened to all the latest records—and so in later years "hire-purchase" would get a special mention in "Someone Saved My Life Tonight," a song that commemorated Reg's split from his fiancée, Linda Woodrow.

To make the best use of their new purchase, the pair went nearly every day to Musicland on Berwick Street in Soho to buy records. Bernie recalls, "We used to hang out there like people hang out in a bar." For a brief time, Reg in fact worked there on weekends just to be around records. Whatever little money they made went into buying albums, well worth it from Reg's point of view.

"It was a wonderful time," he says. "We used to listen to the sounds of the drums, the piano, the bass sounds on the headphone."

To help support his "vinyl habit" and pay off the stereo Reg also performed on cheap "cover versions," Marble Arch label records on which musicians and vocalists tried to duplicate popular recordings. Reg sang backup on Tom Jones's "Daughter of Darkness" and imitated Stevie Wonder on "Signed, Sealed, Delivered."

Lesley Duncan was then part of a female trio that included Kiki Dee (or alternately Dusty Springfield, Reg's teenage pinup) and Madeline Bell. Duncan remembers, "We did not often sing with the guys in those days, but if a big ensemble was needed for any sessions, Reg would be there. He had a zany sense of humor, and we all laughed a lot."

Reg passed most of his time, though, at the DJM studio making demos of the songs he created with Bernie. "All this time I was still in Bluesology," Elton admits. "I was doing all these things behind their backs because I didn't want to give up a steady income until I had sorted out an alternative."

His fellow band members were not the only ones who were ignorant of Reg's activities. Dick James was also unaware of how much use Reg was making of the DJM studio. The Troggs, who would have their first U.S. hit with "Wild Thing," were just one of the groups furious with Reg for hogging the facilities.

A big attraction of DJM was its four-track studio, and through the Graham Nash/Gralto connection, via Williams, Reg and Bernie availed themselves of the facilities there without Dick James's knowledge. Fortuitously, the studio manager and engineer on these sessions was Caleb Quaye, an old acquaintance from Reg's days as a messenger at Mills; Caleb had been working at a competing firm. Caleb had also played with Reg as a guitarist in Bluesology before quitting to take a job as a studio engineer at Dick James Music.

Caleb was a favored DJM employee, and through him Reg booked time, free of charge, in the studio. Once everyone had left the office for the day, they began laying down demos in the studio, frequently working until the wee hours of the morning.

The two men had much in common. Caleb, like Reg, had learned to play the piano by the age of four, though he later became a guitarist. And he, too, had a family musical heritage. Just as Stanley Dwight had played trumpet, albeit in amateur groups, Cab Quaye, Caleb's father, played professional guitar and piano and his wife sang with the band.

It was, of course, Ray Williams who had made it possible, by virtue of the Gralto connection, for Reg to get into the studio in the first place. At this stage Williams appeared in Reg's eyes as something of a savior, and owing to Williams's innocence, there was no written agreement between them. Ray was busy with other acts he had signed to Liberty, as well as his own publishing imprint under its sister company Metric. But he continued to meet with Reg and Bernie and encourage them.

It was not surprising that the DJM studio was in such demand. Dick James had an unrivaled reputation in the music business. A former crooner, James had taken a risk and published the Beatles' music when no one was interested. As a result, he had become a multimillionaire and the most successful publisher in the business. The avuncular James, soft-spoken yet forceful, had the ability to make all those he met believe they were the most important persons in the world.

Over the course of five months, from July to November 1967, Caleb was the recording engineer for Reg on over thirty of his songs, a mixture of ballads, rock and melodic pop with titles like "Watching the Planes Go By," "Tealby Abbey" and "Get Out of Town," with lyrics by Bernie. Another tune, "I'm Just Sitting Doing Nothing," was written by Caleb as well.

It was late one night in November 1967, when Reg and Caleb were recording demos, that "the purge," as it was later called, commenced. Because DJM's offices were above Midland Bank, the office manager of the studio was supposed to notify the bank for security reasons if anyone was using the studio at night. By unfortunate coincidence he happened to be driving by the building and, seeing lights on, went inside and apprehended Caleb, Reg and others in the studio.

The following morning twenty-year-old Steve James, whose job it was to supervise the studio, told his father. Caleb was called in to explain what was going on. "Who the hell are Reg Dwight and Bernie Taupin?" the elder James demanded to know. An ever-loyal Caleb convinced James that he was acting in the company's interests. "I told him how talented they were," Caleb recalls, "and that it was worth giving them a try."

James decided that if they were using his facilities, then he should have the right to listen to their demos before anyone else. When he did so, he liked what he heard, and signed them on the spot. "The tapes were very rough," Steve James remembers, "but I think what we liked was the originality. It was all music that Elton had composed. We felt that it was different from what was around. At the time there was Motown, the Beatles and the Eagles. He did not seem to be emulating the others. We never tried to jump on the bandwagon and just work with people who were copying what was around."

Ray Williams, angered by this arrangement, accused Dick James of "stealing" Reg and Bernie from him. At the very least, he believed, the two men should have been signed to Gralto, the Hollies' publishing venture under DJM. The Hollies, it was agreed, could hold on to the songs recorded by Reg for their label. But as Reg and Bernie appeared to be going nowhere, they did not put up much of a fight. None of Reg and Bernie's songs on the tapes Dick James heard would ever be released.

On November 7, 1967, Reg and Bernie signed with Dick James.

Under the agreement, they assigned DJM world copyright to their songs, to include at least eighteen titles over a renewable three-year period. Further, against a joint advance of £100 ($266) each received a weekly cash retainer of £10 ($27) against future royalties. Reg got an additional £15 ($40) for his other roles as singer and pianist. The royalties were calculated at ten percent of the retail price of each record (after the first 250 copies) and fifty percent of the proceeds from recording, live performance, radio, television and sublicensing abroad.

The contract with Dick James Music, Reg believed, was "heaven-sent." Dick James had the personnel, the studio facilities and the influence in the industry to develop talent. An association with him was an important break for any pop music artist. What might have been the end to free studio time marked the beginning of a new future for them. For Dick James, meanwhile, what had started out as a matter of principle would turn into another pot of gold.

4

And Reg Said, "Let There Be Elton"

"Oh dear, what shall I call myself?" Reg inquired of his traveling companions when he finally told them about the contract he had signed the previous fall with Dick James Music. "They want to record me, but Reg Dwight does not sound much like a stage name, does it?" The Bluesology members were flying back from Scotland in the late afternoon of May 7, 1968, following a performance. It was Reg's last gig with the group.

Now, at thirty thousand feet over the skies of Great Britain in a British European Airways aircraft, Reg, anxious to get past the awkwardness of his parting ways with the band, dwelled on the name change. He wanted to devise a name that had panache and would enhance his appeal as a future solo artist. Any name, he figured, had to be an improvement over the one given to him twenty-one years earlier, at birth.

"A young person's name is not Reginald," Elton says now. "It sounded like a cement mixer. And Reggie is terrible too, a nightmare. It's not so bad in America. Like, Reggie Jackson doesn't sound so

40

bad. But in England it just doesn't make it. Changing my name helped me a lot. I'm still the same person as Reg Dwight, but Elton John gave me a feeling of confidence."

Indeed, in Britain the name Reg Dwight always conjured up images of a rather nerdlike character, suited to his image at school, rejected by his classmates and virtually useless on the athletic field. He believed that his name hobbled him in his career, barring him from a spectacular entry into the world of pop music.

Over the past few months he had made no secret of his desire for a name change. Not only did he mention it to Ray Williams at the Liberty audition, but he had earlier badgered Bluesology's saxophonist, Elton Dean, in private. Reg liked the sound of "Elton." Aside from Elton Dean, there was an aristocrat named Lord Elton and a singer named Elton Hayes who had recorded "The Owl and the Pussycat." But as he knew Dean and not the other Eltons, Reg figured it was easier and more direct just to borrow the name. "Originally he propositioned me for my full name," Dean remembers. "He said, 'I'm going solo and I want to call myself Elton Dean,' and I said, thinking he was joking, 'Oh, forget it, Reg.' " Enamored of the name, Reg did not appear to be bothered that there might be two "Elton Deans" in the same industry, much less the same band.

But Reg was determined. He approached Dean again. "Can I just use Elton?" he inquired, to which Dean shot back, "It'll cost you five percent." Adds Dean, still miffed: "I mean, no one would be happy if someone just came up and said, 'I want your name.' But that was Little Bunter."

Reg backed off, realizing, "I wanted to choose a name that nobody had." Yet to resolve his name dilemma, Reg prodded fellow band members Pete Gavin, Mark Charig, Elton Dean and John Baldry for suggestions. Sipping tumblers of scotch, they made a game out of the search, yelling out different names, including their own, as if they were contestants on a quiz show. An hour later, as the plane began its descent into London's Heathrow, "We all agreed on 'Elton' from Elton Dean and 'John' from me," according to Baldry. Elton Dean, caught up in the camaraderie, did not object this time.

Eventually Reg made the name change legal, inserting Hercules as his middle name. "I wanted to change it legally," Elton says, "because it was such a hassle having two names, like leading two lives. I used to have the middle name Kenneth, which is so useless. No one ever called me Kenneth. I don't know why people bother having middle names anyway—so I thought I'd call myself 'Hercules.' "

In the end Elton Dean had raised no objections, but Reg knew his mother would not be pleased about the name change. "She had a fit," Elton admits. "Everybody had a fit. They didn't think I was serious until I actually did it."

But he had been absolutely serious, and as the plane touched down, he had left the band not as he had joined it, as Reginald Dwight, but as Elton John. Once inside the terminal he said good-bye to his fellow band members. While he would hear little about their careers over the years, in the decade to follow, the name graft they had helped him devise would dominate the press.

In the minds of the two men, Long John Baldry and Elton Dean, whose names he took, Elton John would remain Reg Dwight. But at that moment Reg felt entirely comfortable with his name change. Emboldened by his new persona, he believed that "Elton John" would jazz up his image as he aimed for the top.

5

Positioned to Make His Mark

"They want to record me," Elton had boasted to his fellow band members the previous day after his last gig with Bluesology. It could not have been further from the truth. Elton had not been signed as an artist, as he had told them, but as part of a songwriting partnership with Bernie Taupin. "At that point Elton had not made it known to us that he would like to be considered as an artist," Steve James recalls. "He was just happy to have an environment and the finances to write songs."

Elton had been ecstatic about the contract, but according to Steve James, he was too introverted to express his feelings. "Both he and Bernie were very quiet," he remembers. "Certainly they weren't prone to letting their hair down in front of my father and me." At the signing in November, both Sheila and Bernie's father, Robert Taupin, had been present to countersign the contracts. James remembers Sheila as "very nice. She gave me the impression that she was quite happy for Elton to do whatever would make him happy."

Though it was the originality of their material—the combination of a strong melody and the unique lyrics which were more poetic and eclectic than what was around—that had convinced Dick James to put them under contract, they were expected to churn out lightweight pop songs for other British artists like Engelbert Humperdinck, Tom Jones and Cilla Black, the Liverpudlian ballad singer discovered by Beatles manager Brian Epstein. The association with DJM did not improve Elton's bank account, either.

By now Elton and Bernie had moved out of Sheila's house and into their own basement flat, a decrepit space in the North London area of Islington. Elton was supplementing his income with part-time work at the Musicland record store.

Soon they were joined by Elton's "fiancée," Linda Woodrow. With a small private income from her family's pickles and preserves business, she was able to absorb the greater part of the rent. Initially, Elton was flattered that she had followed him from the north of England. But the distance she had traveled to be with him did not seem to inspire any sexual passion in him. According to Linda, they made love only four or five times during the nine months they lived together. "Though he was never openly gay," she says, "he did admit to being bisexual. He always wore a lot of jewelry and perfume. And he certainly did not seem interested in sex."

After three months their affair begin to spiral downhill, magnifying Elton's depression about his situation at Dick James Music. James had rejected a whole promotional album's worth of songs, among them "Regimental Sergeant Zippo," "The Year of the Teddybear" and "Dandelion Dies in the Wind." The songs had too much of a hippie flavor, reflecting Bernie's obsession with psychedelia. While these songs may have recalled for Elton his not-too-distant days of parading around Carnaby Street in the requisite kaftan, to his boss's thinking they were not commercial and best left forgotten.

By fall of 1968, Elton had figured that he could no longer go on living with Linda and tried to end the relationship, which was heading definitely toward marriage. "If the marriage had proceeded," he says, "it would have been the ruination of me." Linda hated his music and took every opportunity to tell him so, and she also failed to satisfy him in bed. He became increasingly depressed by his situation.

In the drab apartment he shared with her and Bernie, Elton looked at his life and saw little point to it. The stacks of albums filling his tiny quarters were a sorry reminder that despite a childhood spent dreaming about a rock music career, he had so far failed to get a recording contract. He was already twenty-one. As it was, he spent the greater part of the twenty-five pounds (sixty dollars) he earned each week as a songwriter at Dick James Music on other people's hit records.

But most worrisome to Elton at that moment was his impending marriage to Linda. The wedding was less than three weeks away, and Elton had yet to figure a way out of it. Marriage would mean giving up his music and possibly ending up in a basement flat like this one, with its cracked ceilings, primitive plumbing and threadbare furniture, in a suburb like Islington.

Elton used to lie awake in terror thinking about how Linda would react to his calling off the wedding. She often became abusive when she did not get her way. "I was in love with her for the first three months," he says, "but after that she made me completely miserable."

Baldry says that Linda had proposed to Elton, but she insists it was the other way around. She did buy her own engagement ring, though. "He didn't exactly get down on his knees," she confesses. "He just mumbled something about 'Well, we may as well get married.' "

At best the pair serviced the other's neuroses: Elton, according to Baldry, was "having this problem with women dominating him" and Linda obliged by "slapping him around." In later years, Linda denied that she had ever hit Elton or any other man. In fact, she claimed she had been an earlier victim of physical abuse from the Mighty Atom, whom she had left for Elton.

She belittled his music, all that had mattered to him since childhood, the only thing which permitted him to feel special. The idea of marrying Linda made Elton panicky about his future, and as he lay awake, he began to think about suicide as a way out of his problem.

Tormented by these thoughts, Elton got up and walked into the closet-sized kitchen, turned on the gas and stuck his head into the oven. But the fact that he had opened all the windows in the flat, turned on the gas low and expected either Linda or Bernie to wake up and find him momentarily suggested that this was more a cry for help than a serious suicide attempt. As Elton later described the moment, "It was a rather Woody Allen-esque attempt."

Bernie woke up on cue, walked into the kitchen and pulled Elton's head out of the oven. Linda, unaware of the reason for her fiancé's despair, also tried to console him. Then Elton talked privately with his songwriting partner. Though despondent himself about their future in the music business, Bernie convinced Elton that he was too gifted to destroy himself and promised, further, that he would help his friend devise a way out of the marriage.

Even though at that moment a successful career seemed far away, Elton, at Bernie's urging, went to sleep, resolving for the moment to choose life over death. Three days passed. Though Elton moped around, still wanting desperately to cancel the wedding, he reluctantly agreed to spend an evening with Baldry and Taupin in London's West End. Taupin believed this outing might restore his friend to a better frame of mind, but as the evening wore on it became clear Elton was still mired in suicidal despair.

Around midnight the three of them stopped in at the Bag O' Nails club in Soho. The club was an international mecca for rock musicians, and on any given night one of the Beatles or Rolling Stones or even Jimi Hendrix might turn up to relax and mix with other performers. Ordinarily Elton looked forward to having a scotch or a beer and to chatting with other musicians. But this time it was obvious to his two friends that he was not feeling particularly social. Baldry, unaware of Elton's suicide attempt three days before, innocently inquired about the wedding. "I was supposed to be best man," he recalls, "so I said, 'Hey, Reg, have you booked the hall yet?' when suddenly he started to sob. Baldry counseled, "Reg, if you feel that bad about it, just go back to your digs, grab all your things and go back to your mum's home."

It was simple, direct advice, but as Elton would later admit, "I could not bring myself to tell her, and now there were less than three weeks to go." Already the wedding cake had been ordered and the invitations sent out, and Sheila, albeit unconvinced that Linda was the right woman for her son, had nonetheless graciously planned a party for the couple at her home.

As always, Elton had trouble confronting people. "I can make a decision," he admits, "but I lack the courage to communicate it." This night was no exception, and rather than face Linda's wrath alone, Elton enlisted Bernie to return to the flat with him to break the news.

"We rolled home at four in the morning," Taupin recalls. "It was a dreadful scene, but it was all over and done with." Linda, screaming and crying and threatening to commit suicide, grilled Elton about why he had stayed out so late and where he had been. "I'm sorry," Elton blurted out, "I can't go through with it."

Following the showdown, Elton caught a few hours of sleep on the floor of Bernie's room until dawn, when he called his mother. Later that same morning he acted on Baldry's advice and went home to her. His stepfather arrived to collect him and all his belongings. Linda recalls, "That was the last I ever heard from Reg." Bernie also fled with Elton to Sheila's home.

Elton and Bernie expected to live there for only a few weeks while hiding out from Linda. They ended up staying for eighteen months. Seven years later, in 1975, Elton and Bernie's song, "Someone Saved My Life Tonight," graphically chronicled Elton's contemplation of suicide. It was dedicated to Long John Baldry. "It was a narrow escape," Elton says. "I was so relieved it was off. It was as if someone had saved my life that night." Or, as the lyrics went, "You almost had your hooks in me / Didn't you, dear. . . . You nearly had me roped and tied."

Linda had reminded Elton of his father. "She hated everything about me," he says. "It was like my own father all over again. The thing that destroyed me was that she hated my music. Everything I'd write, she'd put down."

And so Reg, at twenty-one, having failed as a child to win the unconditional love of his father and then as a man being browbeaten by a woman, was even more determined to gain the acceptance of the world.

By the spring of 1968, in March, Elton was back on record with an oily ballad, "I've Been Loving You Too Long." Elton wrote the lyrics, but gave Bernie a credit. It was the first record put out by DJM's newly created This Record Company, which was overseen by Dick James's son, Steve. Though advertised on the record sleeve as "the greatest performance on a first disk by 1968's great new talent," the single sank without a trace.

Another flop followed with "I Can't Go On Living Without You," which was selected by Dick James as a prospective British Eurovision Song Contest entry. Performed by Lulu, a popular Scottish-born art-ist, the song ended up in the bottom six in the qualifying final that year. In years to follow Elton and Bernie would confess their embarrassment at the banality of some of their earliest compositions. "Our hearts just weren't in them," says Bernie.

During this period Elton turned to his former acquaintances from Mills, songwriters Roger Cook and Roger Greenaway, who had moved over to Dick James Music. "They said the only way to make it was to work as we found best," Elton remembers, "and we should do what we wanted to do regardless of commercial considerations."

The first song Elton believed worthy of showing his two new allies was "Skyline Pigeon," a smooth ballad that was published by Cook and Greenaway's DJM imprint, Cookaway Music, and recorded by Roger Cook in August 1968. They liked its kindly melody and message. "Skyline Pigeon" was ostensibly about a caged bird longing to be set free, but it was as much a metaphor of the freeing of the creative spirit for Elton and Bernie.

The song would set the tone for Elton's first hit single, the uptempo ballad "Your Song," about the gift of song ("This one's for you"). Amateur interpreters of the lyrics have suggested it was a love song Bernie wrote for Elton: "I hope you don't mind if I put down in words / How wonderful life is when you're in the world." But it was more likely an expression of a shared labor of love than a declaration of passion. Clearly Bernie, since married twice, did not attach any romantic sentiment to the song. "I wrote it when I was having breakfast," he says. "I remember because the original lyric of it still has an egg stain on it. It was one of those set-the-coffee-down stains."

Elton's situation with the company was not helped when Caleb Quaye left after a row with Dick James. In addition to his duties as studio engineer Caleb had his own band, Hookfoot, who were signed to DJM. "It was the days of early R&B fusion," he explains, "and we wanted to forge ahead in that area. But Dick wanted a more straight pop sound. Our differences were philosophical."

Elton now felt somewhat lost. But he soon found a new ally in Steve Brown, who joined DJM's new label as a record plugger. Brown listened to their songs, and though he liked what he heard, according to Elton, "He said that the fault lay in the fact that we were doing things half and half, partly as we wanted and partly as Dick James wanted, and it was coming out a mishmash."

Similar advice came from Lionel Conway, head of publishing at DJM, whose support Elton also enlisted. "Elton was terribly frustrated," Conway recalls, "so I took his tapes home and listened to them myself and I thought, 'My God, we've got a genius here!' " He encouraged Elton and Bernie to be faithful to their own ideas instead of what Dick James was suggesting that they write. What followed, among a batch of songs, was "Lady Samantha," the single that first brought Elton attention.

Though enormously enthusiastic about his new output, Elton was still not happy about the progress in his career. "Elton was paranoid that nothing was happening, and he became a nervous wreck," says Conway, "so I forced the issue by telling Dick James that three or four record labels wanted Elton."

Of course, what Conway conveyed to James could not have been further from the truth. Actually, Elton had been a laughingstock at a gig Conway had arranged for him before thirty major agents. Elton wore to the audition a Mickey Mouse T-shirt and little round glasses, known as "National Health specs" because the government provided them free of charge. "He's got absolutely no chance," said one agent, echoing the opinion of everyone else in the room. "I just can't see him on stage at Madison Square Garden."

Someone else might have overcome the rejection in a few days, but a humiliated and devastated Elton went into a deep depression for weeks. "He withdrew into himself," Conway says. "Some people accept bad news, but he was too passionate about his art to be abused that way."

All the while, Steve James was taking Elton and Bernie's songs around to various record producers without any positive results. "The songs were criticized as too airy-fairy," he says, "and no one could think of an artist to record them." However, Johnny Franz at Philips, who had recorded Elton's teen pinup, Dusty Springfield, came up with a solution. Believing the songs were too stylized for anyone else, he suggested that Elton record them. "The guy's voice on the tape sounds good enough to me," said Franz, who promised to listen to the final product.

Back at the office, Steve James told his father, Steve Brown and Lionel Conway about his meeting with Franz. As he remembers, "We all scratched our heads and looked at each other and someone said, 'Why not? Why not try a master?' " Brown added, "Let me try a few things," and immediately began to assemble some musicians.

About ten recordings were made at DJM's This Record Company, and out of that group, "Lady Samantha," a cynical ballad with a tinny sixties sound about a cast-off woman, was chosen as the single. On January 10, 1967, it was released on Philips, which had previously put out two unsuccessful Bluesology singles. "Lady Samantha" got about 120 airplays on BBC Radio and earned Elton some respectable critical attention. "Professional and musicianly," said *New Musical Express*; *Disc and Music* called Elton a "promising talent." Yet initial sales of under eight thousand copies hardly suggested a mega-star in the making.

What "Lady Samantha" succeeded in doing, though, was to get Elton's name known within the business and thereby convince Dick James to proceed with an album. Elton, unhappy with the single, had not wanted it released. "I thought it was awful," he remembers, "and I told Steve Brown he should stick to plugging." Brown agreed with this review of his producing abilities. Nevertheless, he was a strong advocate of Elton around DJM, and for this reason he was valued as a close professional friend.

Philips, meanwhile, had made it abundantly clear that they were not going to record an album in advance of a hit single. In America there was no interest either. But DJM went ahead with an album called *Empty Sky* in February 1969. Once again Steve Brown was the producer, and Elton knew that he would have to accept whatever terms were laid out.

Fortuitously, Caleb Quaye returned to DJM to put a studio band together for Elton and to play guitar on the album. Among his recruits was a pixielike drummer, Nigel Olsson, who already had a hit song, "Everything I Am," with the group Plastic Penny. He would soon become part of the Elton John Band.

Elton loved the experience of making *Empty Sky*. "It still holds the nicest memories for me—because it was the first, I suppose," he says. "It's difficult to explain the amazing enthusiasm we felt as the album began to take shape, but I remember when we finished work on the title track it just floored me. I thought it was the best thing I'd ever heard in my life."

Whatever the outcome, it was a time that Elton would also treasure because of the camaraderie he felt with Brown and the others. Often they finished work at four in the morning and walked to the Salvation Army headquarters on Oxford Street. Brown's father ran the place and lived above it. Many nights Elton, if he was not kept awake by the euphoria he felt at making his first album, caught a few hours' sleep on the sofa there. But much to his disappointment, no one wanted to release the album in America in the summer of 1969.

Steve James attributed its failure to attract an American audience in large part to the lyrics. "Too introspective and obscure," he explains. "In Britain you can say anything you like if the melodies are right. But in America they pay attention."

Bernie, told of the problem with the lyrics, refused to yield. As James relates, "Bernie suggested that maybe the Americans did not know what they were talking about or they would have to change their feelings about his lyrics. He wasn't going to tailor-make his lyrics to the American market, and I think it would be fair to say that he never compromised."

Prior to the album's U.K. release, Elton recorded a single, "It's Me That You Need," a whiny love ballad with sophomoric lyrics and the endless repetition of "Yes, it's me, / Yes it's me / That you need," his voice an insufferable wail. It was another flop, and again Elton became depressed.

He was soon to be disappointed again when the folk-based *Empty Sky*, heavily laced with flute and harpsichord, sold no more than four thousand copies in the United Kingdom. It was redeemed only by good reviews in the music press and within the industry. Though it did not put money in the bank for Dick James, it was at least some confirmation that the talent he saw in Elton was now being recognized on a larger scale. At the same time, the experienced Dick James knew a lot more work was needed to make Elton a major artist.

Elton was also disgruntled about the gigs DJM was arranging at college campuses in small suburban communities, like Twickenham Polytechnic. At universities he earned £50 ($119) a night. The plan was to give Elton experience performing his own material live. But sometimes he just did not turn up and DJM had to absorb the costs of his no-shows.

Already signed to publishing, recording and managing contracts with DJM, Elton believed he needed the help of someone outside the company. It was an about-face, because he had only recently asked Dick James to manage him.

All along, Elton regarded the tubby and balding James as a paternal figure. Once Elton became famous, he told an interviewer, "To me he's been like a father. If there's a problem, Dick will sort it out." Steve James, whose office adjoined his father's, frequently sat in on meetings. "There were occasions when Elton would say, 'This isn't a music discussion,' and he would ask me to leave the room," he remembers." Elton always had great embarrassment over anything personal, so I understood. I didn't realize at the time that he was gay or had a sexual problem." Elton was also particularly impressed with the fact that Dick James, a former dance-band singer, had recorded the million-selling theme song for the television series "Robin Hood." And James, too, had undergone some show business name changes.

Starting out life as Isaac Vapnick, he quit school at fourteen to become a singer, and three years later, at seventeen, landed his first gig with a dance band. Along the way, he called himself Al Berlin and Lee Sheridan, eventually settling on Dick James when he became a music publisher. In 1963, Dick James and Brian Epstein set up the Beatles' publishing company, Northern Songs. That same year, "Please Please Me" became the first of seven Number One hits that would make James a millionaire many times over.

Nonetheless, Elton, unhappy about his situation at DJM, now turned to Ray Williams, the man who had believed in him and Bernie from the very beginning but whom they had left to sign with Dick James. Williams, meanwhile, had just successfully launched a new band and was looking for a fresh challenge. Harboring no grudge against Elton or Bernie, with whom he had kept in touch all along, he agreed to make himself available.

Williams initially tried to buy out James's management interest in Elton. He sought out several potential backers, to no avail. "The people I went to for help laughed me out of the room," Williams recalls. "They said that Elton would have to earn something like thirty-five to forty thousand dollars a year to make it worthwhile for them."

Nevertheless, Elton continued to want Williams to manage him and pressured Dick James to hire him. Primarily a publisher, James was not particularly interested in the day-to-day chores of a manager. So on May 11, 1970, he signed Williams to a three-year agreement whereby they would share equally the twenty percent management commission. Additionally, Williams drew a salary of forty pounds (ninety-six dollars) a week plus five pounds (twelve dollars) in advance for expenses.

Earlier in the year DJM had decided to proceed with a second album, but its savvy owner knew that changes were needed to make this possible. Because of Elton and Bernie's prolific output, several albums' worth of material was now awaiting the recording stage. They would be divided into *Elton John* and *Tumbleweed Connection*, the album sleeves mirroring the tone of each record. On the former Elton looked like a brooding longhair; on the latter he donned a Woody Guthrie chapeau. The recording was done in January 1970 at Trident Studios in London; the facilities there were thought to be better acoustically than those at DJM.

It was also obvious to Steve Brown that the songs needed a more sophisticated production than he was capable of. Brown initially approached Beatles producer George Martin, but he turned them down because he wanted to be both producer and arranger and DJM wanted to divide these roles between two people.

Elton and Bernie's next choice was Gus Dudgeon and Paul Buckmaster—producer and arranger, respectively, of David Bowie's *Space Oddity*, which had reached Number One in the U.K. charts. Elton was impressed with the uniquely futuristic quality of the Bowie album, considered one of the most technically advanced of the decade, and it appealed to Bernie's fascination with science fiction.

Quite by chance, on a November night in 1969, Buckmaster was at a Miles Davis recital at Ronnie Scott's, London's premier jazz club, when Elton and Steve Brown showed up there. Like Elton, Buckmaster was the product of classical training, having played the cello from the age of six. The son of a pianist mother, he had also spent two years in his early teens at the Naples Conservatory. Steve introduced him to Elton and asked if he would be interested in the project. A demo tape was sent to him, and a week later Buckmaster signed on. Next they approached Gus Dudgeon, who was initially lukewarm but soon came around.

Of the making of the album, completed in two weeks during ordinary nine-to-five working days, Buckmaster remembers, "It was very professional, but it was also done with that sort of brash innocence. We were all flabbergasted that the egg had hatched this beautiful chick. We all had a glow of satisfied confidence. We'd acquitted ourselves very well by doing something that was not really to be imitated."

No one was more thrilled with the album than Elton. Each track was different, each with its own amiable qualities, each sung with conviction. The songs ranged from the surrealistic "Take Me to the

Pilot" to the country parody "No Shoe Strings on Louise" to the
gospel-inflected "Border Song," which was later sung by others, including Aretha Franklin. "Border Song," released as the album's first
single, earned Elton his first appearance on BBC-TV's "Top of the
Pops," then Britain's only chart show. The Buckmaster strings gave
the album a kind of maturity and lushness rare in the early stages of
an artist's career.

As anticipated, the jewel in the album's crown was "Your Song,"
a soft ballad that was a valentine to Elton's fans. Influential BBC
Radio One disc jockey Tony Blackburn pronounced it a "haunting
melody" and predicted the single would become "one of the classics."

For the first time in a long while, a normally reticent Elton behaved in a much more outgoing way, regaling the band over fish and
chips or Chinese dinners with the dry humor that characterized his
personality as much as his dark moods did. "Elton had one of those
minds where, if you picture yourself doing drugs like marijuana, your
mind starts rolling," one session musician remembers. "But he was
straight. His mind just went snap-snap-snap, from one absurd observation to the next. He was a bit like Robin Williams."

Dick James was also much impressed with the final product—so
much so that in March 1970, when a new recording contract was
drawn up, he offered Elton a royalty increase to forty percent from
the original 1967 agreement. In two years it would be increased to
sixty percent. Under the agreement, Elton was bound to DJM's This
Record Company for five years with a proviso that Elton make six,
instead of four, album sides each year.

Most important, the new arrangement symbolized Elton's growing
stature within DJM. By luck, it coincided with the breakup of the
Beatles after manager Brian Epstein's suicide. Soon afterward, James
sold his shares in Northern Songs, and now he was banking on Elton
John to become the second installment of his Beatles success. Because of the orchestration on the *Elton John* album, the cost, originally budgeted at six thousand pounds (fourteen thousand dollars),
neared ten thousand pounds (twenty-four thousand dollars) instead.
James willingly absorbed it. He also bought a van and one thousand
pounds (twenty-four hundred dollars) worth of equipment to put
Elton back on the road.

Delighted though he was with his new contract, Elton again balked
at touring. It recalled for him the boredom he had experienced during

his last days with Bluesology. Steve Brown managed to convince him that this was the only way to promote the album. So Elton became the leader of a trio with drummer Nigel Olsson and bassist Dee Murray, both of whom had been members of the pivotal band the Spencer Davis Group in its last days.

Olsson had already played on the *Empty Sky* album. He introduced Murray, and both men were featured on Elton's third album, *Tumbleweed Connection*. This marked the beginning of a long association between Elton and the two musicians. Murray remembers, "We all had magic together and felt then we had something that could get really big." For each performance Elton got sixty percent of the fee and Olsson and Murray twenty percent each.

In later years, however, Olsson and Murray would come to resent being backup players instead of part of a group like the Beatles or Rolling Stones. "It would have been nice to have had a name other than Elton John, that identified us or was just a name we all created," Murray said in hindsight. "Nigel and I kind of lost our identities along the way."

The Elton John Band made its debut on April 21, 1970, at the Pop Proms at London's Roundhouse. The main act was Marc Bolan and his band Tyrannosaurus Rex, soon to be abridged to T. Rex. Bolan's fame was largely domestic, with two U.K. Number Ones, "Hot Love" and "Get It Out," and the album *Electric Warrior*. To Elton, his music had a "lovely rawness." Bolan, the first pop star whose sex appeal was not limited to women, was also an inspiration to him, and in later years to artists like Boy George. A self-confessed bisexual, Bolan, a former teen model with waist-length curly black hair and a pretty, almost delicate, face, represented sexual freedom.

As a showman Elton was no match for Bolan, who made a grandiose entrance from the wings, clad in satin and with arms lifted to orchestrate the reception. The Elton John Band was received warmly. Still, there were signs of the old shy and inhibited Reg Dwight. On stage he seemed uneasy with himself, but fortunately he could hide behind his piano.

A short time later, however, another gig that had all the elements of a disaster proved to be a prelude to Elton John's future success as a showman. At an outdoor concert in the Yorkshire village of Crumlin, near Halifax, the typically wet British weather dampened the spirits backstage as the artists argued among themselves about who would go on first. Elton himself worried about catching a cold, and Nigel Olsson offered a remedy. As Elton remembers, "Nigel suggested we try moving about on stage. I realized that if I jumped about, not caring about what I was doing, then at least I'd keep my ass warm." And so the making of the uninhibited Elton John came into play, as he leaped on and off his piano and offered brandy to the shivering audience in the first few rows.

It was a memorable and magical performance, and Elton was the unrivaled star of this otherwise inhospitable night. As the audience departed the concert grounds, the name Elton John was imprinted on their minds. Soon fellow musicians were also hearing about him.

One of them was Jeff Beck, formerly with the Yardbirds and a performer with a number of hits. Between sets at London's Speakeasy Club, Beck approached Elton about joining the band. "Obviously I wasn't going to let an offer like this go by," Elton says. "But I was also worried that he might try to turn us into a wailing guitar group, which I was against." Even so, Elton decided to discuss the matter further, until Beck suggested Nigel Olsson be replaced by another drummer. Loyal to his band, Elton flatly refused. A few weeks later, at a meeting arranged by Ray Williams at DJM's offices, Beck's manager proposed a joint tour of the United States with Elton. But when it was suggested that Beck get ninety percent of the tour earnings and Elton only ten percent, Dick James erupted. "Elton John," he declared, "will be a bigger star than Jeff Beck!"

So far there was little indication of much happening for Elton on the other side of the Atlantic, however. Lennie Hodes, DJM's New York representative, had already been turned down by major American recording companies. Were it not for the presence of Elton's staunch admirer and hit songwriter Roger Greenaway when Hodes paid a visit to Los Angeles to meet with Russ Regan, vice president and general manager of Uni, a small recording label under MCA Records, Elton John's future might have ended then and there.

Coincidentally, Greenaway was staying at the same hotel, the Continental-Hyatt on Sunset Boulevard, when Hodes met with Regan. "Russ wasn't really sure," Greenaway says. "He liked the *Elton John* album, but he didn't want to commit himself. Elton was an unknown commodity. He hadn't seen him live. I told him that if he didn't sign Elton John, he would miss out on a world star. Not only was Russ a friend, but Roger Cook and I had been very successful in America, and he respected my opinion."

Those who were around Uni's offices in Los Angeles at the time describe a different scenario. When Regan listened to the tape, they report, he was bowled over by it. "Incredible," he yelled out enthusiastically, and then summoned thirty employees to his office to listen as well. But Regan was not ready to risk any money on an unknown artist whom he had not yet seen perform.

Ironically, Regan was more interested in another DJM act, a new band called Argosy which soon faded into oblivion. He paid a ten thousand dollar advance for them, and Elton was thrown into the deal for free. A decision was made to release one track, "Border Song," and it did well only in Memphis. But at that point, says Steve James, "Russ called my father and said, 'Let's work on this guy Elton. What's he like live? To promote him properly we're going to have to bring him over here and make a big fuss and say he's something special in England.' "

In England, though, *Elton John* was only a moderate success. Favorable reviews and growing interest in the album were no solace to a businessman who had made his first fortune with the Beatles and looked to Elton John as the follow-up act. The only solution, it seemed, was to send Elton to America—and James agreed to absorb the cost of the trip.

Still, the Jameses had second thoughts about their commitment to the John-Taupin partnership. In short, father and son worried whether they would ever see any return on the large sums, now approaching one hundred thousand pounds (two hundred and forty thousand dollars), they had plowed into Elton's career. "Either the album and the trip made Elton," Steve James says, "or we really could not afford to go on after that." Indeed, the money behind Elton was considered at that time to be a large amount to spend on an artist three years in the making.

Elton, now twenty-three, was just as jittery at his forthcoming trip to America, where, it was decided, he would play Troubadour clubs in Los Angeles and San Francisco in late August. "Elton was starting to get a bit desperate," Steve James remembers, "and I would say his tantrums began to manifest themselves around this time because he wanted to make sure everything was done to insure the product was successful." By early summer 1970, "Border Song" and "Your

Song" began to rise on the Billboard Hot 100 chart in the United States. But Elton John himself had yet to come to prominence.

Shortly before his trip to America, Elton lost about fifty pounds during a period in Sweden, and as a result he could get into the fancy clothes his large self had kept him out of until now.

Elton John was well positioned to make his mark. With the counterculture of the sixties fading away, musical imagination, in short, was trying to find a separate peace with various segments of the public. The Jefferson Airplane's shrillness, the Rolling Stones' rage and the Doors' sepulchral edge had dwindled. Music could no longer remain at that pitch. It splintered into fragments, with something for everyone. At one end of the spectrum were the folk-based singer-songwriters like James Taylor, Joni Mitchell and Bob Dylan. At the other was the "heavy metal" sound of Led Zeppelin, a bruising rejection of peace signs and hippies. With the Rolling Stones in tax exile and the Beatles dissolved, Led Zeppelin was the number one group in the world.

It looked as though there might just be room for Elton with his unique balladeer and melodic rock style. And with this in mind he headed toward Los Angeles—aiming for the stars but at the same time expecting very little.

As Elton flew across the Atlantic in TWA economy class, Sheila returned home to find he had filled every nook of the place with flowers. She was still number one in her son's life, even though it was a life consumed by music.

Fantastic Across America

6

Troubadour — Tantrums and Triumphs

August 1970, Los Angeles

"I'm going home," Elton screamed, getting up from the table in a packed Los Angeles restaurant on the eve of his Troubadour debut. "I don't want to be here. I've had enough." Manager Ray Williams could not believe what he was hearing. Here he was with Elton John, six thousand miles from London, awaiting the singer's first American appearance at the legendary club, and the twenty-three-year-old Elton was behaving like a prima donna.

The Troubadour Club was by far the most important showcase in America for top new talent. Every Tuesday night, members of the music press and the record business would turn up at the club at the intersection of Doheny and Santa Monica boulevards in search of a future star. Seldom were they disappointed. The Troubadour seemed to have an uncanny knack for attracting original acts. Bob Dylan, Cat Stevens and James Taylor had all played there. And now Elton John was less than twenty-four hours away from appearing on stage.

As the club's owner, Doug Weston, proudly recalls, "The Troubadour was the only game in town on Tuesday nights in L.A. Most record companies had opened offices on the West Coast, and now it was L.A.—and no longer New York—that mattered most to them. The Troubadour was a great place to test the market."

The club's significance seemed daunting to Elton. The morning after his outburst, however, he emerged from his hotel room as if nothing had happened. But by afternoon, just hours before his show, his spirits were once again low; this time, in a fit of temper, he pushed a member of his entourage into the hotel swimming pool.

Until now his traveling companions had not seen this side of Elton's character and they were totally baffled by it. Only Elton's mother, it seemed, really understood him and could explain his bizarre behavior. Many years later she would blame his outbursts on the pressures of show business: "He was always a quiet type of boy. The darker moods have come since he sort of made it in the pop world. But I don't ever expect him to be ecstatic because that's just not his nature."

Ray Williams, even though he had spent a fair amount of time around Elton, had had no indication until now of his difficult disposition. Elton's fury was triggered by the fact that upon their arrival in Los Angeles, Williams, Bernie Taupin, Steve Brown and album designer Dave Larkham had immediately left for Palm Springs to spend the weekend with some friends. In fact, Bernie met his future wife, Maxine, on this excursion.

Even though Elton had been invited along and declined, choosing instead to remain at the hotel, he was furious about being left on his own. He felt that Williams had no right to be spending the weekend away in Palm Springs. Closeting himself inside his hotel room, Elton became increasingly depressed. Though band members Nigel Olsson and Dee Murray were on hand in nearby rooms, Elton chose to nurse his wounds alone.

For several hours Elton sat fuming over what in his mind had become an unforgivable snub by Williams, who was unaware of Elton's feelings. He watched television and read, but hard as he tried to concentrate, he could not take his mind off Ray Williams's Palm Springs sojourn. Fueled by a mammoth rage, Elton impulsively picked up the phone in his hotel room around seven in the evening, Los Angeles time, and dialed Dick James in London.

As Steve James remembers, "It was the middle of the night when the phone rang, and my father, who was half asleep, mumbled something about, 'Why are you ringing me when you have Ray Williams there with you? That's why I sent him—to look after you.' And Elton said, 'The problem is that he is *not* here—he's in Palm Springs. And I don't know my way around L.A.' Elton then demanded that Ray Williams be fired then and there. But my father told him that they would discuss it upon Elton's return to London." Adds Steve James, "Elton was starting to get to the point where he was ordering people around. He wanted people at his beck and call."

Meanwhile, when Williams returned to the hotel on Monday, the day before Elton's Troubadour debut, he figured Elton's hostility toward him was just a bad case of nerves. "There was no question that Elton was worried that he was not going to succeed," he explains. "And there was nobody hanging around to hold his hand." Williams believed that once the tour was over their friendship would resume as before. He also understood that America, so far away from home, was an intimidating place for Elton.

The decision to send Elton to America had been a difficult one for Dick James. "Initially, the idea was to develop a small trip, primarily for the executives at MCA to see whether they wanted to sign him, and to book him into the Troubadour for a week," says his son. "In addition, we thought it would be a good experience for Elton."

Elton's first record released on Uni was the single "Border Song." It produced a lackluster response. There had been no advance paid to Elton. But Uni executive Russ Regan, convinced that a visit by the artist would increase sales, persuaded Dick James that it was a good idea to send Elton over. The cost of the trip was DJM's major concern. But it was time for the Jameses to decide once and for all whether they were prepared to invest in Elton any further. "My father and I looked at each other," Steve remembers, "and said, 'Look, either this guy is going to make it or he isn't. It's our last shot.' So we agreed to do everything we could do on this project. I remember it was going to cost five thousand pounds [twelve thousand dollars] and we went ahead with it."

Elton was fascinated by America—its movies, music and wide open spaces. But he was also weary. "I wanted to go to America," says Elton, "but I didn't think that the time was right when the *Elton*

John album came out. Dee Murray, Nigel Olsson and myself were earning a reputation as a trio, and I thought it was too soon."

As a measure of just how low Elton's expectations were for the impending trip to America, he confesses, "I went because I thought I could buy some records. . . . I thought it was going to be a joke, a complete hype and disaster."

Yet off he went, a Rocket Man in search of a launchpad which he never expected to find there. Across the Atlantic Uni's Russ Regan had hired a stunt-conscious publicist in Los Angeles by the name of Norman Winter. It was Regan's belief that Winter was the man to orchestrate Elton's arrival.

He was right. Winter put on a show of shows that would rival Elton's own future flamboyance. As Elton's plane touched down at the Los Angeles International Airport, his worst fears about hype were about to unfold before his weary eyes. The trio were met by a London-style double-decker bus. "We'd flown to Los Angeles thirteen hours over the pole in this enormous jet," Elton recalls, "and we arrived to find this bloody great bus with 'Elton Has Arrived' plastered on the side."

Prior to Elton's arrival, Winter had already begun hyping him. *Rolling Stone* writer David Felton had been lured to the publicist's office on the pretense of another interview, but Norm, as he is affectionately known in the music business, only wanted to talk about this new artist from England. "Hey, there's something you gotta hear," Winter said, "This guy's name is Elton John. We just signed him. I wouldn't try to hype you. I just want your opinion. Isn't he unbelievable?"

The record Norm played him was "Your Song," and the journalist was impressed, "It did sound pretty good," Felton later wrote. The next time he popped by Winter's office, on the actual day of Elton's arrival, to pick up tickets for the Troubadour concert, he got more hype. "Hey, did you hear about the bus?" Norm effused. "I picked him up at the airport. The guy's beautiful, man. He just can't believe this is all happening to him. Anyway, get this—we picked him up in an authentic English bus. It just blew his mind. He really dug it." Actually, as it turned out, Elton, embarrassed by this ostentatious welcome, was crouching under a seat.

Norm Winter was clearly working hard on behalf of his latest British import. Local radio stations were playing cuts from the *Elton John* album, until now an underground discovery, while record stores displayed it prominently. The hyperbolic Winter was uncharacteristically mum, though, on another subject—namely, ticket sales of Elton's Troubadour debut. "Nobody wanted to come," he later admitted. "Nobody had ever heard of Elton John, but we did everything we could to get them there because we thought we had a star."

Winter was relentless, even posting himself at the front door of the Troubadour to hand out press kits. The audience that Tuesday night, August 25, 1970, consisted of the Uni team like himself, and the music press, seated around wood-and-wicker tables inside the sparse room with white stucco walls.

There were also many influential musicians in the crowd. Dave Crosby and Graham Nash elbowed with one of the Everly Brothers while Quincy Jones sat up front. Elton's future manager, John Reid, then Tamla-Motown's man in the United Kingdom, was also in the crowd. In all, about three hundred people turned out for Elton's debut.

Publicist Winter had bombarded these celebrities with letters of invitation, follow-up telegrams and phone calls. But the big draw was that American singer-songwriter Neil Diamond, with hits such as "Sweet Caroline" and "Solitary Man" and "I'm a Believer" (recorded by the Monkees), was going to introduce Elton John to the Troubadour audience. "Nobody out there knew Elton," Norm explains, "so they came to see who was this guy that Neil Diamond was introducing."

Because of the moody *Elton John* album cover, with Elton's half-lit face drifting in darkness, and the sentimental songs, the audience was expecting a Randy Newman-type performer on stage. Others, like the *Los Angeles Times* music critic, Robert Hilburn, thought the album recalled both the delicate and sensitive qualities of José Feliciano and the high energy of the Rolling Stones.

What they got instead was Elton John in a yellow jumpsuit and horn-rimmed sunglasses, just being himself, or, as he would later put it, "This was me coming out." The audience roared its approval at his originality and versatility as he displayed his rich bag of assorted styles: country blues ("No Shoe Strings on Louise"), gospel ("Border Song"), a pop ballad ("Your Song") and frenzied rock ("Take Me to the Pilot"). The audience gasped, and applauded each number. Odetta, the folksinger, got up and danced in the last row.

Elton almost blew the last number because he was so nervous with Leon Russell, supreme among his many pop idols, watching from the front row. Kicking over the piano seat in a display of Little Richard and Jerry Lee Lewis antics, Elton performed "Burn Down the Mission," with its relentless rhythmic buildup, sounding at the beginning like a country stroll and ending like a hell-bent revival meeting. The audience—singing, clapping and stomping—gave Elton two standing ovations. Elton, who had already amazed them by what he had just done on stage, leapt on top of the piano in celebration.

"Rejoice. Rock music has a new star," critic Robert Hilburn proclaimed in the August 27, 1970, *Los Angeles Times*. "He's Elton John . . . whose U.S. debut was in almost every way magnificent . . . staggeringly original." And *Rolling Stone*'s David Felton said of Elton's Troubadour debut, "One of the great opening nights in Los Angeles rock."

The following morning at the Hyatt House there were no tantrums and nobody was pushed into the swimming pool. Instead, the newly heralded pop sensation of the seventies was exhilarated by the audience reception. "They clapped *at the start*," Elton told one reporter. "I couldn't fucking believe it. That never happens in England. People over here are ridiculous."

Otherwise, Elton was more subdued, "Friendly, but almost shy, almost fragile," said one reporter among the many who converged on the hotel for post-Troubadour interviews. On the subject of Norm Winter, Elton was quite coy. "Actually, he's worked bloody hard— but that bus, I found that extremely embarrassing. Everyone was sort of getting into a crouch and trying to hide below the windows. I don't know, it seemed a cheap trick. I couldn't believe it. I didn't think it was happening. I mean, I'm a great lover of things that are done with taste, and double-decker buses don't qualify."

Generally, his responses were both measured and modest. "I don't want the big-star bit," he said. "I can't bear that bit. What I want is to just do a few gigs a week and really just get away from everything and just write and people say, 'Oh, Elton John, he writes good music.'"

It is hard to believe, though, that Elton really meant one word of anything he was saying then. After all, at twenty-three he had worked hard to arrive at this juncture, and he loved to be the center of attention. "It was all a bit of a blur," says guitarist Dee Murray.

According to drummer Olsson, "We were all flabbergasted. We knew something really big had happened, but we couldn't believe it." During the week, they all visited Disneyland, in nearby Anaheim, where Elton treated himself to a pair of Mickey Mouse ears.

The afternoon following Elton's Troubadour debut, Leon Russell invited Elton to jam with him at his Hollywood house. Elton felt deeply honored because Russell was the superhero who had led the way for him. Though the wild antics of Little Richard and Jerry Lee Lewis first established the piano's place on both stage and vinyl, it was Russell's boogie-woogie style that helped restore the piano's place as a prominent rock instrument in the late sixties. He had played piano with Mad Dogs and Englishmen, Joe Cocker's band. After seeing Elton at the Troubadour, Russell immediately phoned Bill Graham, requesting that the rock promoter pair him with Elton at Graham's Fillmore East in New York.

Despite the haze of unreality and euphoria that surrounded Elton at this moment, he still managed to focus on Ray Williams's trip to Palm Springs the previous weekend. His anger was unabated, and he began to think now about a new manager, possibly John Reid, a twenty-year-old Scotsman who was the U.K. manager of Tamla-Motown. Elton had often shown up at Reid's London office to wangle free samples of the Detroit-based company's latest releases. A friendship had blossomed, and when Elton made his Troubadour debut, he thought it very important that Reid be in the audience to support him.

Elton would later spend a few days with Reid in San Francisco when he played the Troubadour Club in that city. "I knew there was something weird happening," Williams reflected later, "and I found out afterward that Elton had spent time up there around Reid. So that was the beginning of their friendship. We used to call Reid 'Pamela Motown.' " The play on Tamla-Motown was an apparent reference to Reid's dubious sexuality.

Of his new status as "the pop sensation of the seventies," Elton would say, "It was the perfect instance of being at the right place at the right time. . . . I really became Elton John at the Troubadour Club. After that there was no holding me back." The tour seemed to smooth Elton's final parting with his former self, Reg Dwight,

And so Elton John, attended by standing ovations and rave reviews, moved on to San Francisco to play the Troubadour there. His triumph was not repeated, but it really did not matter, because Los Angeles was the important gig. And thanks to Robert Hilburn's review in the *Los Angeles Times*, Elton John was now a name known throughout much of the West Coast. Songwriter Roger Greenaway, who had attended the Troubadour show and believed in Elton when he was still Reg, even heard about it en route to the Los Angeles airport. On his car radio a local DJ proclaimed, "A new rock-'n'-roll messiah, Elton John, has come to town."

Executives at MCA, the parent company of Elton's label, were ecstatic about the Hilburn review and felt they should jump on it. "They couldn't believe their luck," Steve James recalls. "But they still weren't entirely happy with Elton at this stage. They had a lot of criticism about his personality and looks."

Immediately after his California gigs, Elton gave a special lunch-hour performance for MCA executives at the Playboy Club in New York City. An abbreviated version of his Troubadour performance, it was a disaster from Elton's point of view. He was contemptuous of the venue and the corporate aura, but he managed to be be gracious, paying special thanks to Norm Winter for the publicity he had garnered on his behalf. Despite Elton's personal reservations about the Playboy Club appearance, the MCA executives were very pleased. Still, they remained cautious about whether Elton could duplicate his Troubadour success.

They decided to test his appeal elsewhere, booking Elton into Philadelphia's Electric Factory a few days later. Apparently the industry buzz about the "new rock-'n'-roll messiah" and the "pop sensation of the seventies" had not caught up with the public there. The *Elton John* album had sold only about ten thousand copies in Philadelphia. It had been released in July and now it was already September. While MCA was promoting Elton as rock's new superman, the albums were not moving out of the racks.

The executives were worried, and they told Elton a few hours before he was set to go on at the Electric Factory. Elton did not appear to share their concern. "Don't worry," he said. "Tonight I'm going to burn the city of Philadelphia down. Look out!"

Elton lived up to his promise. Later that night three thousand kids at Philadelphia's Electric Circus stood up and cheered him wildly after a thirty-minute rendition of the tub-thumping "Burn Down the Mission" from his forthcoming album, *Tumbleweed Connection*.

Standing on his piano, he led the crowd in rhythmic clapping and then, leaping on and off the piano, turned his performance into an acrobatic event as well. One MCA executive remembers: "The reaction in that room was like a 6.9 earthquake in Los Angeles." The next day the *Elton John* album sold out in the Philadelphia area.

As a result, when Elton finally boarded his plane for the return flight to Britain, he was a far more confident man than when he arrived. But he was also still festering inside over Ray Williams. Once back home, he vowed to persevere, just as he had with his music, in his ambition to dump the man who had discovered him.

As Ray Williams disembarked from the plane in London, he seemed to have every reason to be pleased with himself. He was elated by Elton's triumphant reception in America. To Ray Williams's thinking, theirs was a friendship that would survive any bumps, present or future, along the way. After all, Elton was the godfather to Williams's baby daughter.

Elton was clearly of a different mind. Fresh off the plane, he stormed into Dick James's office and demanded that Ray Williams be fired immediately. As Steve James remembers, "My father asked him, 'Are you sure?' and Elton answered, 'Yes!' "

It was a bizarre request coming on the heels of his triumph at the Troubadour. But now Tamla-Motown's John Reid was apparently in the picture—and there would be a lot of odd commands from Elton John in the future.

About a week after their return, in mid-September 1970, Ray sensed from Elton's cool demeanor that things were not going to work out between them. At Williams's invitation the two men had lunch. According to Williams, Elton agreed to honor their management contract for nine more months, until the beginning of May 1971, guaranteeing that Williams would receive his commission until then.

Williams then began planning Elton's second U.S. tour. But at every turn he was stymied by Dick James. "He was sending me memos saying that he wanted to handle everything himself," Williams recalls, "and asking me to refrain from making any contacts without his prior approval."

On Elton's second U.S. tour, two months later, in November of 1970, Ray Williams was not part of the entourage. Back in London, meanwhile, Dick James demanded that Williams sign an agreement renouncing any and all claims on Elton John and his earnings. Williams argued that he had an arrangement with Elton to stay on until the spring. At that point James offered him money to leave. Williams refused.

At a further meeting shortly afterward, James made a final offer, which would end up being about fifteen hundred pounds (three thousand five hundred dollars). With a wife and baby daughter to support and no financial resources with which to sue, Williams felt he had to sign the paper. But before doing so, hurt and confused by what he considered to be shabby treatment, he endeavored to contact Elton in America.

But the man he had discovered was no longer taking his calls. Ray says, "I could never get past Steve Brown, Dick James's man, who never put me through to Elton." Having no alternative, he took the money. "I didn't even get a gold disc," he laments. "They all ended up with John Reid."

"Ray always thought it was my father who fired him," says Steve James, "but my father was only carrying out Elton's request." And so the man who had once felt sorry for Reg Dwight and helped him when no one else was interested was now out of work. Ray Williams would not be Elton's only victim: In years to follow Dick James would be another name on the superstar's casualty list.

7

Rock Music's New Messiah

On a windy November day in New York in 1970, as he and Bernie walked along St. Mark's Place to the Fillmore East for a rehearsal, Elton had a premonition. He blurted out: "I think you'd better savor your anonymity now," he told his songwriting partner. "It'll be gone soon enough."

He was right. A gig at the Fillmore East, a funky Old World music theater with velvet seats and superb acoustics, was the apotheosis of Elton's dreams. "If you don't make it at the Fillmore, no matter what the audience is like, you won't make it anywhere," said Elton at the time. "It has the best lighting, the best sound, the best P.A. system. Bill Graham's always been on my side, and I'll work my guts off for Bill Graham."

And so, when Fillmore proprietor Graham, the king of the rock-'n'-roll extravaganza, announced Elton John on stage, Elton knew that he had come an enormous distance in his career. Only three months had passed since his Troubadour concert in Los Angeles, and now he was back in America playing the ultimate insider's showcase and premier New York rock venue.

"Ladies and gentlemen, from England . . ." Bill Graham announced from the corner of the stage. "Dee Murray on bass, Nigel Olsson on drums and Elton John . . ." The roar of the audience drowned out "on piano" from Graham's introduction. Bill Graham had shown great faith in Elton. "I remember I hadn't heard anything like him," Graham recalled. "Here was a guy who could do up-tempo stuff and lovely melodies and ballads. As long as he's alive he's going to make it. He is one of those escapist entertainers. You know when you see Elton you are going to see wonderful entertainment."

Elton's performances at the Fillmore over two nights were sold out in advance. His second U.S. visit was unprecedented in its strenuous touring schedule. In the Los Angeles area alone he gave five auditorium concerts, in San Bernardino, Riverside, Anaheim, and Santa Monica, and at U.C.L.A. In Minneapolis he filled the Tyrone Guthrie Theater. The reception was overwhelming everywhere: In Chicago he had to be hoisted by rope in the air by police and whisked through the crowds.

His *Elton John* album, released the previous July in the United States, had now reached Billboard's Top 25 chart and the second album, *Tumbleweed Connection*, heavily influenced by American country and blues, was expected to be a hit upon its release in January of 1971.

Back in England, meanwhile, *Tumbleweed Connection* had already come out, at the end of October 1970, and received favorable reviews in the press. The record was really an expression of Bernie's love of Americana and the American West, but, remarkably, it had been written and recorded in early 1970, before Bernie or Elton had ever set foot in the United States. Says Bernie, "It was totally influenced by the Band's album *Music From Big Pink* and Robbie Robertson's songs." Elton was enormously pleased with the album. "I don't think there's any song on there that didn't melodically fit the lyric," he says.

One of the songs on the album was "Amoreena," an up-tempo ballad about a man yearning for the puppy love of a young girl who was now far away from the farm. It was dedicated to Ray Williams's daughter by her godfather, Elton.

Elton was fast becoming an exuberant act, leaping onto his piano, flipping, flopping and gyrating as his fingers sprinted across the keyboard. The combination of his unusual songs, the newness of his sound and his dynamic stage act made Elton John the first rock superstar of the seventies. With each live performance he became more confident, adding flamboyance and flash to his act. Jumpsuits, hats and glasses in every rainbow color were becoming Elton John's trademark.

At the Santa Monica Civic Auditorium, Elton wore a Jagger top hat, cape and purple jumpsuit. For a finale he wove a rambunctious rock-'n'-roll medley into the gospel-shouter "Burn Down the Mission." Kicking back his piano stool, he stripped off his jumpsuit and did a series of giant bunny kicks in purple panty hose. Elton's dramatic delivery of "Burn Down the Mission" was a signature piece in his concerts on this tour.

Yet he remained socially ill at ease. At a backstage party after the show, while record company executives and journalists sipped champagne and feasted on catered food, Elton faded into his old shy self, Reg Dwight. He stood in a corner, alone and silent, with a buzz of chatter filling the space around him. "Elton has always been an introvert," Steve James remarks. "The only time he's been an extrovert is when he's gone on stage."

But on that November night up on the Fillmore stage in New York, Elton was once again the consummate performer, showing off a natural stage presence with timing worthy of a veteran stand-up comic. His costumes, like his songs, defied categorization. The songs were from both *Elton John* and *Tumbleweed Connection*.

At one of four Fillmore appearances over two nights he made a grand entrance in a floor-length cape and then peeled down to a star-patterned T-shirt, slacks and a Porky Pig button that lighted up. He also wore a purple hat, a sequined bow tie, a yellow and green and red jumpsuit just below the knees and what could best be described as white Li'l Abner shoes with wings.

Grimacing, gritting his teeth and singing in swallowed tight throat tones, Elton sang the dirgelike "Sixty Years On" with Dee Murray turning up his bass and Nigel Olsson behind a double-barreled kit of thirteen drums, cannonading a melody of his own. Elton, meanwhile, played some delicate solos on the highest octaves of the piano. "Who will walk me down to church when I'm sixty years on?" Elton sang, pausing for dramatic effect after each doomsday interlude. He also performed the gospel-inflected "Border Song" of hope and justice ("Holy Moses let us live in peace / Let us strive to make all hatred cease") and his gift to his fans, the ballad "Your Song," during the two-hour-long concert.

Again he performed some acrobatics to "Burn Down the Mission," climbing on the Steinway and leading the more than two thousand listeners in rhythmic applause. He spun on his piano seat and hopscotched across the stage and pranced on the piano in his winged white shoes and shook hands with the audience surging toward the stage.

But it was not the overwhelming reaction from crowds as he crisscrossed America on tour that certified to Elton that he had arrived at the center of the rock universe. His most important moment of recognition came after the third show at the Fillmore, when a nebbishly rumpled man in a black raincoat and an umbrella appeared outside his dressing room door.

That man was Bob Dylan, a music icon for Elton and Bernie. As Dylan walked in, uninvited, to congratulate them, the dream that had begun three thousand miles away in England came true, for praise from Dylan was almost like a papal blessing. In Dylan's presence the two men stood quivering, awestruck. Their anointment by Dylan as stars produced a headline on the front page of *Melody Maker*. It proclaimed, "Dylan Digs Elton." Until then Elton, caught up in the swirling rush of events, had been unable to fully comprehend what was happening. As he remembers, "We were all too close, too involved, too afraid, still, that it wasn't going to work."

Elton had had a unique warm-up for his Fillmore appearance. Three days earlier he had done a live set for WABC Radio in New York. Aware that Elton would be in town for the Fillmore, disc jockey Dave Herman had approached Steven Brown about getting Elton into the studio. Remembers Herman: "They loved the idea of all that radio exposure and a live concert." So did the radio station. The recording industry was moribund in New York: Everyone had moved to Los Angeles. Elton John, they felt, could drum up excitement here. The broadcast was recorded at the A&R studio in the West Forties in Manhattan.

Elton lived up to their expectations. As 120 fans in their late teens and early twenties sat on the studio floor with drinks and snacks, Elton and Murray and Olsson jammed for an hour and a half—their first live broadcast. Remembers deejay Herman: "It was magical, electrifying. There was blood on the keyboard from the twenty-minute rave-up he did at the end." Thanking the crowd, Elton, his fingers bleeding, said, "Keep smiling—that's the most important thing."

After the performance Elton and his band asked to go back to the station to listen to the tape. "It was their first opportunity to actually sit down and listen to the entire performance," Herman recalls, "and they were very excited hearing it played back."

Elton himself had plenty of reason to smile. He was touted by Herman, among others, as the start of a new generation of musicians. The sixties were dead. The epitaph to that era was written at the rock festival at California's Altamont Speedway in San Francisco in December of 1969, when a fan was stabbed to death while the Rolling Stones played. By the fall of 1970, as Elton toured America, Jimi Hendrix and Janis Joplin were already dead of drug overdoses; and a few months later, in July 1971, Jim Morrison collapsed and died, either from drugs or drink or both. Each of them was only twenty-seven. Young people were now less interested in rock as a stoned-out communal experience and more excited by what an individual artist might have to say. The Beatles had split up, and the fretful Jefferson Airplane were reinventing themselves. Out went the superbands of the sixties. The search was on for a seventies superhero with a low-keyed, protest-free approach to life.

That person, it seemed, would be a tousle-haired Englishman named Elton John, who, at twenty-three, eschewed drugs, cigarettes and serious drinking. Even his increasingly outré outfits seemed harmless, like gimmicks bought from a theatrical warehouse or suburban party store. Unlike other rock stars, who wore undershirts and chewed gum on stage, his look was neither defiant nor obscene.

Elton John's music caught the first wave of pop nostalgia in 1970. Brought up on almost two decades of music, from Elvis and Jerry Lee Lewis to the Beatles and the Rolling Stones, Elton drew from a grab bag of styles that included rock, pop, gospel and soul. To these rich reserves he brought the technique of a classically trained pianist and, from his pub days, the gusto of a saloon player. From Bernie Taupin came story lines that were both personal and poetic. There was no lead guitarist driving the music and drowning out the lyrics. The piano-led trio with Nigel Olsson on drums and Dee Murray on bass was altogether unique.

And so as 1970 came to a close and Ray Williams looked for work, Elton was well along on his Yellow Brick Road to fame. He was voted top male vocalist in the 1970 *Record World* magazine poll, and he and Bernie were celebrated as best composers at the New York-based International Music Critics Awards.

The Rocket Man had finally conquered both coasts of America. Yet while he was happy with his stage act, Elton still wanted to make more changes behind the scenes. Having successfully disposed of manager Ray Williams, he believed it was time to add a new person to his entourage.

8

Musical Chairs

"I want John Reid to manage me," Elton told Dick James in early 1971, after his second American tour. The music publisher was not surprised. Reid had seldom been out of Elton's sight since the Troubadour concert, and he had even moved into an apartment with Elton in the West End of London. Having successfully disposed of Ray Williams, Elton clearly needed someone to look after him, and feeling closest to Reid at the time, he was adamant about getting Dick to hire him.

Dick James and his son Steve were naturally concerned. They had developed Elton as a songwriter and singer, and by their own accounting had invested heavily in him. They felt that Reid would eventually steal him away. "Elton and John Reid were obviously having a relationship," says Steve James, "and when Elton brought John Reid in, I didn't take to him much. I felt that he was only out for himself and that we weren't going to get any loyalty from him."

In recent days they had observed a change in Elton's personality. "He would come into the office and start being confrontational," remembers Steve James. "It could be about anything. If we said 'black,' he'd say 'white.' Someone was obviously churning up his mind." They suspected it was Reid.

Elton had seemed to pull away in recent weeks from Dick James, whose personal, as well as professional, advice he had so often sought. "My father was aware that Elton was having sexual problems," says Steve James, "though he never breached Elton's confidence by telling me any of the details—and certainly not at that time. What my father tried to point out was that there was nothing particularly wrong with Elton, and if he wasn't attracted to or could not perform with a girl, he probably had not met the right one." Dick had also helped Elton obtain the apartment he shared with John Reid by acting as guarantor with the landlord.

Dick James had to make a decision. Elton wanted a new manager, and Reid, in his capacity as head of U.K. Tamla-Motown, certainly knew the music business. At twenty-one, he was also energetic and enthusiastic. Though Reid would probably not be loyal to DJM, Dick James reasoned, at least he would have Elton's interests uppermost in his mind on account of their close relationship. As Dick remarked to his son, "Who else can we rely on to get Elton out of bed in the morning than the guy he's in bed *with*?" James gave up twenty percent of Elton John to Reid and, unlike his predecessor Ray Williams, Reid was also paid a yearly salary of four thousand pounds (ninety-six hundred dollars). Further, when DJM's management contract expired, in March 1973, Reid would manage Elton exclusively. Reid arrived at DJM in August 1971—and from day one he lived up to the Jameses' suspicions of his disloyalty.

The previous September 1970, DJM had used its option to renew the publishing agreement, then nearing expiration. Out of several options offered to them, Elton and Bernie accepted a three-year term and royalty rise from fifty percent to sixty. Elton gratefully accepted the increase, which he viewed as a goodwill gesture from Dick James. An associate of Dick James had recommended a lawyer for Elton and Bernie to work out the details of his contracts with DJM. Reid would devote the next few years to unraveling and discrediting them.

Of particular concern was James's holding of the copyright to Elton and Bernie's work for the rest of their lives and for the fifty years after their deaths. Through their lawyer, Elton and Bernie asked if James would permit the copyrights to revert to them. James rejected this outright. To do so, he said, would be tantamount to functioning as a mere agent. Apparently he had learned a bitter lesson from his experience with the Beatles: James only owned the copyrights to two of their early songs, "Please Please Me" and "Ask Me Why."

Another area of contention concerned foreign royalties, as Elton became more popular around the world. The Jameses had set up an elaborate network of subsidiaries. Some, like DJM USA and those in Australia and France, were wholly owned by them. DJM also controlled territories which local publishers managed for a fee. There were also third-party publishers with varying royalty scales.

To mitigate Elton and Bernie's income tax burdens (now at Britain's whopping eighty-three percent maximum rate) a mazelike plan was devised to divide domestic and overseas earnings and then funnel these earnings through companies with which Bernie and Elton had "employment contracts." Unknown to the Jameses, as part of his "on-the-job training," Reid began trying to sniff out irregularities in royalty payments to Elton; he was even seen by one employee photocopying documents.

John Reid's launch in the music business had been like Elton's climb up the charts, a combination of dedication and hard work. Born September 9, 1949, in Paisley, a low-income town near Glasgow, Scotland, he was the second son of a welder and a housewife. At ten, Reid moved with his family to New Zealand, where his father, John, had been sent to work by an engineering company. Two years later, Reid and the family returned to Scotland because his mother, Betty, was homesick.

There he was enrolled in St. Mirin's School, where the slightly built lad became a model student. His piercing eyes projected a fierce intelligence and gave him a hawklike appearance. Even back then he was enterprising, managing two other pupils at the school as a potential singing act. When the two boys were beaten up by a local gang, Reid jumped into the fight and ended up being pummeled as well. Certainly it was not the last time he would be involved in a physical fight: In later years some people even called him the Boxer on account of his violent outbursts.

Inspired by his voyages to and from New Zealand, young Reid initially decided on a career in marine engineering. But after two years, and fired up by the rock music of the day, he quit college at seventeen and made his way south to London. There he worked as a salesman at Austin Reed, an elegant men's clothing store, while he looked for a job in the music business.

A few weeks later his break came, when Ardmore and Beechwood, a small publishing subsidiary of EMI, hired him as a record plugger. One of their songwriter-artists was Neil Diamond, the American star who later introduced Elton at the Troubadour. Swiftly, Reid climbed the corporate ladder at EMI, and within two years was promoted to label manager for their franchise, Tamla-Motown, in Britain. It was in this capacity that he had first met Reg Dwight, who kept turning up at his office for free samples of the latest Motown releases.

A friendship grew between the two, though initially no one suspected anything out of the ordinary. Reid, in his conservative pin-stripe suits, went out of his way to project a straight businessman's image. Elton, the increasingly bizarre dresser, could be forgiven. He was, after all, a rock star, and it was assumed that he had his coterie of females.

After Elton's Troubadour debut in Los Angeles, he wanted to tell Reid of his success. Elton's manager-to-be was in San Francisco for a Motown convention and caught his act there. By this time Reid was well aware that Elton's talent was unique, and he believed strongly in him. Together they had an amazing journey to make. Reid, a man of fierce ambition and a short fuse, would guard Elton in future years like a high-strung terrier. Never before had the saying "opposites attract" been so true. Elton, in all his rock-'n'-roll splendor, and John Reid, the straight businessman, were an unlikely combination. But, oh, what a couple they would make.

Shortly they moved into an apartment together close to Marble Arch in London. It seemed logical that there would be little time for girls, just time to build careers and futures inseparably linked.

By April 1971, Elton's sound track for a film called *Friends* had come out, along with the live recording *17.11.70*, made from his New York radio concert back in November. *Friends*, an inane movie about two teenagers who run away from home, live together and have a baby, had been recorded before Elton was internationally known. It was the last project in which Ray Williams was involved as Elton's manager. The thinking behind the movie sound track was that it was a good way to expose Elton to a larger audience outside the United Kingdom.

The plan backfired, and Elton felt overexposed and exploited. The

Friends album was promoted more as an Elton John album than a sound track for a movie. As Elton recalls bitterly, "It was harrowing work, which we did in four weeks. The album should have been released to coincide with the movie, but the American company [Paramount] put it out earlier to cash in on my name. We were so brokenhearted when we saw the sleeve, though. We'd always been in charge of the artwork, but then Paramount said, 'Don't worry, we'll come up with a great sleeve.' And they came up with dross. I mean it was hideous."

Signs of Elton's perfectionism were beginning to show. Disappointed also with the live album, in this instance he blamed the bootleggers who had made unauthorized recordings during the performance and had indirectly forced its release earlier than Elton wanted.

"I agree that the live album is not very good," Elton admitted to critics, "but I think it's valid despite the fact that its sales were a disaster. It did mean that I had four albums in the American Top Thirty at the same time—something which had not been done since the Beatles." Even *Empty Sky* had outsold the live broadcast album in Britain; in America it sold only 325,000 copies, compared with over two million for *Elton John* and *Tumbleweed Connection*.

Neither album was considered by critics to be the appropriate follow-up to *Tumbleweed*, which Tom Zito of the *Washington Post* described as being "right out of the so-called new romanticism; love songs, songs about old soldiers and inherited guns. Yet beneath all this is a real feeling for the universal."

Earlier in the year, in January of 1971, Elton made his first Continental splash at the annual MIDEM pop festival in the south of France. DJM thought that this was the place to launch him in Europe and hopefully duplicate his dizzying success in America. A black-tie event, MIDEM was attended by the international movers and shakers in the industry and broadcast live throughout Europe. Six full months of planning and negotiation had gone into Elton's appearance there. Radio air time had been blocked out for the first of two shows, and the broadcast could not extend beyond the allotted time. So it was more than worrying to Elton that, with only one hour of airtime left, Eric Burdon and his band War went on . . . and . . . on . . . and on.

Elton never got airplay that night for his songs, and his curses were furious. "Eric Burdon, you're a fuck-up!" Elton screamed from off-stage, where he, Cat Stevens and Richie Havens were waiting their turn. "Get off the stage."

Remembers Richie Havens: "Elton and I had been backstage talking about English clubs like the Speakeasy. We were all excited about the festival until Eric Burdon and War went on . . . ten minutes, fifteen minutes, twenty, thirty. . . . It went from worse to worst. Elton was pacing offstage. He was not only fuming, but screaming some nasty curses that were definitely going out across the radio. He was mad because it wasn't fair, and then he refused to go on. So did Cat Stevens. It started to get really crazy backstage. My roadie, this seventeen-year-old kid, said to them, 'Hey, wait a minute, you're all artists, you're going on.' Cat Stevens, Elton and I agreed to take less time and did about four songs each." Though they were robbed by Eric Burdon of airplay, they at least honored their professional responsibilities.

Havens agreed to let Elton go on before him, and Elton thanked him for his generosity and suggested that Havens close the show with his signature song, "Freedom." The audience, by now aware of how Eric Burdon had hogged all the time, jammed the hall and gave Elton a standing ovation before he had even sung a note. Elton then went on to give them one of the most inspired and emotional sets of his life. Though Elton did not get airplay for his set, the night was still a triumph. The audience was on its feet singing along with every number.

On the stage at MIDEM, Elton had once again demonstrated his confidence as a showman. But privately, he was still shy, reserved Reg. The next day, as Elton walked along the Croisette in Cannes, Elton saw his former boss from Mills Music, Cyril Gee, in a restaurant café with his wife and a few other people. Tentatively, he approached Gee, who remembers, "He introduced me as his first boss to everyone at my table. But he still called me 'sir,' not that I insisted on that. Elton wasn't quite sure whether to call me 'sir,' 'Mr. Gee' or 'Cyril.' He agonized for a second and then apparently decided on 'sir,' which was for him the most comfortable."

For much of 1971, Elton toured relentlessly, starting with performances in Scandinavia. In the United States and Canada he gave performances in fifty-five cities, including two nights at New York's Carnegie Hall. That earned him a rave review in the *New York Times*.

In what was described as "the best-produced rock concert there in a long time," Elton soloed at the piano for the first half with numbers like "Your Song," "Skyline Pigeon" and, from *Tumbleweed Connection*, "Talking Old Soldiers," a song that likened growing old to rusty flowers. He felt these songs were not suited to a full rock treatment. For the second half, joined by his band, he sang "Country Comfort," about the pleasures of farm life; the hard-rocking "Honky Tonk Women" by the Rolling Stones; and "The King Must Die," among other hits.

Drummer Nigel Olsson also got a rave. A critic noted, "Mr. Olsson's drums were amplified perfectly, and he gave a performance that was often beyond breathtaking." Remembers Lionel Conway, who had been an early believer in Elton at DJM and later left to join Island Records: "Nigel lived with my wife and me at our home for the first five years he was with Elton. He never knew where he stood with Elton. He could be fired and reinstated by Elton from one day to the next. A bad performance could do it . . . 'You're fired.' " For the moment, it seemed, he was in Elton's good graces.

Often the concert venues were within driving distance, and Elton and the band took turns at the wheel. "We were just like a little family," remembers bass player Dee Murray, "traveling around together in a station wagon. Usually we drove to smaller venues like gymnasiums and colleges in the Midwest. It was great. We were young, we were playing wonderful music together and we were very excited."

He adds: "John Reid was the one factor that was always a little thorn to everybody, but I think most managers are. He kind of controlled stuff."

They also toured Japan and Australia that year. "In Australia they thought we were a bunch of freaks," Murray remembers. "They'd stare and say things like, 'What's this, a traveling circus?' at airports. Of course, Elton's hair was orange then, with green dye behind his ears. He has always been outrageous. Ever since the Troubadour he got his confidence up."

But once back in London at his flat at 384 The Water Garden, which he shared with John Reid and thirty pairs of boots, Elton loved to relax in front of the television catching up on the latest soccer scores. His fondness for the game had not abated. And all the while Elton continued to build his record collection. In America, his first stop upon arriving in Los Angeles or New York was a record store, where he often filled a whole shopping cart with the latest releases. By now the collection Elton had started as a young boy back in Pinner had grown to five thousand albums, twenty-five hundred 45's, a hundred EPs (extended plays), sixty 78's, five hundred eight-track cartridges and three hundred cassettes.

Otherwise, in the privacy of his own home there were few signs of the flamboyance that was now so apparent to his fans when he appeared on stage. Instead, here in his luxury flat, domesticity was part of his repertoire. At home Elton enjoyed cleaning up, vacuuming, polishing furniture, even ironing. As he told one reporter at the time, "I enjoy ironing to take my mind off things."

In many ways Reg Dwight still lived inside Elton John. Rather than party the night away at a club or disco like many of his fellow performers, Elton was still happier in the company of one or two friends.

"I'm not on any rock-star circuit," he said at the time. "I don't mix much, and I'm not involved in any of these supposedly hip things. I don't do drugs, I don't even smoke, and I'm giving up alcohol. I don't want to behave like a star or be thought of as a star to my audiences. I want to be more like the guy who lives next door."

But this was no ordinary guy. Elton was fast becoming a one-man industry, and the pressure was causing him to behave erratically. By November 1971, DJM had released Elton's sixth album in less than two years. It was called *Madman Across the Water*. Steve James remembers: "We had a real slanging match over one of the tracks which we thought had somehow lost its way and could have been better. We wanted Elton to rerecord it. He was furious and started yelling, 'I know what I'm doing. Why are you telling me this?' He stormed out and didn't come back for a week."

John Reid, on James's orders, persuaded Elton to do the track over. About a week later Elton showed up at the office and, according to Steve James, "sheepishly asked me if my father was still mad at him. I told Elton, 'Why not go and knock on his door and have a cup of tea,' which he did. And all of a sudden out of his pocket Elton produced a cassette of the rerecorded track and said, 'Tell me what you think.' "

Dealing with Elton's by now famous moods often proved difficult for Steve James, who was about the same age: "Elton was a perfectionist who sometimes found it hard to take criticism that he could so easily give other people."

Madman was not well received by the music press, and its sales were disappointing. Elton's explanation was that American singer-songwriters Carole King and James Taylor, who appealed to a similar audience, had cornered some of his market. Carole King's *Tapestry* album had stayed at Number One on the U.S. charts for fifteen weeks, and James Taylor's rendition of "You've Got a Friend," written by King, also landed there.

Madman also showed just how busy Elton and Bernie's schedule had become. When they went into the studio to record the album, instead of the customary twenty to twenty-five tunes to choose from, they had only eight. This time there had been no leeway for change.

Still, the LP spawned two singles, "Levon" and "Tiny Dancer," the latter a tribute to Bernie's new wife (and Elton's sometimes seamstress). Bernie had met Maxine the year before during the infamous weekend in Palm Springs that had spelled the beginning of the end of Ray Williams's association with Elton. At the wedding in early 1971 in Bernie's hometown of Market Rasen in Lincolnshire, Elton served as best man and a contingent of DJM staffers arrived by train for the ceremony.

Dick James had bought his star lyricist a silver Mini. But as Bernie had never learned to drive, Maxine, an earthy blonde with California Valley Girl looks and the daughter of a successful inventor, took the wheel. The couple honeymooned in Hawaii and then traveled together through America, visiting Civil War battlefields that fascinated Bernie, before settling into a rural, albeit quaint, life in Lincolnshire.

All of *Madman* had been written during Elton and Bernie's hectic touring. One track, "Holiday Inn," was a witty takeoff: "You ain't seen nothing until you been in a motel, baby, like the Holiday Inn."

To those who dismissed the album's lyrics as too self-involved and childish, Elton shot back, "People still tend to forget that Bernie's not even twenty-one yet." Elton, twenty-four, hardly displayed maturity himself. The relative slump in sales already had him giving interviews about retiring.

Still, it had been a remarkably prolific year for Elton. He was the subject of cover stories, including one in *Rolling Stone*, and he also made television appearances, including one on "The Andy Williams Show." While Elton's Troubadour tour had lost ten thousand dollars, one month later the second U.S. tour netted $65,666. By the end of 1971 Elton was on his way to the million-dollar mark.

In June 1971, James had made a deal for Elton, whose career was now flourishing in America, with MCA Records for five years. Elton would get a $1 million advance and another million the following May. Under the agreement Elton would receive a fifteen percent royalty on the retail price of each record sold. It also called for DJM's This Record Company to provide MCA with seven Elton John albums at agreed-upon intervals.

Between his transatlantic hops, Elton managed to find time to help old friends Lesley Duncan and Long John Baldry. He played backup all the way through Lesley's LP, *Sing Children Sing*. "Elton was very big news at the time," she says, "and yet he asked to work on it. Elton's being on it really helped me get a lot of radio and TV exposure. He was very generous." Elton also sang "Love Song," another Duncan composition, on *Tumbleweed*.

Similarly, Elton coproduced *It Ain't Easy*, which was an attempt by Long John Baldry, the former lead singer of the now-disbanded Bluesology, to try to revive his R&B roots and also his recording career, to no avail. "When I was asked to do the Baldry thing," Elton remembers, "I said yes right off the bat." Rod Stewart, who was becoming rich and famous in tandem with Elton and who had once shared vocals with Baldry in another band, was the coproducer of the record.

But the year 1971 had also been an exhausting one. Now, having ended one phase of his development with the *Madman* LP, Elton knew more changes were in order, and he was thinking about adding a guitarist to his band's lineup.

As the year drew to a close, Elton looked forward to what had every indication of being a grand finale. The Royal Festival Hall in London was a modernistic and grand venue for Britain's latest star to give a year-end concert. The opportunity of appearing with the Royal Philharmonic Orchestra also appealed to this former junior pupil at the Royal Academy of Music. The concert was, above all, a chance for Elton to show how far he could stretch his talents and the range of people who would listen to him.

Though the audience in their tuxedos and evening dresses did not go away disappointed, Elton was upset as he stepped off the stage. What he had expected from the event is still not clear even to this day. But the lack of respect and encouragement he felt from the orchestra angered him. As a classically trained pianist himself, he believed that their attitude toward him was unjustified, and he gave them a tongue-lashing in public.

"I thought the orchestra were a bunch of cunts," he told one interviewer. "I just thought they gave me a quarter of their best and they did not take the event seriously. I felt so tense because I was uncomfortable with them. They made snide remarks. I sunk a lot of money into that concert and I'll never do it again."

Elton believed that he was a victim of rock snobbery. "Now I've made it," he remarked at the time, "it's become very hip to put me down."

By next year, 1972, Elton would gross $1.1 million from his U.S. tour. Remembering his father's desire to please the establishment, Elton was determined to win everyone over. He looked forward to the New Year with a new band lineup and a sound that would never be forgotten.

9

The Homecoming

Nineteen seventy-two was a momentous year for Elton. His *Honky Chateau* album turned to gold and gave him his first Number One hit LP in America. In Britain it climbed to Number Two. It was his seventh album in less than two years and boasted two hit singles, the Bowie-esque "Rocket Man," which was destined to become an Elton John classic, and the jazz-stomper "Honky Cat," a somewhat caustic send-up of American rednecks: "Get back, Honky Cat, drinking whisky from a bottle of wine. . . . You better quit your redneck ways."

Elton, twenty-five, now had six gold albums—all of them except the *Friends* movie sound track in the Top Ten—and six chart-making singles. Elton also made his film debut with a guest appearance in *Born to Boogie*, which was a documentary about Marc Bolan's pop group, T. Rex.

Elton's success also brought him a major change in lifestyle as well. Gone was the Hillman Imp he used to drive to Bluesology gigs and in its place came a powder-blue Rolls-Royce convertible, a Ferrari and, just for good measure, a Bentley. And his new home was a mansion with a swimming pool on seventeen acres in tony Virginia Water, Surrey, just outside of London.

Elton had definitely come a long way, but even so, he had yet to realize it fully. He needed to make a pilgrimage to his past to grasp how much he had achieved in such a short span of time. And so, in December 1972, he went back to his old school, Pinner Grammar, where his peers once took his cap and rejected him on the athletic field. The theme song of this concert might well have been "If They Could See Me Now." Many of his former classmates still lived in the area, and surely they would hear about his triumphant return to Pinner Grammar.

He gave a concert and toured the school to observe any changes. Of course, in his purple suit with matching eyeglasses and a fox cape with an animal-shaped diamond broach, he really did not need to look beyond himself to see changes. Pausing outside his old class-room, he tried to imagine his former self, Reg Dwight, sitting at a desk and wearing gray trousers, white shirt, brown jacket and tie with a yellow stripe—the school uniform. But he couldn't. Only seven years had gone by since Reg attended Pinner. But to Elton it seemed like a lifetime ago.

Back then Elton had felt so alone and uncomfortable with himself that he'd almost wished he were invisible. But he had never been the sort of fat kid who harbored grudges against the better looking and more popular boys or hoped that they would grow up to be failures. Throughout those years he had been too consumed by his music to allow himself such mean-spirited distractions.

His devotion to the music had paid off. Liberated by his phenom-enal success and the trappings that went with it, including his Ferrari, which he parked on the school grounds, Elton could afford on this December day to be generous with his time and attention. He asked questions of and listened to his old teachers about changes that had taken place there. He was mobbed by his fans in the hallways, and a group of students and teachers had to form a human chain to usher him into the student lounge. There, when asked what he wanted, Elton said simply, "I'd like a cup of tea, please."

Elton performed for over two hours at the school. The biggest hit of his show was "Crocodile Rock" from his soon-to-be-released LP *Don't Shoot Me, I'm Only the Piano Player*. Fittingly, it was a nos-talgic song evoking the high-spirited, rollicking innocence of fifties and sixties rock 'n' roll. An amalgam of hit tunes like "Little Darling," "Oh Carol" and some Beach Boys as well, it was exactly the kind of music that Elton wanted to make: "I remember when rock was young / Me and Susie had so much fun," he sang with relish. "But the biggest kick I ever got / Was doing a thing called the Crocodile Rock / While the other kids were rocking round the clock, / We were hopping and bopping to the Crocodile Rock . . ."

"Crocodile Rock" became Number Five on the U.K. charts. By February, it would become Elton's first Number One single in America, knocking Stevie Wonder's chart-topping "Superstition" back to Number Three. A week later the LP from which it originated, *Don't Shoot Me, I'm Only the Piano Player*, also went to Number One. Both album and single were his first releases on Elton's new label in America, MCA, the parent company of Uni, on which he had recorded until then. The original pressing was black; later came the collector's version in rainbow-colored vinyl.

Elton needed to make this trip back to his past to try to exorcise the demons that preyed on his feelings of self-worth. As he remembers, "I never realized I was a success until I went back to my old school to do a concert. All the masters who taught me were there, and they were very nice and they just said, 'Well, you've done very well. You've got on.' They looked just the same and I thought, 'What will they think of my act?' because it was a bit wild. But they were really nice. And when I drove away, I thought, 'You've made it. You've arrived.' It was a nice feeling."

Though Elton had yet to resolve the pain he felt from his father's rejection, at least at this moment he had the respect and affection of surrogates, including the music master who had scorned Elton's decision to drop out of school to join Mills Music as a messenger.

A few days later Elton returned to Pinner Grammar to donate a color television set. As a newly minted millionaire, Elton was already showing a largesse for which he would become legendary over the years. But Elton's charitable spirit began at home. He bought his mother and stepfather, Fred Farebrother, a £15,000 ($35,172) home in Ickenham, near Pinner. They called it the Gingerbread House. He also traded in Sheila's Mini and bought her a white MGB sports car. Elton always provided for his family first, and in return they looked after him and his houses when he was away on tour. His stepfather, for example, was something of a jack-of-all-trades around Elton's properties, and his uncle, Reginald Kenneth Dwight, for whom he was named, spruced up his gardens.

The interior of Elton's new house in Virginia Water, named "Hercules," was fixed up by Farebrother, a painter and contractor, who amused his business associates by turning up in bright scarlet boots with enormous heels. The boots were a gift from Elton. The house was painted white inside as a backdrop for a profusion of plants that created a junglelike effect, the chandeliers and the black Steinway. The pièce de résistance was a jukebox that lit up when it played the old rock-'n'-roll 45's on which Elton was weaned.

John Reid also moved into the house, which had cost an estimated £50,000 ($117,525). Hercules had the requisite collection of pricey cars in the driveway. There was Elton's Rolls-Royce Phantom IV, which he used for touring, a Rolls-Royce Corniche hardtop, a Ferrari Boxer and a Mini GT. In the trunk of one Rolls Elton kept a moped that he used in London traffic.

In recent years arriviste rock stars had been migrating in droves to this Surrey stockbroker belt around the town of Virginia Water. But unlike some of their messy music industry colleagues, Elton and Reid were as meticulous as two spinster aunts. Nineteen seventy-two also saw the marriage of Sheila and Fred Farebrother, and they used Hercules as their official residence on the marriage certificate. When Elton and Reid were away, the newlyweds lived at the house.

But even when Elton was home, Sheila still did his bookkeeping, sorted his laundry and looked after his spaniel, Brian, and German shepherd, Bruce. As for John Reid, Sheila accepted him as a family member, just as she had earlier embraced Bernie. At least it appeared that way on the surface—but one friend of Elton's wondered if there might be some hidden meaning in the Christmas present she gave Reid every year: an electric carving knife.

Elton also came to depend on a Virginia Water neighbor and his wife as his cultural gurus. They were actor-turned-director-and-producer, sometime bookstore owner and aspiring novelist Bryan Forbes and his actress-author wife, Nanette Newman. Their home, Seven Pines, appeared to Elton to be the apotheosis of good taste, and he enlisted the couple as his official advisers on home furnishings and objets d'art. An avid reader, Elton frequented Forbes's bookstore and came away with tomes to fill his shelves.

The couple accompanied Elton that year on his first foraging of Cartier's. However, the tacky rock-sized ring that Elton numbered among his other purchases did not strike his two new shopping companions as something either of them would decorate *their* fingers with. Elton himself acknowledged that the ring was more an amusement than a serious candidate for his jewelry collection. Elton loved campy things, and as he twirled the ring on his finger he remarked that it would be perfect for some blue-rinsed lady in Miami.

In July 1972, when Elton took his first real vacation, the Forbeses and their two daughters joined him, John Reid, Bernie and Maxine in a rented beach house in Malibu. This vacation at the sprawling house also marked Elton's arrival on the Hollywood scene. Among the guests who came to dine were Groucho Marx and Mae West. That summer, easy and breezy, with friends coming and going, allowed Elton to recover a lost childhood.

For much of 1972 Elton's mood was as expansive as his generosity. The year had begun on an upbeat note with the addition of a new band member, Davey Johnstone, a multitalented lanky blond Scotsman. Johnstone played not only guitar, but also banjo, mandolin and assorted other stringed instruments. Elton wanted a different sound—more rock-'n'-roll band than lush orchestration, and more spectacle than sensitive singer-songwriter.

It was time, Elton believed, to add a guitar to the lineup, in which his piano reigned supreme. On the recommendation of Elton's record producer, Gus Dudgeon, Johnstone had played on three tracks of *Madman Across the Water*. Though respectful of Johnstone's musical gifts, Elton still was not sure he was right for the live band, because Davey had been in the vanguard of folk music in the late sixties as a member of the group Magna Carta, which Dudgeon had also produced. As it would later turn out, Johnstone outlasted the original members of the Elton John Band, bass player Dee Murray and drummer Nigel Olsson, by remaining for almost two decades.

Early in the year Elton, Bernie and the band traveled to France to record *Honky Chateau*. At the Strawberry Studios in Château d'Hérouville in the countryside about thirty miles outside of Paris, Elton found a satisfying ambience. There was a communal feeling among Elton, Bernie and the band.

At times, Elton tried out songs on his keyboards on the chateau's spacious lawns. Band members, relaxing under a willow tree, listened to Elton make the final revisions on a song. Crossing the Channel to France had lifted Elton's dejection about his recent work, allowing him distance from the stagnation he felt after *Madman*. The new surroundings sparked an enormous period of creativity that culminated in the double-album *Goodbye Yellow Brick Road*, which was recorded there, along with *Honky Chateau* and *Don't Shoot Me, I'm Only the Piano Player*.

Of the making of *Honky Chateau*, Elton remembers, "It was like a Motown hit factory. Bernie was upstairs writing. Maxine, Bernie's wife, was rushing downstairs, correcting the spelling, throwing the lyrics on the piano, then me working on them and the band wanting to play as soon as I'd finished."

Typically, Taupin composed lyrics in less than an hour. Once twenty to twenty-five accumulated, they were given to Elton, and he placed them, one at a time, on the piano. After reading the words, he struck a chord and began softly playing alternative chord structures until he completed the song. If Elton could not complete it in thirty minutes, he discarded the sheet of lyrics in favor of another in the stack. Some albums can be written, arranged, recorded and mixed in a matter of weeks: *Honky Chateau* took ten days.

The sound on vinyl this time was as exuberant as Elton's live stage act. In addition to the two hit singles "Rocket Man" and "Honky Cat" there was the doo-wop of "Hercules" and the funky fun of "I Think I'm Going to Kill Myself," a terrific riff on "getting bored being part of mankind" because of not being allowed to use the car and having to be in by ten at night.

On the album sleeve Elton sported a mustache and beard and dark glasses, in contrast to the melancholic shadings of the *Elton John* album. Whereas Bernie's lyrics from the early period were suffused with childlike longings for the English countryside and a fascination with the American West, *Honky Chateau* offered not only country comforts, but also an urban landscape disturbingly real and uncomfortable. The song "Mona Lisas and Mad Hatters," for example, portrayed New York as a place where "rose trees never grow" and people say "good morning to the night." This time Bernie had actually been on the scene to record his impressions—in contrast to *Tumbleweed*, where his evocations of the American West were the product of his imagination and reading. Bernie wrote the lyrics of "Mona Lisas" during a stay in a midtown Manhattan hotel where a man was shot in the street just below his window.

In June 1972 Elton returned for a second time, just before his Malibu holiday, to Strawberry Studios to start his eighth album, *Don't*

Shoot Me, I'm Only the Piano Player. The sleeve was Hollywood-style poster with a movie marquee announcing the title. It was accompanied by a ten-page libretto. Elton was now identifying himself as a performer in the Glam Rock style. David Bowie, Marc Bolan and Rod Stewart, the flamboyant lead singer with the Faces who eschewed the progressive rock of the period, were all part of that genre.

Also at this time Elton took to wearing jumpsuits trimmed with feathers, stack-heeled silver boots and personally customized glasses. "People knock me for wearing tailed pink lamé suits that glitter and those insane platform shoes and the whole electric Liberace bit," he remarked. "And they're really going to groan when they see my new glasses that cost five thousand dollars each and light up. I cannot believe they take it seriously."

In October 1972, he fulfilled a boyhood dream by coming face to face with one of his heroes, Liberace, for the first time. It was backstage at the Royal Variety Show, an annual charity event in London. As they waited to go on, the two performers chatted about their costumes. "See this suit?" Liberace camped. "It's wonderful. I press this little button and it lights up in the dark."

Jimmy Horowitz, who played second keyboard on "Crocodile Rock" for Elton that night, observed the two performers. He remembers, "It was as if Elton and Liberace had known each other for ever and ever. Elton, no doubt, got a lot of ideas from him."

Elton had interrupted his Stateside tour that fall to appear at this charity event. But despite his encounter backstage with Liberace and the coveted opportunity to perform before the Royal Family, it turned out to be a fiasco. That night Princess Margaret, the Queen's sister (and an avowed Elton John fan), and the Queen Mother were in the audience. But when Elton arrived at the London Palladium, where the show was taking place, he wondered if he had made a serious mistake by flying back for the event.

The facility was totally inadequate. "Poor sound equipment, too many acts crammed into four hours . . . it was carnage," Elton remembers. "I am not a violent person but I came close to punching Bernard Delfont [the show organizer] right on the nose." Though disgusted with the incompetence involved in the production, Elton participated in the show. But the moment his performance was over he stormed out of the Palladium. Publicly he vowed that he would never perform again at this event unless, he qualified, "one of the Royal Family specifically asks for me." Elton was so livid about the event that he broke a confidence of the Queen's sister to argue his case. "Princess Margaret has told me she thinks it's four hours of boredom," Elton squealed to the press. "I know what she means. When artists like Carol Channing are singing 'Diamonds Are a Girl's Best Friend' and throwing imitation diamonds at the Royal Box— what can you expect? The only reason the Royal Family puts up with it is because the money goes to a charitable cause."

But disgruntled as he felt, in the near future Elton would participate again in another Royal charity event. This time it was a favorite cause of Princess Margaret's, disabled children. "When you get to know Princess Margaret," said Elton, "you find that she is very down-to-earth. She holds a genuine interest in my music."

Elton became a proud Royalist, proclaiming at every opportunity his love for Britain's First Family. "I think the Royal Family are marvelous," he says. "Beneath all the façade they are real human beings. But I wouldn't like the life, having to cope with so many official engagements, particularly if they're a yawn like the Royal Variety Show."

Having resumed his Stateside tour, Elton was back again at New York's Carnegie Hall by late November. While Elton performed "I Think I'm Going to Kill Myself," a story of a world-weary youth suffering the teenage blues, a man in a bridal outfit with a silver helmet topped with wedding cake broke into a manic tap dance to Elton's percussive piano playing. The dancer, and the two midgets holding up his long flowing train, were part of the stage act.

A *New York Times* headline of November 22, 1972, read, "Elton John, Rock Singer, Decorates His Performance," which was surely an understatement. "There are rock singers and musicians who believe that art is enough," wrote Ian Dove in the *Times*, "standing unadorned onstage, paying homage to their material as if it were the latest tablet down from the mountain. Not Elton John."

The review also noted: "With his partner Bernie Taupin, Mr. John has managed to write some of the best rock songs of the last five years. . . . Therefore Mr. John has less need than most to decorate his concert appearances. But decorate he does, and he did at his Carnegie Hall concert on Monday evening. . . . Mr. John does not really need the frills—his own stage dress was a glittery silver, green and red suit of lights—but it's nice that he takes the trouble."

The dancing man in the bridal outfit, Legs Larry Smith, a member of the former British satirical rock group Bonzo Dog Band, enhanced Elton's American tour with these surrealistic touches. For his final appearance of the evening he dressed in green, with wax fruit on the shoulders. A chorus line of young women kicked its way across the stage Rockette-style. Unbridled theater now matched Elton's virtuosity note for note.

Elton gave value for money. "I've always thought rock 'n' roll was people's music," says Elton. "It's always been a thing people should enjoy as far as I'm concerned. I don't see why performers should bring the moodiness into it. I hate all that sort of moodiness. So David Bowie's inaccessible and he's got mystique and he's got great stage presence. I also think it's very sick. I also know David has always wanted to be Judy Garland. Well, I'm the Connie Francis, then, of rock 'n' roll."

The prima donna business was best left at the office—namely DJM back in London, where Elton was becoming increasingly foul-mouthed and unpredictable. Steve James remembers: "Elton had an uncontrollable temper. The four-letter words, one after the other, and the nasty things he'd say about people! He'd get personal about them. He'd basically call you a fucking idiot. Usually it was spur of the moment and afterward he couldn't remember that he'd said anything."

Elton and James argued over the song "Daniel," a ballad about a Vietnam War veteran who moves to Spain to spare his family the pain of his life. Elton was insistent that this song, the first track on *Don't Shoot Me, I'm Only the Piano Player*, be released as a single. Dick James disagreed, even issuing a statement, "We are releasing 'Daniel' as a single solely because of the pressure from Elton. It is also against the wishes of MCA, who distribute Elton's records in America."

Elton hit back, blabbing to the media, "It's one of the best songs we've ever written. I don't care if it's a hit or not . . . I just want it out." Elton was so adamant on this point that he paid for all the advertising himself on the condition that he would be reimbursed if it reached the Top Ten. Elton was proved right. "Daniel" hit Number Four on the U.K. charts and for a time looked like it would become his second Number One hit, after "Crocodile Rock." By the following year, in June 1973, it peaked at Number Two.

Daniel was a rare "message song." Erroneously perceived in the strife-torn United States of the early seventies as political thinkers, Elton and Bernie were in reality anything but. "What positive reaction can you get from stoned ramblings of someone screaming a political message?" Bernie remarked then. Said Elton, "I can't stand some half-stoned junkies coming on stage to yell out their political ideas." Some fans had even said, incorrectly, that the "Madman Across the Water" was Richard Nixon.

Bernie's lyrics were pretty much straightforward—on occasion poetic or fantastical—but almost never political. The song "Burn Down the Mission," the signature piece of the first tour, was not, according to Bernie, an exhortation to political violence. "We try to make our songs timeless," he explains. " 'Burn Down the Mission' was just about the poor fighting the rich in a song incorporating a lot of aggressions. It had no specific target."

Back in England, however, "Burn Down the Mission" once cleared out a hometown gig at Watford Town Hall, in a London suburb near Pinner. Elton was halfway through the song when a police inspector suddenly appeared on the scene, grabbed Elton's piano stool and announced that a caller claiming to be from the IRA had said there was a bomb under the stage. One thousand fans were evacuated for twenty minutes while police searched the hall.

The song "Daniel" ("Oh I miss him so much . . .") created further controversy. The Daniel of the song, like Elton, did not seem to have any girlfriends, fueling rumors that Elton might be homosexual. At that stage Elton had yet to make his famous declaration of bisexuality in *Rolling Stone* magazine. That would come four years later, in 1976. Nor did Elton seem to engage in the usual sexual rites of rock artists with female groupies. Not that the groupies weren't trying: As Sheila reported, "Elton has all sorts of pressures—right to his losing his glasses when a crowd of girls chased him and he had to run away from them without seeing where he was going."

Elton knew that he could not rely on his own physical attributes to lure fans. "Sex appeal?" he said when one interviewer brought up the subject. "I've got to own up—it's a bit of a mystery." Elton also remarked on his thinning hair: "The reason my hair isn't long is because it's falling out. Yeah, I'll probably be the first bald pop star. Ha!"

There was also his weight problem. Steve James recalls, "We were always trying to get him to look like a pop artist. Elton tended, when he was uptight, to turn to food, lots of hamburgers and ice cream. I would tell him to try to keep his weight down. My father would tell him. Steve Brown would tell him. MCA Records would tell him. The photographers would tell him. And Elton would say, 'Don't worry about it. Yes, yes, I know, I'll take care of it,' which was rarely what he did."

Hardly a heartthrob, Elton still managed to attract enormous crowds. Elton's version of Glam Rock was not about self-love, but more a devotion to pleasing his audiences with sustained outbursts of talent and showmanship. He would become a legend in his own time—but not in his own mind. At the Philadelphia Spectrum, nineteen thousand people turned out to see him, breaking a house record set by Elvis Presley. Elton personally invited singer Patti LaBelle, who lived in the city, to his show.

In the mid-sixties as a member of Bluesology, Elton had accompanied LaBelle and her group, the Blue Belles. Back then he was Reg Dwight, of course, and their paths had not crossed for the past several years. Elton, who adored LaBelle, was eager to impress her. One of his all-time favorite records was LaBelle's rendition of "Somewhere Over the Rainbow," on which, as Reggie, he had sung and played keyboard.

He picked up the phone and dialed her home number. "Hello," said a euphoric Elton. "May I speak to Patti LaBelle?"

"Speaking," she said. "Who's calling?"

"Elton John. I want you to come to my show tonight at the Spectrum."

LaBelle, who had heard Elton's music on the radio and liked it, could not figure out why this twenty-five-year-old phenomenon was calling to invite her to his show. She mumbled, confusedly, "Your show?"

"Patti," Elton pleaded. "It's me—Elton John—Reggie."

"Reggie!" LaBelle exclaimed. "What are you doing being Elton John? It's so wonderful. I'm so happy for you."

Remembers LaBelle: "I was shocked. I mean, this guy who used to play piano and I used to beat in cards was now Elton John."

Because of a prior commitment, she says, she had to decline the invitation, but within three years they would work together again, this time with LaBelle on backup, on Elton's *Rock of the Westies* album.

Back in Pinner, Horace Sewell was equally confused by Elton's enormous celebrity and increasing fortunes. Horace, Elton's maternal step-grandfather, was a gardener. Seven years earlier, Sewell had complained to one of his employers, "I worked hard all my life for very little money. Not like my grandson. He's tinkering away at the piano. He's eighteen and he ought to be doing something other than tinkering away at the piano. When I was his age I worked from sunrise to sunset for ten shillings a day."

The employer, Ethel Seaford, the wife of a local physician, asked, "Doesn't he do any work?"

"No," said Horace, "he just tinkers away at that old piano."

Now, eight years later, in the spring of 1972, Horace reported that Elton had just bought a mansion. "Oh, he must be doing well, that grandson of yours," said Seaford. "Is this the grandson who tinkered away at the piano?"

"He don't do a lot in this country," Horace said, "and he don't play under the family name. He's playing in America, Las Vegas . . ."

"What's his name?"

"Elton John."

Remembers Mrs. Seaford: "It was an absolute stunner to me. To Horace, Elton was just a name, someone tinkering away at the piano. Horace was a lovely, simple man. He rode to work on a bicycle. He carried a sack over his shoulder and was the best man with a spade I ever met. He only missed work if it was really blustery because he had a peg leg from the War and couldn't balance himself on the bike then."

By Christmas 1972 Elton was spotted arriving at his grandparents' home with a large color television set for them, and within a year their grandson's "tinkering at the piano" earned them a new cottage.

Elton's spending was not confined to himself or his family. As his fortunes increased, he lavished pricey cars, artworks, expensive jewelry and holidays on close friends and associates. His gift giving was not always grandiose, but no less thoughtful for that. In New York during one American tour, guitarist Davey Johnstone had his heart set on a mandolin, but could not make up his mind to spend $800 on it. He visited the New York store Manny's a few times to look over the instrument. Once Johnstone finally decided to purchase the mandolin he showed up at the store to learn that another customer had beaten him to it. Disappointed, he walked back to his hotel room to find the mandolin waiting for him there. Elton, aware of Davey's desire, had gone out and bought it for him.

At year's end, Elton's family eagerly awaited his homecoming. Sheila and Fred had a cake for him with a rocket on it to commemorate his hit song "Rocket Man." The message on the cake read, "Congratulations on Your Success." On the eve of Elton's return from America, Sheila told a reporter, "The first thing he'll do when he gets home is sit down at that desk and write out a dozen checks. He loathes the feeling of owing anybody any money."

At heart Elton John was still the dutiful and responsible Reg Dwight whom he went back to visit in a sense at his concert at Pinner Grammar. Sheila worried about the pressures on her son. "I hope it will ease," she said. "But he still rings at times and says, 'I've got the day to myself, Mum, come on over and spend it with me.'"

Despite the pressures, Elton, now twenty-five, looked on his achievements with pride. The previous year he had told *Rolling Stone* magazine reporter David Felton, "I've got to do everything in three years. After three years you just have to assume it's gonna go down. Realistically, I don't think I can be any more popular than I am now."

Elton was wrong. The best was yet to come. The Yellow Brick Road still lay ahead for Reg Dwight from Pinner. "I know you're not really supposed to say this about your own," Sheila told an interviewer from the local Pinner paper in December 1972. "But he's an amazingly nice boy, that Elton John."

10

Island Man

In the spring of 1973 Elton decided again to record outside of England. High on his recent experiences at the Château d'Hérouville, he believed that a change of scenery was good for the creative soul. Elton liked the idea of placing himself in a distant setting where, removed from the details of daily living, he could concentrate solely on his music. Though the chateau's studio facilities had not met his standards, the ambience there had made up for it, unleashing an outpouring of songs, including Elton's first Number One hit single, "Crocodile Rock."

Elton was inspired to travel. But there was a major stumbling block. There were not many good studios in the world, which left Elton with limited options of where to work on his next album. Even so, feeling adventurous, Elton made a suggestion. "Hey," Elton rallied Bernie and the band, "let's go to Jamaica," and he and his entourage headed for the Caribbean.

Jamaica seemed like the perfect place. The Rolling Stones had just finished recording there, and to Elton's thinking that was a good enough recommendation. Any technical problems, he reasoned, could be resolved by producer Gus Dudgeon, in whom he placed full confidence.

Arranger Paul Buckmaster, however, who had invested Elton's earlier albums with a mature orchestral sound, was gone. Many people believed that his dismissal was a case of Elton bowing to the press. *Rolling Stone* had printed a review suggesting that Elton would sound so much better "without these huge smudges of whipped cream strings that arranger Paul Buckmaster piles on . . ."

The review angered Buckmaster, who says, "I did not want to be labeled a string arranger when I was an all-around arranger. I considered it a sort of stigma." Buckmaster, who went off to work with jazz great Miles Davis, was glad for the opportunity to involve himself in what he called "more hard-edged, exploratory, out-there" music. Elton wanted a more toned-down, simplistic rock-'n'-roll sound devoid of complex instrumental ensembles.

As the plane touched down on the island of Jamaica, Elton felt he had his winning team with him. With the island's palm-fringed white beaches, colorful flowers and transparent blue waters, Elton figured on this, his first trip to the Caribbean, that Jamaica would prove an agreeable place to work on his next album.

More important, it was an exciting time for a musician like Elton to be in Jamaica. A new sound had been discovered there. It was called reggae. Reggae was really a rhythmic variant of socca, and socca (calypso) music, originating largely in Trinidad but indigenous to the entire Caribbean region, had been around for generations. But the Jamaicans, with the help of Englishman Chris Blackwell and his Island Records, had just recently found a way to harness the local talent and market it worldwide. Bob Marley, a Rastafarian, was the high priest of this musical genre.

But while the dulcet strains of "Oh, Island in the Sun" and "Jamaica Farewell" continued to captivate tourists on calypso nights at their hotels, elsewhere on the island Third World revolutionary messages issued from this new band of reggae artists.

Kingston, the capital city of Jamaica, was not only central headquarters for reggae, but also a hotbed of political ferment. The locals' favorite "tranquilizer," ganja (the local name for marijuana), tended to have a reverse effect on some of its users: It often triggered outbursts of anger. Kingston, with its shantytowns and groups of unemployed men hanging around on street corners smoking ganja, had many characteristics of an "inner city."

Elton was quick to sense the undertones of rage and violence there. He remembers, "I was afraid to go out of my room at the hotel."

For three days Elton locked himself in his room with his keyboard. However, unlike three years before at his Troubadour debut, he was not sulking or ringing up Dick James to tell tales out of school. Instead, now twenty-seven years old and feeling more confident of himself, Elton just worked on the new album. Writing under self-imposed detention, he managed to complete most of the songs.

One of the tracks was definitely island-inspired. Titled "Jamaica Jerk-Off," it was a celebration of sun and music and island indolence. Ever the mimic, Elton sounded as though reggae were his mother tongue. But considering the circumstances of his stay on the island, "Jamaica Nightmare" might have been a more appropriate title. When Elton eventually left his hotel room to go to the Dynamic Studios, he found the place surrounded by barbed wire and armed security guards. He quickly realized there there was a strike going on. "When we'd go in, the picketers would blow crushed fibers through blowpipes at us," he recalls, "and we'd come out of there with rashes."

It soon became apparent that no album would ever come out of the studio sessions. The equipment was poor, and the only song Elton got to record was the hard-rocking "Saturday Night's Alright for Fighting," and even that was unusable. "It sounded like it had been recorded on the worst transistor radio," he sniffed.

Elton was appalled. Here he had traveled over three thousand miles at great expense, lugging equipment, and he had not even one track to show for it. Elton, who was then in the process of setting up his own recording company, Rocket Records, had just received a quick, albeit unhappy, course in the business. He decided to flee the island and make his way back to the chateau in France. But his departure was not easy. After the anxiety-ridden events of the past few days, Elton believed that he would not get out of Jamaica alive. "They impounded our equipment," he remembers, "and when Bernie and I left, we had a taxi ride to the airport that took us through sugarcane fields. I thought I was going to be killed."

Elton's disdain for time wasting, often interpreted as impatience, was one of the few positive legacies of his Royal Air Force squadron leader father. Discipline and responsibility, the virtues of middle-class respectability, had been imparted to the boy, and as a result Elton approached the making of every one of his albums with great earnestness.

Once back at the Château d'Hérouville, Elton worked feverishly on the album, recording as many as five songs a day. As drummer Nigel Olsson remembers, "It had such a great atmosphere and it was such a good place to work." Indeed, Elton was like a maniac at the chateau, getting up early every morning, playing at the piano with Bernie's lyrics. Within half an hour a new song would be finished.

As a result of his commitment to work, it would take him only fifteen days to complete the album *Goodbye Yellow Brick Road*. Luckily, the album did not seem to suffer from the problems experienced in Jamaica. In fact, it surpassed Elton's expectations, yielding his second Number One hit single in America, "Benny and the Jets."

The single also earned the fat, flamboyant Englishman entry onto the R&B charts. An ecstatic Elton told *Rolling Stone* magazine, "I'm such a black record fanatic that to think I'm actually in the R&B chart means that if it doesn't get any higher than thirty-four I'm gonna stick it up and frame it." Elton made an appearance on the TV show "Soul Train" and sang "Benny and the Jets." Ultimately he would hang a Number Fifteen R&B record on his wall.

The title track, "Goodbye Yellow Brick Road" ("You can't plant me in your penthouse / I'm going back to my plough"), which expressed a yearning to escape the life of celebrity, was the first single to be released. It went gold, and ended 1973 as Number Two. The follow-up was supposed to be "Candle in the Wind," but after a black soul station in Detroit started giving "Benny and the Jets" heavy airplay, MCA made a decision, over Elton's protests, to release it as a single. Elton, who frankly could not see its appeal as a single, put MCA executives on notice that if "Benny and the Jets" flopped, they would be wholly responsible.

In Britain, meanwhile, "Candle in the Wind," released by DJM Records as a single, reached Number Eleven. "Benny and the Jets" was on the B side. Because of its opening lyrics, "Goodbye, Norma Jean," "Candle in the Wind" was interpreted by fans and the music press alike as a eulogy for Marilyn Monroe. But according to Bernie, the song really transcended Marilyn and addressed the larger issue, as he saw it, of Hollywood myth-making; in particular, the ease with which the system could destroy just what it set out to create.

Though the song still remains one of Elton's most popular ballads, recording it was not easy. "It was so hard to record," says Elton. "The only way I recorded that in the end is that we put the piano on afterward. It was the first vocal I'd ever recorded standing up, and after that the piano, guitar, drums were put on. It was such a hard song to do because it's not a typical piano number and I actually sang the number leaping around the microphone and going crazy."

Clearly, *Goodbye Yellow Brick Road*, Elton's first double album, had something for everyone, from the hard-edged rock of "Saturday Night's Alright for Fighting" to the fuguelike instrumental, "Funeral for a Friend," unusual for Elton, which segued into "Loves Lies Bleeding" ("Can't face another day / Wonder if the changes have left a scar on you"). For doo-wop fans there was the track "Your Sister Can't Twist" ("But she can rock 'n' roll") which sounded like the fifties hit "At the Hop." Though in some ways a derivative composer, Elton was at the same time staggeringly original in the way he blended all these influences into a style that was distinctively his own.

Despite Elton's doubts about double albums—because "ninety percent of them are padded with long jams, eight-minute cuts and the like"—he felt that he had surmounted his own objections. "*Goodbye Yellow Brick Road* is like the ultimate Elton John album," he says. "It's got all my influences from the word *go*. It encompasses everything I ever wrote, everything I've ever sounded like."

At twenty-six and at his peak, Elton was still very much Mr. Goody Twoshoes from a London suburb, eschewing hard drugs and sex with groupies. "I've seen what cocaine can do to people," he moralized in a *Daily Mail* interview. "And hash just gives me a headache, although they get a bit funny in America when I refuse a joint. And groupies . . . well, I'm really not into one-night stands."

In interviews, at least, he managed to come off as wholesome. But his stage wardrobe got weirder and weirder and his outfits continued to turn heads. Elton now trotted out on stage in platform shoes with five-inch heels, custom-made glasses with his name lighted up on them, bell-bottom trousers and sequined jackets. Even his civilian clothes could be described as costumes.

"I'm making up for lost time," said Elton, whose father had forbade him as a boy to wear the popular mohair sweaters and Hush Puppy shoes. "It's an expression of myself. It's like I'm being a teenager now, and I'm just having a good time." Patches of Elton's thinning hair as well were tinted green with splotches of orange.

Luckily for Elton, in the seventies celebrities were allowed to look tacky. Ordinary people, after all, were also wearing ridiculous bell-bottoms, platforms and wide collars. Polyester was king then, and the gaudier the better. If the sixties were about changing the world, by the seventies—with Nixon still in office, the widening of the Vietnam War into Cambodia and the Kent State killings—all the marching and protesting were starting to look futile. Now it seemed, the agenda was "changing outfits," and Elton was definitely the leader of the pack. If there was little to be done about altering the body politic, there was at least one personal freedom over which one had total control—the choice of what to put on in the morning. Fat or skinny, it did not make a difference. The peer pressure to diet and exercise was still nearly a decade away, in the eighties, when rock videos emerged and image sometimes superseded talent. Wedged between the self-immolating sixties and the self-aggrandizing eighties, the seventies were simply, to paraphrase one of Elton's future songs, about "growing some funk of one's own."

Elton was at his most outrageous in September 1973 at the Hollywood Bowl; it was part of an American tour that ran from August to October. A billboard on Sunset Boulevard announced a sellout of the concerts, with a portrait of Elton in top hat and tails. All forty thousand tickets had been snapped up as soon as they went on sale.

Introducing Elton that evening was the star of the pornographic movie *Deep Throat*, Linda Lovelace, dressed up like a Las Vegas moll. As she stepped toward the microphone, a huge backdrop of Elton was unveiled. The stage lights went up to reveal full-grown palm trees bordering a huge, glittering staircase and five pianos of varying colors.

"Hi," Linda gushed. "I'd like to introduce some of tonight's guests, very important people and dignitaries from around the world who wouldn't dare have missed this gala evening." Out came actors disguised as the Queen of England, Elvis Presley, Frankenstein, the Pope, the Beatles, Batman and Robin, Groucho Marx and Mae West, all of them bounding over the staircase and lifting the piano lids to reveal the giant inlaid letters E-L-T-O-N—and releasing a flock of one hundred white doves. "Here he is," Linda said, whipping up the audience, "the biggest, largest, most fantastic man, the costar of my next movie . . . Elton John!"

At that moment the *enfant gauche* of rock music materialized on stage, wearing a five-thousand-dollar pair of glasses that had fifty-seven tiny light bulbs spelling "Elton." The sound man was enlisted at one point to appear on stage in a crocodile costume as a visual accompaniment to "Crocodile Rock." The space cowboy costume Elton wore for his other prestigious gig that tour, at New York's Madison Square Garden, appeared subdued by contrast.

Elton would explain his Hollywood Bowl experience this way: "I like to lift them up, drop them down, lift them up again. It's the same as having an orgasm. You try to save the very best till last. It's like two hours of . . . I don't know. It's like fucking for two hours and then suddenly finding out there's nothing you can do after that. It's so emotional and so physical, you don't ever want to do anything else."

The traveling Elton John extravaganza extended to MCA leasing its own private aircraft, the forty-seat *Starship*, outfitted with a "hippie room" for relaxation. The *Starship* also ferried Stevie Wonder to a Boston gig to jam with Elton. The event marked Wonder's first appearance after a car crash. In later years, when Elton was sidelined because of an operation, Wonder returned the favor, enlisting Elton to jam at one of his concerts.

The *Starship* made it possible for Elton to ground himself in one place, a home away from home as he flew in and out of cities for concerts. His hotel suite often housed an elaborate stereo system and hundreds of records, from Pink Floyd to Mendelssohn, that he liked to listen to. A television set or two was always on.

Film director Bryan Forbes, his friend from Virginia Water, went along on tour to film a documentary on Elton titled *Say Goodbye to Norma Jean*, taken from the line in "Candle in the Wind." Included in Forbes's eighteen hours of filming were the recording sessions at the chateau and interviews not only with Elton and Bernie, but also with members of the band. Forbes also did the narration, which *New York Times* TV critic John J. O'Connor described thus: "When not verbally smothering his subject, Mr. Forbes is cloyingly cool. His self-consciousness about possibly not being hip is so unhip that it becomes a self-destruct mechanism. Mr. Forbes seems to be convinced that he is reporting the Second Coming."

Forbes and his actress-author wife, Nanette Newman, were now firmly part of Elton's widening circle of friends. Nearly a decade later, Elton's manager, John Reid, to the complete amazement of his cronies, was rumored to be romantically linked with one of the Forbes daughters; there was even talk of an impending marriage, but that never materialized. One of the Forbeses' houseguests, Katharine Hepburn, looked after Elton's swimming pool when she came to visit, scooping out a frog and other debris with a butterfly net. According to Long John Baldry, it was Hepburn who got Elton interested in tennis, and before the year was out, Elton was taking a few lessons from Billie Jean King, who would also become a personal friend. He was also close to rocker Rod Stewart, for whom he and Bernie composed a song, "Let Me Be Your Car" on Stewart's *Smiler* LP the following year. Elton also played piano and performed in the chorus line on that project.

Elton, it seemed, could do no wrong, garnering praise from many quarters. Despite Forbes's stilted narration, Elton on film managed to impress the *New York Times* critic as "refreshingly free of trade jargon" and "a talented composer and a marvelous pianist." At his self-effacing best, Elton called himself a "tubby little singer" who saw himself twenty-five years hence as "bored, aging and playing piano in a pub somewhere."

For the moment, however, Elton was doing everything possible to craft an image that would ensure his longevity. He made himself more accessible to the press than almost any star of his stature. Bob Dylan, for example, had given only one interview in six years. Elton, on the other hand, gave interview after interview. As he explained to *Honey* magazine, "I wouldn't hide for two reasons. First, because I think it would damage my music. Musicians who have become recluses have shut themselves away from the influences that made them good musicians in the first place. And second, I'm really having a good time. All the publicity, all the hype, is enjoyable in its own way."

Elton cultivated disc jockeys as well. "Elton has always been a good public relations man," says Guy Farrow, Elton's promoter. "It's not as if he ever went away and buried his head in the sand. He's always been active and he has always kept very friendly with the DJs and producers. He always had time for them."

The press also became a vehicle for Elton to air his grievances about Dick James Music instead of confronting James directly. In several interviews he bellyached about the double album *Goodbye Yellow Brick Road* being counted only as one LP under his contract, which called for two albums a year. Two albums annually, he moaned, damaged his creativity.

All too often James would first learn about Elton's complaints in the press. It was with few regrets that James, who was becoming increasingly irritated by Elton's disloyalty, decided to turn over full managerial responsibility to John Reid. That same year, 1973, the publishing agreement between Elton and DJM ended, and in another two years the recording contract would expire, too. It was obvious to James that Elton was not aiming for any gold watches at DJM.

The evidence was never more visible than in the start-up of Elton's own record label, Rocket Records, for the moment an outlet for artists other than Elton, but intended as a berth for him once he left DJM. Elton declared, "I have seen so many artists bled by businessmen with little regard for their music that I just wanted to do something to help."

Launched to give artists more leverage over the record company, Rocket offered higher royalties than the industry average. Instead of the customary to nine percent of retail price, Rocket artists would get ten to fifteen percent. Though Elton billed this royalty formula as novel, David Geffen had already offered these terms, when he lured Bob Dylan from Columbia to Elektra/Asylum for seventeen percent, which proved a disaster. Other similar quixotic ventures had ultimately ended on the verge of bankruptcy: The Beatles' Apple Records was one example. Their mission had been to showcase embryonic artistic talent, but they also signed a considerable number of useless acts which drained Apple's reserves.

By then Reid had already left DJM, having resigned in mid-August 1972. A month later, on September 20, he incorporated himself as John Reid Enterprises. He did so with a five-thousand-pound (ten-thousand-dollar) bank loan, using his management contract with Elton as collateral. Reid and his father John were listed as the two directors. All the while, Reid was mindful of how Elton and Bernie wanted to own the copyrights they had signed away back in 1967.

And a month after starting his own company, the twenty-three-year-old Reid confronted fifty-two-year-old Dick James about Elton's royalties from DJM USA.

Elton and his savvy manager had a very practical vision of how Rocket and its publishing arm, Pig Music, could best serve their interests. The creation of these separate companies would ensure that Elton received the largest cut of his earnings without having to tolerate, for example, a fifty-fifty split on a composing royalty with a publisher. Further, there would be extra income for Elton from directorships and shareholdings from publishing as well as from recording. Elton owned one quarter of Rocket Records, which would be manufactured and distributed by MCA in America and Island in England.

During its first year, in addition to Elton and Reid, Bernie, Gus Dudgeon and Steve Brown were involved in the administration of the business. Reid also ended up luring away Steve James's secretary of seven years. If Elton and Reid were bold about how they used and raided DJM to launch this enterprise, they were the opposite when it came to rounding up talent for their new label. The roster of artists they signed hardly suggested they were aiming to be in the vanguard of the music business.

One of the first to be signed was British singer Kiki Dee (born Pauline Matthews), whose career was stalled at the time. John Reid figured he could recycle her as a major talent. Reid had known her in his days with British Tamla-Motown. Although talented and attractive, Dee had only one chart single, "Love Makes the World Go Round," from her 1971 Motown LP.

Elton also had a history with Dee. They had sung backup together in the mid-sixties, when both were associated with Philips. Rocket invested about £50,000 ($117,000) in Kiki; Elton and Bernie wrote for her. "We've always refused when people asked us to write for them because we didn't think it would work," Elton said in 1973. "But we decided to write for Kiki to change her image from the sort of 'bouffant Latino-type singer' to what she really is."

Nothing made him happier, Elton professed, than Kiki's breakthrough with "Amoureuse," which landed in the Top Twenty on the charts. The success of this single restored Kiki to prominence after nearly a decade and portended a bright future for Rocket as well.

Kiki would enjoy a relatively short-lived success, with another hit single, "I've Got the Music in Me," in 1974 and, two years later, in 1976, her first Number One hit, "Don't Go Breaking My Heart," a duet with Elton which also resulted in *his* debut at the top of the singles chart in his native England. Ultimately, Kiki gave up recording altogether to become an actress.

Meanwhile, across the Atlantic, Rocket signed up singer-songwriter Neil Sedaka. On Sedaka's two Number One hits with Rocket in 1975, "Laughter in the Rain" and "Bad Blood," Elton sang backing vocals.

Sedaka's heyday had been in the early sixties with hit songs like "Calendar Girl" and "Oh Carol" and "Breaking Up Is Hard to Do," before hitting a dry spell as an artist; for the middle and latter part of the decade he concentrated largely on writing for others. By the time Rocket signed him, Sedaka had already returned to recording under RCA.

The atmosphere at Rocket's American office, a two-story brick building on Beverly Drive in Beverly Hills, was more adventurous than the talent the company signed and indicative of the flamboyant character who owned it. Much of the artwork on the albums was done in Rocket's suite of eight rooms next door to the offices of Hollywood superagent Irving "Swifty" Lazar. Bernie was intensely involved in plugging his ideas for the album covers, particularly for *Goodbye Yellow Brick Road*. Rocket's president, Tony King, an Englishman, Elton, and others liked to roller-skate in the building. "Once, Tony wore a dress," remembers staff artist Ron Wong, "while he skated up and down the hall." This LP (*Goodby Yellow Brick Road*) was the last one for which DJM owned the publishing rights, but Elton was still under a recording contract until 1975 with them, though Rocket was producing and recording his albums.

By this time Elton and his cronies, gay and straight, liked to cloak themselves in girls' names. Elton, for example, was Sharon Cavendish, after a fat lady who played piano in England, while Reid's alias was Beryl. Privately, among his gay cabal, they free-associated, as in "Oh, you're a Jill" or "You're a Barbara," with other men.

But Elton managed to keep this aspect of his life a secret. Questions about his relationships evoked vague but entirely believable answers from Elton about settling down and having children one day or about having little time for a family of his own because of his punishing schedule. Bolstering his pronouncements was the mileage he gained from dredging up details of his near-miss marriage to Linda Woodrow. Nearly every magazine or newspaper profile contained a reference to his aborted wedding plans.

By year's end, Elton gave his fans a traditional family entertainment with the release of a single, "Step Into Christmas," a bouncy fifties-type tune, which he had written and recorded in a day. A throwaway song that sounded like a jumped-up version of "Jingle Bells" (or, as Elton admitted, like something by the sixties girl group the Ronettes), it still made the charts in the United Kingdom.

Indisputably, Elton had much to celebrate as 1973 drew to a close, and the merry lyrics of this seasonal song seemed to sum it all up. "Welcome to my Christmas song," Elton sang effusively. "I want to thank you for the year."

11

Down Under and Out

The evening of February 27, 1974, started out most agreeably, for Elton in Auckland, New Zealand. Rose gardens surrounded the gracious white villa where a press reception was being held in his honor. About one hundred people, sipping champagne and vintage New Zealand wines, turned out for the party at the Parnell Rose Garden Lounge ten minutes from downtown Auckland.

Though completely exhausted, Elton was buoyed by the affectionate greeting he received from the guests and the news that his shows were completely sold out. On the eve of his performance, Elton savored his good fortune as much as the soft summer air laced with the aroma of roses. He was also feeling relieved, because Auckland was the last leg of a tour that had already covered Japan and Australia.

This tour was the last one to be arranged by Vic Lewis, formerly of the NEMS agency, which had been Beatles manager Brian Epstein's firm and later became a DJM subsidiary. Lewis, to Reid's thinking, was part of the Dick James cabal, and as such he had to be banished from Elton's circle. The ex-bandleader shared with Elton a love of cricket, soccer and tennis. Lewis was also heartbroken about

Elton's personal relationship with Reid, believing as he did that Elton might have married and had children.

How much longer Elton could keep up this whirlwind was a question that the center of all this activity had neither the time nor the inclination to ask himself at this stage. Elton wanted to capitalize on his spectacular career while it lasted. He was Mr. Frantic, aware that no one could sustain this level of success forever.

At that moment, Elton's latest album, *Goodbye Yellow Brick Road*, had sold over two million copies, and overflow crowds vied for tickets to his concerts. There was no waning of his popularity in sight. By now Elton was also the vice president of Britain's National Youth Theater and a director of the Watford Football Club, a soccer team near London.

Elton's love affair with soccer had begun in childhood when he accompanied his father to football games at Vicarage Road, the home of Watford, his favorite team. Attending the games was one of the rare pleasures shared by father and son. Elton had ambitions to play professionally like his cousin Roy Dwight, but realizing his limitations in this area, he settled for the role of spectator. Over the years his passion for the game had not abated, and while away on tour he always kept up with the latest scores of his beloved team.

By the early seventies, soccer teams, especially those in the fourth division, were not considered to be great money-makers. Far from being glamorous, these teams lost money, and were unable to attract large crowds, apart from die-hard fans. But Elton's devotion to the Watford Football Club was not diminished by its lack of success. When he was made vice president of the Watford team in 1973, he considered this election a great honor.

Elton's election came as a surprise to some observers who regarded him as a dilettante in this area. Elton proved them wrong, and the following year, 1974, he was made a director. There were big drawbacks to Elton's new appointment. The team was in extremely poor financial condition, owing the bank nearly two hundred thousand dollars and the directors another three hundred thousand dollars. But Elton did not see himself as a philanthropist, and he made that quite clear when he agreed to do the job.

"This is not just a happy little bandwagon with me picking up the bills," he declared. "The board are working hard to make the club pay for itself. If Elton John puts two thousand people on the gate I shall be pleased. But I don't believe in gimmicks."

Now, however, thousands of miles away from Watford, as Elton and his entourage mingled with members of the press and other Auckland dignitaries, his soccer team back home in England was not uppermost in his mind. Instead he was focusing on the next day's event, feeling the usual preconcert tension. So, too, was John Reid, who everybody said was visibly exhausted by the most recent stage of the tour, Australia. His job as Elton's manager was a demanding one. For at least a year Reid had been negotiating a new contract for Elton with his American recording label, MCA. Reid, though a hard-nosed businessman, was still learning about the industry. "I had to take each stage slowly," he says. "I was dealing with people who had considerably more experience than I had."

The twenty-four-year-old Reid would tell people that he felt as though he had aged ten years from the pressure. A demanding perfectionist, Reid was known as much for his volatile personality as for his business acumen.

Among the people at the party on that summer night in February was Judith Baragwanath, an Auckland model and fashion columnist for the *Sunday News*. Like the other guests who had gathered at the Parnell Rose Garden reception, she was eager to meet Elton John. As events transpired, however, she would come face to face with Reid's furious temper and her only remembrance of this night would be a black eye.

She had observed Reid belittling her friend Kevin Williams, the party's organizer. "You're an incompetent!" Reid screamed at Williams after being told that a particular brand of liquor he requested was not available. Reid then hurled the contents of a glass of champagne in Williams's face. Baragwanath, a friend of Williams, confronted Reid a few minutes later, saying she could not believe that anyone could be so cruel. "How could you do that to anyone?" she demanded. "You rotten little bastard."

Reid, by now beside himself, thought he had heard someone say, "You little poof," and, as he would later maintain, "in a reflex action" he struck her in the face, injuring her left eye. He said he was blinded by rage and did not know the identity of his victim.

Later that same evening, as Baragwanath was being treated at a hospital emergency room, Reid was making the rounds of Auckland nightclubs with Elton and nineteen other people in their entourage. At one stop, where a postconcert party was being held for pop star David Cassidy, Reid beat up another journalist, David Wheeler, who was also with the Auckland *Sunday News.*

Apparently Wheeler had been talking with a woman in Elton's party and had expressed his dismay overe earlier events at the reception. Seconds later, Elton, Reid and two other men pounced on him. "You have threatened my manager," Elton said, grabbing the journalist's collar and shaking him. Wheeler was completely baffled. "I don't know what you're talking about," he protested. Suddenly, Reid jumped in and started punching Wheeler, who fell to the ground. Then he kicked him in the mouth. Wheeler suffered chipped and cracked teeth, a black eye and facial bruises.

With another victim now on his way to the emergency room, John Reid and Elton went back to their hotel. David Cassidy's security chief reportedly rang Reid to warn about a possible retaliation against Elton, himself and others in their group.

Indeed, the next morning there was trouble: It was not another round of fisticuffs, but an appearance by Auckland police to arrest Elton and Reid on assault charges and to escort them to Auckland Magistrate's Court.

Elton, dressed soberly in a gray suit with a dark open-necked shirt and yellow-tinted spectacles for his appearance at the court, did not speak other than to plead guilty to collaring Wheeler. The judge acquitted Elton on the grounds that the pop star, believing initially that a threat had been made against his group, had acted on a false factual basis, and at worst was guilty of being anxious and indiscreet. Elton was released and ordered to pay fifty Australian dollars (seventy American dollars) toward the cost of the prosecution. During an adjournment Elton signed autographs for fans in the courthouse.

But the judge meted out much harsher punishment to Reid, noting "the continuity of the offenses," which went beyond a mere misunderstanding or anxiety. Reid was sentenced to a month in jail: three weeks for the attack on Wheeler and one week for punching Baragwanath. Additionally, the model received an out-of-court cash settlement of $2,500 Australian ($3,714 American) from Reid. Reid, the judge scolded, displayed "an ill-mannered, arrogant indifference to people in the way he dealt with them."

Reid requested, but was first denied, bail. What should have amounted to a straightforward concert date in Auckland, New Zealand, was fast evolving into high drama: Just ninety minutes before Elton was to appear onstage at Western Springs, an open-air arena, his manager was locked inside Mount Eden Jail.

It was beginning to look as though the show would not go on. But a special appeal meeting between Reid's attorneys and a Supreme Court justice at the latter's home saved the day. Pending a hearing of Reid's appeal of his sentence, scheduled to be heard within a few days, the justice freed him on $5,000 Australian bail. The conditions of bail were that Reid had to report twice daily to the police and temporarily hand over his passport to them.

Reid managed to attend Elton's show. But his freedom would be short-lived. Within days his sentence was upheld and he was locked away in jail. Ultimately he served twenty-one days, with his sentence reduced by one week for good behavior.

Highly embarrassed by the ordeal, once back in London Elton defended his manager on television. Elton claimed that members of his group had been threatened by a local Auckland journalist and that they had acted out of fear. "I went up, seized him by the collar and was just about to clock him," Elton related, "when my manager stepped in and hit him for me."

Elton also remarked on the tour: "We got the largest crowd in New Zealand history for one show, thirty-five thousand people, one percent of the population," he said. "And yet that one incident ruined it." Exhausted by the experience, Elton then proceeded to cancel a seventeen-date schedule of concerts in Britain, except for two live appearances: a performance at the Watford Football Club and a fundraiser for disabled children at the Royal Festival Hall.

The events in Auckland did have one positive effect, though. Realizing that a rest was long overdue, Elton took his first vacation alone in four years. Elton needed time all to himself. He went to John Gardner's Tennis Ranch in Scottsdale, Arizona, for a month of dieting and nonstop tennis. "When all the trouble started and my manager was sent to prison, I had time to think," Elton acknowledged. "The thought of going on another tour, for the time being, was impossible. If we didn't stop now, I think it would have been the end."

12

Making Rock History

"I don't want that track on the album," Elton warned producer
Gus Dudgeon. Even before the New Zealand disaster, the start of
1974 had been difficult for Elton. He was under fierce pressure to
complete his album *Caribou* to accommodate his tour schedule. He
was busy beyond belief, and the pressures were clearly bearing down
on him. He had to record *Caribou* in eight days, and because of
technical problems at the studio the tracks had to be rushed and cut
in three days.

Elton was angry about this, and especially unhappy with the backing vocals on the track "Don't Let the Sun Go Down on Me," a Roy
Orbison-inspired ballad with harmonies reminiscent of the Beach
Boys. Initially, the track was supposed to feature an ambitious lineup
which included the Beach Boys, Dusty Springfield, Danny Hutton
of Three Dog Night, and the group America, all of whom had been
assembled by Dudgeon.

But the outcome proved too chaotic and unwieldy, and Elton was
now nearly coming to blows with Dudgeon over it. Shrieking and
cursing, Elton warned him against including the track on the album.
Fortunately, the soft-spoken Dudgeon was able to salvage the song,

The Elton John band. (AP/Wide World Photos)

John Reid in trouble in Rome. (AP/Wide World Photos)

Rocket Man Elton returns from Russia—
1979, Heathrow Airport. (AP/Wide
World Photos)

A friend of the stars—with Elizabeth Taylor backstage in Philadelphia, July 7, 1976. (AP/Wide World Photos)

Fit for a prince. Elton meets H.R.H. Prince Charles at Wembley, 1986. (AP/Wide World Photos)

Elton the football fan—Los Angeles, 1976. (AP/Wide World Photos)

With Andy Warhol at Xenon disco in New York, June 13, 1978. (AP/Wide World Photos)

A sailor in Rio, February 1978. (AP/Wide World Photos)

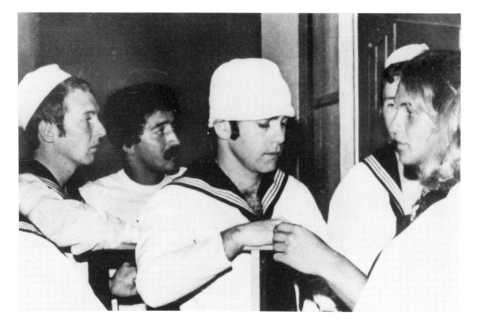

Bride and groom—Elton and Renate Blauel, Sidney, 1984. (AP/Wide World Photos)

Elton and Bernie Taupin at re-
signing with MCA Records, Los
Angeles, July 1987. (Kevin
Winter/DMI)

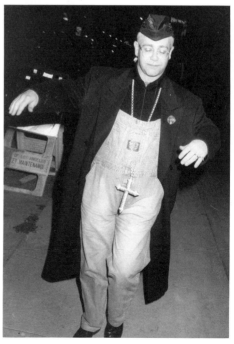

Elton cavorts outside Hollywood
party, November 1989. (Kevin
Winter/DMI)

"Reg Strikes Back." A dressed down
Elton, backstage at Madison Square
Garden, New York City, October
1988.
(Albert Ferreira/DMI)

Liberace Redux. Elton struts his stuff at the Garden, New York City, September 1986. (David McGough/DMI)

Elton with casino king Donald Trump and his then wife Ivana at a party at El Morocco, New York City, October 1988.
(Albert Ferreira/DMI)

Over the top. Elton notches a record for thirty performances on the Garden stage, October 1989. (Albert Ferreira/DMI)

paring down the ensemble to the Beach Boys' Bruce Johnston and Carl Wilson, and thereby calming Elton.

"Don't Let the Sun Go Down on Me" would turn out to be the outstanding track on an otherwise mediocre album that included some losers, "Dixie Lily," written by Bernie during the dog days of a Mississippi fishing trip, and the inane "Solar Prestige a Gammon," which was supposed to be a joke. An example of the latter's inscrutable lyrics: "Kool Kar Kyrie Kay Salmon / Hair ring molasses abounding."

Though lyricist Bernie Taupin was by now being billed as something akin to the poet laureate of rock music, when the lyrics were examined without the melody behind them, they often seemed to amount to little more than a catchy line. Often, Elton's masterful composing elevated Bernie's sometimes pretentious or pedestrian lyrics and gave them intonations and shadings. The poetry seemed to come from the music, not the words. On their own, many of Bernie's lyrics could be mere scribblings—jottings in some notebook consigned to a desk drawer. Of course, it could be argued that without Bernie's lyrics to fuel Elton's musical imagination there would be no songs in the first place. However, Elton's gift of composition, marvelous piano playing and dramatic delivery really made all the difference.

Yet in the public's mind, Bernie was the "poet" and Elton the "performer," a perception mirrored by their respective living circumstances—Bernie residing in his country cottage called Piglet-in-the-Wilds with his wife, Maxine, and Elton in his lavish home Hercules, a split-level mansion within reach of London. With Elton's pack-rat tendencies, the place was starting to resemble Elvis's Graceland—except that Elton was obsessively neat.

Elton's rendering of "The Bitch Is Back," the only other single to come off the *Caribou* album, was an example of how he could take a moronic phrase, "Bitch, bitch . . . the bitch is back," sound almost onomatopoetic. Lashing out with his voice, practically annihilating the lyrics with his scathing and violent delivery, Elton managed to convey the essence of the word *bitch* better than Bernie's lyrics could ever do.

There were few outstanding tracks on the *Caribou* album. But at the very least Elton had found an enchanting new place to work, the Caribou Recording Ranch in Nederland, Colorado. Owned by James

William Guercio, who had managed the jazz-rock group Chicago, the ranch was set on the last slope of the Rocky Mountains, at an altitude of about eighty-six hundred feet. Caribou was vintage Western, with even a dinner gong summoning the British boys in the band to meals. The food was usually Yankee fare served by comely members of the staff.

Elton liked the place so much that he titled the album created there *Caribou*, and he returned to work there twice. To this Englishman, the Rocky Mountains were a spectacular setting, and the *Caribou* album sleeve showed Elton, wearing black trousers, a leopard jacket and pink-tinted glasses, against a painted backdrop of tall mountains and blue skies. But as much as he reveled in the natural beauty of the Rockies, Elton was consumed with worries about the album. It was time, he figured, for the critics to pounce.

Elton had other concerns on his mind as well. At twenty-seven he was definitely getting bald, as was visible in the photo on the *Caribou* sleeve. He was worried as well about his fledgling record label, Rocket, which had so far done nothing more than stumble on a few forgettable acts. Kiki Dee was an exception: Her debut single on Rocket, "Amoreuse," had landed in the Top Twenty, suggesting a good future for the company. Neil Sedaka would not debut on the label until January 1975.

But it was difficult to envisage any hits from any other artists within the company. Longdancer, a folk-rock combo signed to the label, had limited appeal even though the brother of Elton's drummer, Nigel Olsson, was a member of the group. "Longdancer is not mind-shattering yet," Elton remarked at the time. "They've got a long way to go yet." Almost a decade later, however, in 1983, the band's guitarist, Dave Stewart, teamed up with Annie Lennox of the Eurythmics for a Number One hit, "Sweet Dreams (Are Made of This)." And there was also the thirteen-year-old Welsh boy soprano Maldwyn Pope Thomas, whom Rocket signed to a lengthy contract. The boy had come recommended by BBC Radio 1 disc jockey John Peel, but once inside the studio ready to record, his voice changed. Along with the chaos at Rocket and the breakneck speed of the *Caribou* album, Elton was experiencing further anxiety from impending contract negotiations with his American recording label, MCA.

"It's a miracle the *Caribou* album came out," Elton says, "because of all the pressure within the group; especially with me. We'd been on the road for four and a half years and we all looked like just unbelievable zombies, felt like death warmed up and we were just at the point of breaking up." Then came the fracas in New Zealand that landed John Reid a monthlong jail sentence, interrupting his negotiations on Elton's behalf with MCA.

The pressures were taking their toll on Elton's physical health as well. "I'd put on forty-five pounds because I was drinking at least half a bottle of scotch each day," he said. "I just felt awful and I looked at myself—'At twenty-seven your hair's going, your body's going, *you're* going.'"

"I mean, I was just becoming an alcoholic," he admits. "It was just ridiculous. The worst thing is the next day. I got to the point where I was taking things to get me over getting up, and feeling like that you just feel like, 'Ahhh.' So I thought, 'That's it. It's gonna be health from now on.'"

It was then that he canceled the seventeen-date British tour and went off to John Gardner's Tennis Ranch in Arizona. If Elton had been using the wardrobe department and flamboyant costumes to make up for a lost and unhappy youth, he was now doing the same in the athletic arena, playing tennis with Wimbledon winners Jimmy Connors and Billie Jean King.

The previous year Billie Jean King had started World Team Tennis in an effort to make the sport, still very starchy and largely lily-white, more egalitarian. Well-intentioned as the idea of team tennis seemed, it never really caught on, and probably its major legacy was altering the dress code from all-white to a rainbow of colors. It was an idea that appealed to Elton. He became a fan of the Philadelphia Freedoms and attended their games whenever he was in town. Courtesy of Billie Jean, Elton was rewarded with a Freedoms warm-up suit custom-made by the sport's premier designer, the Englishman Ted Tindling.

Elton was thrilled by this new addition to his wardrobe. As Billie Jean remembers: "We gave it to him and as we were in the limo coming back from the matches he said, 'Billie, I'm going to write a song for you.' I said, 'Sure you are,' and he said, 'No, I mean it, just wait and see.'" That song was "Philadelphia Freedom."

Elton, who had given up alcohol and sweets, now gorged himself on athletic events. He was unhappy, for example, if a gig got in the way of his watching "Monday Night Football" while in America. Unabashedly, Elton admitted, "I'm an absolute sports groupie. I always feel sorry for the team on the bottom. I was never any good at sports—and I remember one year at school everybody had teams. On "field day" they would compete against one another. Because I was fat they used to put me into the shot put. And the first time they put me into the shot put, I went to it and the ball spun off my chin and fell on my foot and broke my toe. I was only good at soccer and tennis."

Elton was becoming like the archetypal fat kid who finally gets some attention and respect and now has an opinion on everything: "It's been said there's a parallel between sports and rock people because they come from the same background," Elton expounded in an interview. "No way. Sports people go through hell. You have to be far more dedicated. It's not a question of physical ability, because if you've got it, you've got it, like playing the guitar. If a tennis player loses his concentration for one minute, it can blow the whole game." Elton even talked about baseball: "I hate the fucking Oakland A's and they win it every year. I'm a Mets fan."

Elton's tennis vacation had been both a tonic and an elixir. Once back in England, a now-refreshed Elton gave two magical performances in London. His concert at the Royal Festival Hall raised more than £10,000 ($24,137) for disabled children. Elton, in turn, took home a pair of stuffed leopards from Princess Margaret, a friend whom he would soon be accompanying to a movie premiere.

The other concert took place at the Vicarage Road grounds of the Watford Football Club. Attended by forty thousand people, it was the largest crowd in the club's history. Elton, suitably dressed for the event in Watford's colors, yellow and black, raised £40,000 ($96,548). His old friend Rod Stewart, also a football fan, sang "Country Comfort," from *Tumbleweed Connection*. Elton thought Rod's rendition was better than his own—and so he had stopped singing it. But the big surprise of the day was Elton's own version of the Beatles' "Lucy in the Sky With Diamonds," which, unknown to the audience, he would soon record.

Performing for Watford pleased Elton enormously. "Soccer really does mean a lot to me," he explained. "I need it for the fact that it brings me into touch with some kind of real world." Proud though he was of his directorship of the Watford club, he also saw some peril in an association with the sport, namely the players' tendency to drink. For the time being, at least, he had sworn off alcohol.

The results of his abstinence were evident in June 1974, when he breezed in to New York to launch Rocket artist Kiki Dee and to publicize his *Caribou* album as well. He was forty pounds lighter after the strict regimen of dieting and exercise that he had begun in Scottsdale.

But if his frame had shrunk, his mood was expansive as he gave interviews in a cheap hotel room rented for the purpose. On the trip to New York Elton stayed with friends on Central Park West because, as he explained, "I hate hotels. For the money I spent even in Los Angeles in the last four years I could have bought a house." His favorite Los Angeles stopping place was a bungalow (actually a small luxury house) on the grounds of the Beverly Hills Hotel, because, he explained, "I've got a lot of luggage. I couldn't just stay anyplace. I wouldn't be able to fit it all in." Elton always registered under various aliases. More recently, at the Beverly Hills Hotel, he had used "Frank N. Stein."

The shabby hotel room used for interviews this time seemed a curious economy on Elton's part because everything else about the twenty-seven-year-old star screamed of profligacy. His piano-thumping fingers were adorned with diamonds and ivory, and, calculating the excess-baggage charges on tour, Elton came up with the figure of ten thousand dollars. He even carried a special suitcase for his fourscore glasses in every conceivable style and tint.

"My theory about spending money," he explained to one interviewer, "is that I could walk in to this hotel and the maid could come up to me and suffocate me with a great big pillow and I'd be dead. So many people are miserable with success. I can't be that way. People are really morbid. They become successful and hide away. I can understand the hiding, but I refuse to stop going and spending money or having a good time. I like to consider myself an eccentric."

Frivolous as his purchases appeared to be—they included three pairs of mink-trimmed glasses—they did not mirror his taste in fine art. Superb antiques and examples of French art deco filled every inch of his mansion in England. "It would look like the British Museum," Elton said, "except I've got gold records on the ceiling."

Elton had traveled to America aboard the luxury ocean liner *France*. During the five-day crossing he wrote an entire album's worth of songs. He was in high gear, creatively and physically. Straight off the boat, Elton hightailed it to Philadelphia to play with comic Bill Cosby at an exhibition tennis match.

"Usually they get three thousand people at the Spectrum," he recalls. "But they had nine thousand that night. It's one thing to go out there and play rock 'n' roll, but to play tennis like a schmuck is another. I lost the first two games. . . . But I knew I could beat him."

He did win the set, and indeed he seemed to be scoring on all other fronts as well. By June "Don't Let the Sun Go Down on Me," which had caused Elton so much aggravation, became his fourth gold single, at Number Two, in the United States, only two months after "Bennie and the Jets" reached the top. The single also earned Elton a Grammy nomination for Best Vocal in 1974. The next month, the *Caribou* album hit Number One in the United States, staying there for four weeks, and also topped the U.K. charts. By September, "The Bitch Is Back" peaked at Number Fifteen in the United Kingdom and Number Four in America. Granted, the critics were lukewarm, but in view of Elton's low expectations for the album, he was able to live with the reviews.

By July, his manager John Reid, sprung from his jail cell, had concluded his months of final negotiations with MCA. Under the new terms, Elton, the boy from Pinner, was guaranteed $8 million annually.

"I don't have anything to do with the business," Elton said. "I can't bear it. If I've got a buyer's meeting, I think, 'Oh groan.' This is completely John's baby." But he was also quick to point out, "Basically, he's got no choice about *how* I am. If he didn't like what I wore onstage—and sometimes he doesn't—he's got no chance of changing it, because I'm my own boss. My ideas, what I want to do, they're paramount. Obviously, he wants the best deals for me, but if I don't want to play a particular hall, say, it doesn't matter if it's the biggest hall. I won't play it."

Despite his extraordinary wealth, with personal earnings from record sales, publishing and performing fees and royalties reaching the $25 million mark, Elton still carried some old habits from leaner days. Though armed with credit cards, he rarely used them because he was terrified of paying the bills at the end of the month. And outrageous and egregious as his spending appeared to be, it was also

true that Elton John made his megamoney the old-fashioned way—
he earned it.

Throughout most of June and July Elton was back in Colorado
recording at Caribou his *Captain Fantastic and the Brown Dirt Cowboy* album for release in spring 1975, as well as a spate of singles that
included a cover version of the Beatles' "Lucy in the Sky With Diamonds" and "Philadelphia Freedom."

Once a rough mix of "Philadelphia Freedom" was cut, Elton could
hardly wait to play it for Billie Jean King. In fact, he turned up in
nearby Denver, where her team was in the playoffs, to play the song
for her. Rushing into her dressing room, where she was preparing
for a match, Elton was highly excited, telling Billie Jean, "You've got
to listen to this tape. This is it, the song I wrote for you. Do you like
it? Listen to this part. Hear the beat? That's when you get mad on
the tennis court."

Billie Jean loved the track, and before the year was out Elton
brought his new muse out onstage at a Philadelphia concert to dance
to "Philadelphia Freedom" while he hit tennis balls into the audience. Predictably, two years down the line, in 1976, those fans who
liked to invest Bernie's lyrics with heavy political and spiritual messages explained the song as a bicentennial tribute to the City of
Brotherly Love and the home of the Liberty Bell.

The cover version of the Lennon-McCartney song "Lucy in the
Sky With Diamonds" from the Beatles' 1967 album *Sgt. Pepper's
Lonely Hearts Club Band* was the highlight of Elton's second visit to
the Caribou Recording Ranch. "I said to John," Elton relates, " 'I'd
like to record one of your songs. Which one would you like me to
do?' And he said, 'No one's ever done "Lucy in the Sky" . . .' "

This marked a change for Elton because, aside from his Bluesology
days "Love Song" by his friend Lesley Duncan, and the Rolling
Stones' "Honky Tonk Woman," he had not released a single by anyone other than Bernie and himself. Early in 1975 "Lucy" would become Elton's third Number One single. It was only the second Lennon-McCartney song not sung by the Beatles to top the charts. Peter
and Gordon's "A World Without Love," which reached Number One
back in 1964, had been the first. Elton's "Lucy" took the title of the
most successful Beatles cover version of the modern rock era. The
"Dr. Winston O'Boogie" who was listed on the credits as a guitarist
was John Lennon himself.

Later in the summer of 1974 when Lennon was making his *Walls and Bridges* album in a New York studio, Elton sang backing vocals and played piano and organ on a new song, "Whatever Gets You Through the Night," Lennon had written. Recognizing the song's appeal, Elton predicted that it would reach Number One. Lennon, who believed he was out of favor in America, disagreed. Elton insisted otherwise and wagered that if he was proved right Lennon would have to appear with him in concert at Madison Square Garden. Never believing the single would top the chart, Lennon accepted the bet.

Elton would later explain that he made the bet as much for John Lennon as for himself. "I knew it would be great fun for me," he says, "but I also did it for John. I thought it would do him good to get out of his shell."

Lennon was going through a bad period. He was separated from Yoko Ono and living a fairly dissolute life in Los Angeles with his sometime personal assistant May Pang. He was also being hounded by United States immigration authorities, who were denying him the green card that would enable him to work in America.

John Lennon was Elton's hero. "He's the only person in this business that I've ever looked up to, the only person," Elton says. "I've met people who are great, like Mick Jagger and Pete Townshend, whom I admire tremendously, but they are not in the same league. I'm sorry. He is the only person in this business who is one hundred percent sacred to me." Elton had by now retired Bob Dylan as his ultimate hero.

On Thanksgiving Day, November 28, 1974, Elton and his hero would make rock history together at New York City's Madison Square Garden. Less than two weeks earlier, "Whatever Gets You Through the Night" had hit Number One and Elton called in his bet. The reclusive ex-Beatle did his part. For Elton the historic event was the culmination of a ten-week, forty-five-concert tour that had broken house records elsewhere in the country—including at the Los Angeles Forum, where tickets for three October concerts had sold out in minutes and a fourth performance had to be added. By November 1974, Elton also had another Number One LP, his *Greatest Hits*.

A few days before his appearance at Madison Square Garden, Lennon turned up in Boston to watch Elton's show there. "When he saw all the equipment," Elton recalled in an interview during which he was clad in a chocolate box cover, "he said, 'My God, is this what it's all about?' "

Lennon was a nervous wreck backstage at the Madison Square Garden concert. Elton and the band were also experiencing a bad case of nerves. Midway through the show, Elton was still not sure that Lennon would actually turn up. Kiki Dee and her band, the opening act, came and went, followed by an intermission that seemed to the audience interminable. Then came an animated cartoon of the song "Teenage Idol" ("I'm gonna grab myself a place in history / A teenage idol that's what I'm gonna be"). By now the Garden was abuzz with rumors of Lennon's appearance, and fans were giddy with excitement.

Five minutes later Mr. Teen Idol himself materialized for his show of shows. His grand piano sparkled with paneled mirrors, and Elton himself was dripping with a half million dollars' worth of insured gems. Ed McCormack in *Rolling Stone* described Elton as "banging away at the piano in some kind of cockamamie papal purple robe" with "a four-foot ostrich plume slanting and swaying up from his glittering top hat at a wild angle" and looking "for all the gawking world . . . like the bastard offspring of some unthinkable tryst between Leon Russell and Liberace."

Elton opened with the instrumental "Funeral for a Friend" and then, lifting the top hat to show off his feather-framed glasses, turned to face the audience to wish them a happy Thanksgiving. He presented a platter of their favorite songs. But midway through the concert Elton and his band started to become concerned. John Lennon had yet to appear. Elton called out his name, and on hearing it, Lennon made a detour to the bathroom to throw up. Then, suddenly, to wild applause, John Lennon himself wandered on stage.

As if in deference to Lennon, Elton had already removed his flashy outfit, at least the top half of it, revealing his hirsute chest, all slimmed down and adorned with suspenders. It was a subtle way to shift the focus away from the glitz of Elton's act to the stage-shy Lennon whom Elton admired so deeply.

Together they performed three numbers, "Whatever Gets You Through the Night," "Lucy in the Sky With Diamonds" and "I Saw Her Standing There," a song for which Paul McCartney was primarily responsible. Ultimately it would be released on the B side of "Lucy." Elton had wanted Lennon to sing "Imagine," but Lennon had turned him down because, as he put it, "I didn't want to come on like Dean Martin doing my classic hits," and furthermore, this was Elton's show.

The cheers that greeted Lennon brought tears to Elton's eyes. Deeply moved by the tribute to his hero, a choked-up Elton murmured to his audience, who had set the Garden aglow with sparklers, candles and matches when he sang "Don't Let the Sun Go Down on Me," "Thank you. You're all incredible."

As Elton remembers, "It's hard to describe how wonderful it was to see Lennon back onstage, loosening up, beginning to enjoy himself, in the end revealing the persona of John Lennon all over again. So much so that later, at a postconcert party, when I said to him, 'You must be tired of hearing this, but your music changed my life,' he smiled kindly, his face aglow, and said, 'You're right, I do hear that a lot, but I never get tired of hearing it.'"

As a gesture of thanks Elton gave Lennon a black onyx pendant trimmed in gold and encrusted with several diamonds.

The historic significance of this night did not unfold, however, for another six years, until December 1980, when John Lennon was assassinated outside his New York City apartment building. That Thanksgiving concert with Elton, on November 28, 1974, was the last time John Lennon appeared onstage.

For the moment, though, the irony of Lennon having to elbow his way through a crowd to get to Elton at the postconcert party was not lost on either man.

The bash that night at the formal Pierre Hotel turned out to be as stormy as the concert itself. Elton, in a swirling tease, called an overdressed woman, a complete stranger, a "slag," cockney for an unattractive woman of low morals, and then spirited himself away to another location in the room.

Elton had a razor-sharp tongue and often his sardonic observations could be very hurtful to an unsuspecting person. The boy whom nobody paid any attention to at school was determined not to go unnoticed. An outrageous remark or an outburst of temper or a grotesque costume promised him attention.

In December, "Lucy in the Sky With Diamonds" hit Number One on the singles charts. But even with that hit, another gold single, "Don't Let the Sun Go Down on Me," and two chart-topping albums, *Caribou* and *Greatest Hits*, all in the same year, Elton still had not made peace with his past.

13

Rock Music's Newest Midas

On a sunny morning in late June 1975, a brown chauffeur-driven Rolls-Royce Phantom pulled up outside Cartier's on London's fashionable and exclusive Bond Street. The car's tinted windows hid the identity of the passenger. A crowd, gathering on the sidewalk, seemed to think the gold crest on the door might mean a glimpse of a member of the Royal Family.

Much to their puzzlement and disappointment, a short, roundish man in high-waisted green trousers alighted from the car. Clearly this was no prince, though the reception accorded him by Cartier employees suggested otherwise. The doorman bowed before him and a chorus of eager and solicitous salesmen chirped, "Good morning, Mr. John. Can we help you with some gifts?"

Royal spender Elton John, the Captain Fantastic of customers, was on a gift-buying mission for his band and staff. There were eleven names on his list and potential presents next to each one. With his personal assistant, Bob Halley, and two salesmen in tow, Elton charged past displays of gold paper clips and platinum letter openers to pick out more expensive items.

By now Elton's generosity had reached mammoth proportions. On his manager alone he had recently lavished an $80,000 yacht and a $10,000 Fabergé clock. Elton's secretary received a $2,300 red fox coat. Earlier in the year Elton had sent a Dutch Master etching to Rod Stewart for his thirtieth birthday.

One of Elton's more amusing extravaganzas was a party he hosted in early 1975 at the now-defunct Le Restaurant in Beverly Hills to celebrate Rocket artist Neil Sedaka's chart-topping "Laughter in the Rain." Elton made a grand entrance on a horse rented for the occasion. Remembers Sedaka, "Elton galloped into the place and Mae West was sitting right next to us with her bodyguards."

It was customary for Elton to reward his band and staff members after a major concert or tour. And there were just three days to go before his only major appearance of the year at Wembley Stadium in north London. It promised to be a huge event. More than seventy thousand people had paid more than £200,000 ($480,000) to attend his concert there. In less than five years Elton's personal earnings from record sales, publishing and performance royalties totaled $25 million, and his annual income was now $7 million.

Rock's newest Midas would put on quite a show at Cartier's for *Time* magazine correspondent David DeVoss, who was reporting a cover story on Elton. The journalist watched as the tab rapidly mounted for purchases, which included a gold necklace, a bracelet, one duffel bag, four briefcases and three gold cigarette lighters.

"What are we going to get for Skunk," Elton asked his assistant, referring to guitarist Jeff "Skunk" Baxter, whom he had recently lured away from the Doobie Brothers. "Does he smoke?"

"I don't know," replied Halley. "But we simply must get that burgundy bag for Ray. It just matches his Bentley."

The burgundy bag was meant for Ray Cooper, the manic percussionist and beanstalk of a man who had been recruited during the making of *Caribou* and whom Elton believed might relieve him in the acrobatics department. "He takes a lot of work off me as far as visuals go," Elton explained. "I can have a rest every now and again because I know he's having a bit of a leap about."

Elton purchased the bag for Ray over the protest of another customer, an expensively dressed woman, who insisted that she had expressed "active interest" in the bag the day before. But the sales-man ignored her wishes and removed the bag from the display case and put it in Elton's pile. The woman scowled at Elton. Elton, smiling slyly, wrote out a check for $7,000 to cover the bag and the rest of his purchases. "Being interested," Elton snorted, "is not the same as buying it."

Even if Elton never sang another note, he could still afford to put his money where his mouth was. Under the new contract negotiated by manager John Reid, MCA advanced $8 million over five years for distribution rights to his albums. He was now the world's highest-paid artist, and the owner of two Rolls-Royces equipped with tele-vision sets and two tape decks, and a Ferrari, a $250,000 home in a London suburb and a $925,000 mansion in Benedict Canyon in Los Angeles.

"The only thing I really crave," said Elton, a collector of Rembrandt etchings, Magrittes and art deco, "is an original Toulouse-Lautrec or an Hieronymus Bosch."

For MCA the deal was equally beneficial. If Elton's albums, av-eraging two a year, continued to sell at the current rate, the company would recoup its investment after two albums. His newest LP, *Captain Fantastic and the Brown Dirt Cowboy*, the ninth of his twelve albums to sell more than a million in the United States alone, turned platinum before it even hit the music counters, with advance orders for 1.4 million copies.

It slotted into *Billboard*'s Number One the day of its release, a feat never achieved by Elvis or the Beatles. Within a week it topped all three U.S. charts — *Billboard, Cash Box* and *Rolling Stone* — and hit Number Two in the United Kingdom. Over the past five years, Elton's worldwide sales of forty-two million albums and eighteen million singles had generated $300 million in retail sales.

The MCA agreement also allowed Elton time to pursue other projects. Steve McQueen, a close friend, had repeatedly encouraged Elton to take up acting. Elton, who was never comfortable with him-self, resisted at first, eventually accepting director Ken Russell's offer of a cameo role in the rock opera *Tommy*. Elton's three-minute ap-pearance as the Pinball Wizard in the film established him as a box office draw. Many movie houses showing the film even gave him top billing. "You're gonna die when you see *Tommy*," Elton told one interviewer. "Ken Russell made me pull more faces in that movie than I've done in my whole life. Pulling the worst faces of all time. I get beaten in the movie."

Back in Bond Street, Elton, having won the battle of the burgundy bag, was on his way out of Cartier's when it suddenly occurred to him that he had forgotten to buy *himself* something. Quickly, the salesmen obliged, opening this display cabinet and that box of jewelry to try to interest him in a ring or some other trinket. Nothing particularly appealed to him, though, and minutes later he charged out of the store and climbed back in the Rolls.

Not one to stint on himself, he directed the chauffeur to an art deco gallery nearby. Darting in and out of rooms there, Elton selected three posters, "Subway Symphony," "Miss Wurlitzer" and "Fading Star," and two small statues. Fifteen minutes later, he wrote out another check, this time for $4,300.

These latest art acquisitions were supposed to go into the game room of Elton's Virginia Water mansion, except that every inch of wall space there was covered with silver, gold and platinum records and other awards. Though Elton knew this ahead of time, he did not have any reservations about his purchases. As he explained, "Inanimate objects have been my friends for years. I actually talk to paintings."

14

Stage Cloak and Dagger

On the eve of the release of *Captain Fantastic and the Brown Dirt Cowboy*, Elton picked up the phone and dialed Nigel Olsson at home. His drummer had expected a phone call to find out when rehearsals were set to begin. The Wembley Stadium concert, at which Elton planned to preview the album, was no more than a month away.

But Olsson was taken totally by surprise when he heard what Elton had called to tell him. He and bass player Dee Murray had been fired. And so they would now not be part of the lineup at Wembley. As Olsson remembers, "Elton called me himself to say he wanted to change the band. He was ringing from Richard Chamberlain's home in Los Angeles."

It was a rare act of bravery on Elton's part. "Usually," said Olsson, "his lackeys—record plugger Steve Brown or personal assistant Bob Halley—did the dirty work." Normally, in the mercurial world of the rock music business, firings arrived by way of an intermediary. But there had never been a chain of command separating Elton from his band, who were more like family than mere business associates. At the very least they had expected Elton to tell them in person that they were no longer needed.

Murray received the bad news while on holiday in Barbados. "It was a disappointment," says Murray, "because there were things going on that I didn't know about. If people had the courage to just come out in the open with it, then it would have been more understandable." Likening the band to a family, Murray acknowledges, "Things happen when people live together and get older. But too many people take the easy way out."

According to Murray, Elton tried to soften the blow by telling him he had consulted John Lennon, who had advised against the sackings. Murray recalls, "Elton said Lennon told him he was a fool for breaking up the band. But Elton wanted to change." Elton now counted Lennon as a close friend, and in November 1975, he became the godfather to John and Yoko's newborn son, Sean.

Olsson, oblivious to his imminent firing, had spoken affectionately about Elton and the band to an interviewer earlier in the year. "We're so close it's like a family thing. We don't really feel that we're under his shadow because of the family thing. . . . And now people know there's more people than Elton John. Kids go to see Elton, but they know the other guys as well. We have our own separate part of the audience and it's great. But I can't see myself leaving Elton, because we're too close, like a family."

The pixielike drummer with his teen-idol looks made no secret all along of his desire for personal stardom, but this was always secondary to his commitment to the Elton John Band. During the *Captain Fantastic* sessions Olsson had recorded his own single, "Only One Woman," an old Bee Gees tune, which he sang. It was released in January 1975, and he was looking forward to a singing career in the future. The previous February he had gone into Ringo's studio outside of London to cut an album. "I think if we [the Elton John Band] had been promoted the right way in the beginning," he would say later on, "we could have now been in the same class with the Beatles—I mean, everybody knows who Ringo is."

Olsson had also envisaged the Elton John Band recording an album of their own and going on the road together during lulls in Elton's touring and recording. The lineup was to be Olsson, Murray and Davey Johnstone. Defending his actions in the press, Elton hinted that Johnstone knew about the sackings and had given his tacit approval.

However, if Elton thought he had a conspirator in Johnstone, he was wrong. According to Kiki Dee, Johnstone's girlfriend at the time, "Having been kept on, Davey was in an awkward position. Obviously he felt sorry for Dee and Nigel, yet didn't want to antagonize Elton. I didn't know, and still don't, the ins and outs of the situation, beyond Elton's wanting a change. What was questionable was the way it was done."

Both Olsson and Murray felt betrayed. Loyal to Elton for five years, they had just returned from a grueling tour of America, Japan, Australia, New Zealand and England. The timing, too, could not have been more brutal. They had contributed their talents once again to what would become Elton's biggest-selling album to date, *Captain Fantastic and the Brown Dirt Cowboy*, and now, all of a sudden, they were no longer needed. Three days hence, at Wembley, Elton was planning to showcase his new band and preview the *Captain Fantastic* album without them.

Elton himself offered a few different scenarios. One claimed that the original band members might have been resentful about the addition of percussionist Ray Cooper and guitarist Davey Johnstone to the lineup back in February 1972. Quite to the contrary—they had all adjusted happily to the change. Elton also suggested that Murray had balked at the volume of concerts. But if this were the case, then Murray would have quit of his own volition and certainly would have reacted altogether differently to the firing. In fact, Murray icily rejected a dinner invitation from Elton as a balm for his hurt feelings.

Olsson, on the other hand, was more forgiving. Elton had promised him a song for his solo career. Diplomacy was also required because Olsson was signed to Rocket Records and John Reid was also his manager.

Though Elton publicly stated how awful he felt about the sackings ("I'd never fired anyone in my life before"), privately, of course, he had instigated the dismissal of Ray Williams years before. In fairness to Elton, though, riding so high in his career and terrified that a fall might be imminent, he believed that it was time to take a few risks. "The *Captain Fantastic* album is great," he said, "but I'd be a fool to believe I'm the biggest cheese in the world."

Despite his enormous commercial success and the diversity of his songs, he had yet to gain the respect of many rock critics. For the most part they regarded Elton and Bernie as purveyors of commercial middle-of-the-road music. Those critics, accustomed to "message songs" and extended guitar riffs that could only get airplay on FM stations, sniffed at Elton and Bernie's melodic tunes, each a little over two minutes, neatly packaged for AM radio or piping into elevators.

"Middle-of-the-road—I like that term," Elton said. "It means that my music appeals to a wide variety of people, which is what's important." Later on he would invest his music with another description, "ultra-melodic pop," to defend against his critics. Elton's simple four-chord songs, while identifying him with a distinctive style, also gave rise to the notion that he was just recycling the same tunes.

A more severe criticism was that Elton borrowed too heavily from other artists—hard rockers from the Rolling Stones, harmonies from the Beach Boys, ballads from Joni Mitchell and Leonard Cohen. However, a suit brought by Pat Boone alleging that the "la-la-la-la" passages at the opening of "Crocodile Rock" were stolen from his 1962 hit song "Speedy Gonzalez" was nothing more than a nuisance.

Adding heft to Elton's lightweight image was his well-publicized party-hopping and outré outfits, including the tight leather pants with a simulated erection sewn into the lining which he wore to his post-Hollywood Bowl concert the year before. For a performance of "Lucy in the Sky With Diamonds" on the TV show "Cher" he wore $4,200 glasses with cloud-shaped lenses suspended by gold hooks from a gold and platinum frame encrusted with 103 diamonds.

Offstage his outfits were no less outrageous and were still a camouflage for his shyness. "He wears garish clothes onstage and off and hides behind costumes," his friend Cher said. "I saw him at a party where he came in wearing a bright pink wig and a magenta-colored suit." It was also a way for Elton to disarm people. Before anyone could poke fun at him by virtue of his bizarre attire, he beat them to it. Such fashion statements were also an act of rebellion against the sartorial restraints Elton's father had imposed upon him as a child.

Elton could also defend himself with his quick wit. Zingers were his form of martial arts. "I thought I was pretty strong," says Cher, noting, however, that "Elton can really throw darts. He calls me 'an old tart' or 'the queen of the supermarkets.' But it is always a tease, never really unkind." Except the previous year, when Elton appeared as a guest, along with Bette Midler, on Cher's television show. "Elton made me cry," Cher says. "He said some very unkind things about a song we were rehearsing. I got very upset and I began to cry.

'Damn it, Elton,' I said, 'I asked you [two] on this show because you're close friends. But who needed this aggravation?' "

The next day Elton, feeling terrible about his vicious tongue, arrived on the set with a star sapphire on a gold chain which he gave to Cher along with his profuse apologies.

If Elton could dish out the barbs, he bristled at any attacks when it came to his own work. He was vehement about being taken seriously. "People may come to see what I wear or what my glasses look like," he insisted, "but they don't buy records for their looks. Melody sells the record. People buy for sound, melody and song, along with quality. The music has got to be there."

Captain Fantastic marked a departure for Elton. The album's greatest success was musical. Instead of his four-chord songs like "The Bitch Is Back" and "Daniel," the title track, "Captain Fantastic," for example, was a tightly structured tune foiled against a subdued chorus in a minor key.

An autobiographical album, it was the story of a dirt cowboy (Bernie) from the north and a suburban scrambler (Elton) struggling for recognition as artists. Chronicling a thirty-six-month period—from their meeting to Elton's Troubadour debut—the end of most of the songs led musically to the start of the next. It was a sequence as much as a theme album.

The album covered their meeting on London's Tin Pan Alley ("Tower of Babel"), their signing with Dick James ("Meal Ticket"), early frustrations writing commercial tunes ("Bitter Fingers"), Elton's contemplated suicide over his impending marriage ("Someone Saved My Life Tonight"), Bernie's yearning for the Lincolnshire flatlands ("Tell Me When the Whistle Blows"), the first successes signaling a profitable future ("We All Fall in Love") and a confessional ("Curtains") of early naïveté and mistakes.

This time critics had to wonder about the apparent arrogance of twenty-eight-year-old Elton and his twenty-five-year-old partner Bernie writing an autobiography. It seemed a bit premature and presumptuous at this stage in their careers. Steve James, for one, found the album too introverted. "*Captain Fantastic* was indulgent," he says, "instead of being an album written and recorded to entertain." DJM asked Elton to cover the cost of the album sleeve, with an illustrated libretto inside a scrapbook of clippings from the sixties and a four-page cartoon strip of Elton's life.

Greil Marcus was one critic who shared James's view of the album. Reviewing *Captain Fantastic* in New York's *Village Voice* in June 1975, he described it as "flat, painfully slow, and filled with the kind of self-awareness that in rock and roll so often comes off as mere self-pity."

To this day James wonders whether the American atmosphere at the Caribou Recording Ranch, where the album was recorded, contributed to Elton's musical introspection. "Americans tend to analyze things much more than we do," James explains. "We English tend to accept things much more on face value. The environment in the States and American musicians around him probably made him feel a bit more introverted."

Convinced that *Captain Fantastic* was his best album, Elton brooded over a negative review in *New Musical Express*, and he even went to the extreme of wanting to sue the magazine for libel. When that proved ridiculous, Elton picked up the phone and called the editor to complain. "He made a big fuss," remembers James, "yelling at the editor about how could he do this, how could he criticize him when this was his best album. The *New Musical Express* was very influential then, and Elton actually ended up creating more animosity. But John Reid and all the sycophants around Elton were telling him how great the album was."

Elton's moods were so wayward that one minute he was mouthing off about how the English refused to give him the approval he deserved, and in the next how he would never forsake his homeland to become a tax exile in America. "You pick up the paper in England and you read who are the biggest stars in America and they say Bowie, Jethro Tull, and they never mention me," Elton complained. "That's real bullshit."

Fuming over what the tabloids printed about him, Elton maintained, "If anyone is going to be picked on, it's always me. With the money situation in England and everybody moving out, so everybody says (I never said it in an interview; I mean, Rod [Stewart] says it in interviews), but the big headline will be 'Elton Leaving England: Deserting a Sinking Ship. Well, We Don't Need Him!' I take the can from so many people."

Elton, now in an eighty percent tax bracket, decided, against the advice of his attorneys, not to follow the rock-star exodus to Europe and the United States. "There is nowhere like Britain," he declared.

"And I will pay through the nose to live here." The previous year, 1974, Elton had paid £1.8 million (a little over $4 million) in British taxes for the pleasure of living there.

America, however, seemed more suited to his showy spending than his native Britain. "My old friends think I'm used to such luxuries that I wouldn't accept their humble fare," Elton lamented to *Time* magazine. "There's a lot of resentment. I used to resent successful people."

Sheila worried that others begrudged her son his wealth. "People tend to shy away from him now," she said. "His old school pals are trying to pay their mortgages and they think Elton doesn't care."

Meanwhile, as his old friends were growing more envious, Elton had spent money unabashedly, drinking the finest wines, dining at pricey restaurants and jetting off to parties anywhere in the world if he fancied being there. He also frequented casinos to play blackjack, and even then he had a knack for coming out ahead or at least breaking even after a night of entertainment.

Elton's popularity had never been as great in Britain as in the United States. Though the duet "Don't Go Breaking My Heart," performed with Kiki Dee, would top the charts in the United Kingdom the next year, Elton would have to wait fifteen years, until 1990, before he had a solo Number One hit single in the United Kingdom. Then, it was only after Elton promised to donate the profits from it to his favorite cause, AIDS. In view of his lesser appeal in England, Elton was understandably nervous about the Wembley concert.

It was his only major appearance in England in 1975 and he would have to share the bill with other artists. More important, it marked the debut of his new band. In years to follow, the firings of Olsson and Murray would come back to haunt Elton. "I know people have said this band doesn't sound as good as the old band," Elton said, "but it's going to take time."

In addition to Davey Johnstone on guitar and Ray Cooper on percussion there were two new American musicians, Kenny Passarelli on bass (formerly with Joe Walsh, and taking Murray's place) and session keyboard player James Newton-Howard. Replacing Nigel Olsson on drums was Roger Pope, formerly with Kiki Dee's band and before that with Roger Cook's Blue Mink; he had played on Elton's earliest recordings. Another recruit from the past was Elton's pal, guitarist Caleb Quaye, whose support had led to Elton signing with DJM.

The new group rehearsed for ten hours daily in a studio outside of Amsterdam. In the days leading up to Wembley, Elton, chafing under the criticism of the sackings, was in a somewhat defiant mood. "It's an important concert for us," he explained to a *Sunday Mail* reporter. "Every detail must be right. Every note, every chord. When you are on top of the tree—and I suppose we are at the moment—you are always the target for cynics. But I will not give them the opportunity to tumble me. It is an attitude that only makes me dig in my heels."

Elton, who wanted to project a more subdued image, decided at the last minute to wear a simple blue suit with decoration only on the trouser cuffs instead of the tight black jumpsuit with silver studs, mirrors and sequins that had been specially designed for this event.

Elton's nervousness would prove to be well founded. The event was completely sold out, with seventy-five thousand in attendance, a cadre of celebrities. Paul and Linda McCartney, Harry Nilsson, Dean Martin's son, Dino Martin, Jimmy Connors and Billie Jean King sat on padded wicker chairs inside the stadium's royal box, above the audience. Concert crowds normally preferred the old standards to new unfamiliar material, but Elton had decided to preview *Captain Fantastic* throughout much of his one hour on stage. Elton had come on last after a full bill—the Eagles, Joe Walsh and, just before his set, the Beach Boys, who stole the show with their breezy California harmonies.

In fairness, the crowd's loyalties were divided among all the artists, and coming on at the end of a long afternoon of entertainment did not help Elton. He found the less-than-enthusiastic reception unsettling. Here he was at the top of the charts, his *Captain Fantastic* album edging out McCartney's *Venus and Mars* for the Number One slot on the U.S. charts, and it was hard to accept being upstaged.

Fiercely competitive, Elton always kept himself informed of where he stood on the charts, and he liked to know ahead of his rivals. To this end his Los Angeles office phoned every Monday morning to report the ratings to Elton and later in the day air-expressed the trade papers to him.

If Wembley portended a plunge in popularity, it would not come in 1975. In July, "Someone Saved My Life Tonight" hit Number Four in America, but reached only twenty-two in Britain. Once again Elton deflected inquiries about his social life by reprising the story of his aborted marriage to Linda Woodrow that was the inspiration for this song.

"Of course I felt for her," he said. "But what could I do? Would she have suffered an unhappy marriage?" Elton sang the lyrics ("You almost got your hooks in me / Didn't you, dear?") with such ferocity that the concern he expressed about his ex-fiancée seemed false. To one British reporter he claimed that he was dating "two or three girls in Los Angeles, but in England the score was blank. . . . One day, though, I want a wife and kids, but that's when I'm no longer a rock-'n'-roll singer."

By June he was back in America, recording his next album, *Rock of the Westies*, at Caribou. There the slimmed-down ugly duckling from Pinner dressed up like a cool dude in a Wyatt Earp hat and gem-studded western shirts. Somehow the sweatpants, silk evening socks and pastel Mary Janes that complemented Elton's rhinestone cowboy clothes gave him a ridiculous look.

At the Caribou ranch Elton enjoyed the camaraderie of the band, producer Dudgeon and manager Reid. It seemed to allay the loneliness and detachment he was feeling more and more often. Whooping it up like a bunch of teenagers, Elton and his cronies put the music up to the highest decibel while they boogied, bopped and bumped to playbacks of the tracks. "Un-REAL!" and "Dynamite!" they yelled. Elton liked to hear music the way kids listened to it.

Elton was a fan as much as a superstar. "The great thing about rock-'n'-roll," he said, "is that someone like me can be a star." Elton, much like a teenager, also had the habit of latching on to a song and listening to it or singing it in the car, at parties, on the tennis court, everywhere, until he drove his friends to distraction.

Though Elton had continued to watch his weight since his stay the previous winter at the Arizona tennis ranch, he was starting to drink again after giving it up in the wake of the New Zealand fracas. He fueled himself with scotch and water. Elton dedicated *Rock of the Westies*, his thirteenth album, to ex-band members Nigel Olsson and Dee Murray. Ironically, one track was titled "Hard Luck Story." By November the LP, just like *Captain Fantastic*, entered the charts at Number One.

Rock of the Westies also yielded Elton's third Number One U.S.

single of 1975, "Island Girl," along with "Lucy in the Sky With Diamonds" and "Philadelphia Freedom." It was his fifth Number One single all together. The album itself, originally titled *Bottled and Brained*, was more a throwback to the up-tempo *Caribou* than a sequel to *Captain Fantastic*, and critics hacked it to pieces. Later on, Elton would admit to *Rolling Stone* that it "probably doesn't have much depth to it, but I kinda like it."

At this stage in his career Elton could have recorded Lawrence Welk's favorite tunes and rocketed to the top of the charts. Everything he touched in 1975 turned to gold. He even managed with "Island Girl" to depose "Bad Blood," by his own Rocket artist Neil Sedaka, from the top of the charts. Because Elton owned the label and also sang backing vocals on "Bad Blood," it was as if he were succeeding himself.

The lack of privacy that attended Elton's celebrity was starting to rile him. "I'm getting really cheesed off," he moaned to *Rolling Stone*. "A couple of years ago I would deal with three or four fans outside the hotel and walk off down Lexington Avenue. Now it's impossible. I can't cope. I don't want to end up my life like Elvis. I want to be somebody who's active and involved with people, and that means going outside. I even tried one of those disguises, but that just doesn't work. I went to an amusement park on the tour and thirteen people surrounded me for protection. I felt like the pope."

Even in England Elton felt invaded. Two years earlier it had taken him two hours to escape from a concert hall in Newcastle, and the following year one hundred fans had surrounded a Liverpool radio station and refused to leave until Elton appeared. Concert crowds were one thing, but having fans surrounding him on the street was altogether unacceptable.

On August 25, 1975, Elton returned to the Troubadour in Los Angeles to commemorate the fifth anniversary of his triumphant debut there. It was a charity event for the Jules Stein Eye Institute, and his performances raised $150,000 for it. Only five years earlier, on the eve of his Troubadour debut, publicist Norm Winter had to pull out every public relations trick in the book to lure people to the show. Though the less-than-plush Troubadour had fallen into disrepair in more recent years, this time celebrities, including Mae West, Tony Curtis, Hugh Hefner, Cher and Ringo Starr, paid $250 each to attend Elton's opening night. About one hundred thousand people were unsuccessful in buying twenty-five-dollar tickets for his other sold-out appearances. Police, meanwhile, had to close off Santa Monica Boulevard to traffic because of the crowds outside the club.

But the Troubadour appearance dredged up guilt feelings in Elton about his firing of Olsson and Murray, and at his shows he publicly thanked both men, now nowhere to be seen.

Elton, on the other hand, seemed to be everywhere. He was voted Rocker of the Year by all the trade papers, and his cherubic face was all over CBS-TV when he cohosted with Diana Ross the first annual Rock Music Awards, in which he was a nominee in four categories. He was also elected to *Playboy*'s Jazz and Pop Hall of Fame.

On November 21, 1975, Elton was awarded a star in the sidewalk of Hollywood Boulevard's Walk of Fame as Los Angeles declared Elton John Day. For the first time in the history of 1,662 such ceremonies, the whole street had to be closed off because of converging crowds. Elton, deeply moved by the honor, remained the showman America loved. He was characteristically British in his droll remarks, confiding that it was hard "to think of things to say to the bloody pavement."

Elton John had now achieved movie star status and all that went with it, including a Benedict Canyon Moorish-style mansion with a swimming pool and a tennis court and lots of greenery. It had once been home to Greta Garbo, and the garden had a gazebo she had built to sleep in when it rained, and a waterfall, too, because she liked the sound of running water.

One morning Elton woke up in his Los Angeles home and saw a female fan sitting on the bed next to him. "Who are you?" Elton asked. To which the girl replied, "You don't know me." Christ, Elton thought to himself, the CIA should have the sources these kids have; she could have been somebody with a gun. Elton had always gone to great lengths to protect himself. Only eight people had his unlisted phone number, and even then it was changed every two weeks. Actually, Elton had never felt comfortable in the dark and eerie mansion, near the house in the canyon where the Manson murders had taken place. Now a complete stranger was sitting in his bedroom. His elaborate security system appeared to have failed him. Elton told her to get out and, fortunately, she obeyed.

These days Elton spent more and more time in Los Angeles, playing tennis on his own court, sitting up all night talking with friends or playing backgammon. Occasionally, he would also dance the night away with his good friend Cher.

From an onlooker's point of view, Elton appeared to have it all. But with all these fancy trappings, his life sometimes seemed to be spinning out of control. His increasing despair was obvious on one occasion while he was touring America: He had disappeared to his hotel room where he swallowed a fistful of Valiums and then reappeared to tell everyone. As he remembers, "I just wanted someone to put their arms around me and care."

Though it was a mock suicide, Elton's feelings of despair were very real. For while it seemed the world embraced Elton John the performer, he was privately a deeply lonely man. Reg Dwight still inhabited Elton John, and he continued to search for connections to his past. In November 1975 Elton hired a private plane to bring 130 friends, family, staff and journalists from London to Los Angeles for a week of celebration. Each person received a gift bag which, among other holiday treats, included a camera. They were put up at the Beverly Hills Holiday Inn.

The highlight of their stay was the weekend. The group was split in two—half the revelers going to a party at the marina where the yacht *Madman*, which Elton had bought for John Reid, was berthed, and the rest going to Elton's concert at Dodger Stadium. The next night the two camps switched places.

It had taken over a year to negotiate the concerts at Dodger Stadium. No other artist had appeared there since the Beatles rocked the place in 1966. But the Fab Four were history. Elton John was now the man of the hour, omnipresent, tossing out new hit singles month after month. As soon as one slipped off the charts, another climbed on it. Over a two-night period more than a hundred thousand people turned out for this event.

Inside the stadium, anticipation was in the air. Elton's imminent arrival on stage was regarded by many fans as something akin to the Second Coming, with 110,000 people holding their breath for the man they had all come to see. Fittingly, the stage was an altar, and as Elton appeared on it, thousands of worshipping fans rushed toward him but were intercepted by guards.

For over four hours Elton sang songs of his comic-book heroes, of innocence lost, of loves lost, of dead-end lives of loneliness and despair, mixed in with felicitous and bouncy up-tempo tunes. As always, he leapt on his piano, he ran across the stage, he strutted, he jumped up and he even fell down. He was a cheerleader, a clown, a messiah. He changed into costume after costume. But his sequined Dodger uniform told the whole story. The number on his back was 1. The baton was truly his now—he had taken over from the Beatles as the top British musical export.

The concerts at Dodger Stadium meant a great deal to Elton. It was hardly surprising that the enormous energy he put into his performances had led to his domination of the industry in a short five years. No other performer could put on this kind of show, spectacle and festival all in one.

But for all this success, Elton was near collapse four days later. Visibly tired and ashen, Elton decided to take four months off on the advice of his doctors. The touring and recording demands he placed on himself were, by any other artist's standards, inhuman. Apparently the lessons of the previous year, when his frayed nerves sent him packing off to a tennis ranch for a month, were still to be learned. Now exhaustion overwhelmed his compulsive work habits.

Elton knew that a year like 1975 could never come again. It was only a question now of how far and how fast he could fall in the fickle world of pop music. The weary twenty-eight-year-old superstar remarked, "I don't want to go on kicking piano stools over forever." Elton now longed for the past, which seemed like a century ago, but which was, remarkably, a mere eight years gone by.

"When I met Bernie," Elton told *Time* magazine's David DeVoss in June 1975, "I wanted to sit home and write records. But it was easy to give in to the image. Things shiny and clean came so quickly. But in the winning, something was lost. Five years ago I wondered if I'd ever get to Spain for a holiday. Now I whiz around the world. I regret losing touch with reality."

Elton found some reality when he brought the planeload of people to Los Angeles for the weeklong festivities. Among them were members of the Watford team, the sister of Kiki Dee and Bernie's gardener. "The really nice thing about it is that he took people who didn't have the money to jet off for a week in L.A.," says Dee. "I remember going to Disneyland and seeing the Rocket accountants wandering around in a trance trying to figure out what was going on. But it was a lovely gesture."

Elton's wild spending habits had now approached Presley-like proportions. "I guess it's gotten a little out of hand," he admitted. "People are starting to call me Old Moneybags."

Of course, there was always Sheila to remind her son, who cruised Cartier's as if he were doing his grocery shopping, of his middle-class origins. "I bought my mum a handbag," he said, "and when she found out how much it cost, she took it back and got a cheaper one."

15

A Royal Night Out at the Cinema

It seemed impossible that Elton could find anyone more famous than himself to escort for an evening. But one night in January 1976, as Elton emerged from his brown monogrammed Rolls-Royce on Shaftesbury Avenue in London's West End, all eyes were fixed on the lady in his company. Unlike Elton, a child of middle-class suburbia, his companion this evening was a woman who was born famous, and it was only because she had an older sister, the Queen of England, that she was not the best-known woman in the world.

Not even his Hollywood friends could compare socially to this woman, and here was Elton, a child of suburbia, from Pinner, taking her to the movies. Two friends, film director Bryan Forbes, who had made the documentary of the superstar's life, and his wife, actress Nanette Newman, were also along. This was a gala performance for Elton. He was escorting Princess Margaret.

Notwithstanding his bell-bottoms and platform heels, in his plain gray suit, Elton John, the prince of glitter, looked remarkably subdued alongside the princess, who was wearing a dazzling gold-encrusted gown. But on this night the occasion was the film premiere of Neil Simon's *The Sunshine Boys*.

The four patrons of the A.B.C. Cinema on Shaftesbury Avenue took their two-pound (four-dollar) seats in the last row of the cinema and then laughed their way through the film comedy. Emerging from the theater, Forbes remarked to the paparazzi, "We loved the show," and then the party of four squeezed into the back of Elton's car to be whisked away to dinner.

By now Elton had forged a friendship with the Royals. Recently Princess Margaret had told Elton over tea, "You are louder than Concorde." As a tribute to her, Elton titled his world tour later in the year Louder Than Concorde.

Though Elton was becoming the Royals' favorite performer, his behavior during much of 1976 would hardly qualify as a command performance. There seemed to be no protocol, palace or otherwise, for what Elton felt he needed to announce to the world.

Rocket Man Falls to Earth

16

Elton the Confessor

"If you are listening now, you asshole," a seething Elton announced over the airwaves, on Friday the thirteenth of August 1976, "come down here and I'll destroy you. I'll rip you to bits on the air. . . . The *New York Times* really has delusions of grandeur." Elton was a guest on deejay Scott Muni's live radio show over WNEW-FM in New York City.

Accustomed though he was to the critics pouncing, Elton was now in one of his doomsday moods. The slightest negative press was viewed by him as a threat to his entire career. At such times he either hid out with his depression or made some bogus retirement threat. At this moment, however, Elton refused to allow John Rockwell's review of his opening night at Madison Square Garden to go unanswered. In response he unleashed a vicious personal attack on the critic. "I'd like to see John Rockwell," he lashed out. "I hope he comes down. I bet he's about four foot three. I bet he's got boogies up his nose. I bet his feet smell."

In his review, Rockwell, a highly respected music critic at the *New York Times*, had described Elton's concert as "a smooth show that offered wallpaper music of the most banal sort." But he had also praised the evening's "technical elegance, its pace and decor" as well as Elton's "strong voice and charm."

But at this stage Elton felt that he was above any criticism. Further, the sellout crowds during his sixteen-day East Coast tour that had begun in Washington, D.C., during Bicentennial Week and concluded at the Garden told another story. The Garden concerts alone grossed $1.5 million and established Elton as the biggest single draw ever to appear in the giant arena, with one of his seven performances breaking the house record. No one—not Rockwell or any other critic—was going to diminish this achievement.

Critics were not the only ones aiming darts at Elton. In a *Playboy* interview, Glam Rocker David Bowie had called him "the Liberace, the token Queen of Rock," adding, "I consider myself responsible for a whole new school of pretensions—they know who they are, don't you, Elton." But Elton dismissed Bowie as a "silly boy."

With members of the press, however, Elton was something of a collector of injustices. He believed that many critics belittled him by questioning both his popularity and his musical significance. Elton had struck a bitter note when he told another *New York Times* writer in the weeks leading up to the concerts, "I'm the person rock critics love to hate. And I quite revel in it. You see, there is currently a trend among rock critics: Only if you are genuinely bad will they love you."

Now, on this steamy Friday the thirteenth, with the temperature climbing past ninety degrees, Elton was boiling mad. From the studio he lashed out at John Rockwell. "If you don't like me," Elton yelled into the mike, "just come out and say, 'Listen, I hate the guy.'" It was apparent that Elton was overreacting because Rockwell was mostly indifferent to his music. "I did not dislike his music," Rockwell remembers thinking in the early seventies. "I just found his sensibility brittle, arch and nervous, with not much melodic interest. I was more indifferent to it than anything else." He adds, "During the 1974 concert, when John Lennon appeared on stage with Elton, it just lifted the whole evening to another level and put Elton John in perspective."

A week after the broadcast, according to Muni, one of New York City's major radio personalities and something of a rock music scholar as well, Rockwell telephoned him. "He said he had heard about what

Elton had said and that he was surprised that Elton even knew who he was or that he existed."

No one was more aware of every aspect of the music industry than Elton, and this included knowing the names of critics and what they wrote about him. Muni marveled at Elton's knowledge of rock 'n' roll. "Elton was turned on by the twenty thousand records in the studio," Muni remembers, "and he would know from just the shape or color of the album spine what it was." "EJ the DJ" was how Elton billed himself, and, says Muni, "Elton was like a cat at play. Frivolous, zany, always on the wild side."

But on this particular visit to Muni's show Elton behaved more like a raging bull blindly attacking anyone he believed had wronged him. The customary magnums of champagne he brought along for these appearances only fueled his tongue.

Appearing on the radio show ended his virtual silence during his Garden appearances. The man who had been more accessible to the press than any other rock star in recent memory had been refusing all interview and photo requests. Instead, he locked himself away in Liz Taylor's old suite at the Sherry Netherland Hotel on New York's Fifth Avenue. And his bodyguards, including former Mr. America muscleman Jim Morris, were under strict orders to keep reporters away. They were said to be ill-tempered, in fact, by some members of the press.

For the balding Munchkin who leapt around the Madison Square Garden stage in sequins and red sneakers, commandeering Muni's chair meant breaking his self-imposed seclusion and facing yet another crowd waiting outside the studio. He obliged his fans with autographs. But once inside the station, as the microphone went live, it was clear that Elton was not there to please. "Welcome to the only transvestite station in New York," Elton twitted his audience. "What we're going to do is play some disco for all you people out there who are straight."

So in between some serious record-spinning, Elton attacked others besides Rockwell over the next three hours. "If Robert Stigwood [producer of the LP and film *Saturday Night Fever*] is listening," he said, "I'm fee-urious with you, Robert. I just want to tell you I've seen your film *Survive!* Robert, and just like your label, it's the biggest piece of shit I've ever seen."

Clearly amused by his guest, Muni urged Elton on, inquiring of him, "Do you go out in disguise?"

Elton retorted, "If I go out in a wig, which I do often, and a tight skirt and a pair of stilettos, people have still got to spot my ass anywhere."

It was sort of a running joke between Elton and Muni for Elton to make some renegade remark. After Muni introduced him, Elton talked about the disc jockey's designer dress, a product of Elton's invention. Elton would then fawn over the dress that he dreamed up, using descriptions like "lovely black sequined." Elton, a.k.a. Sharon, enjoyed these gender games, dressing men up in his mind as females or assigning them girls' names.

Many observers, meanwhile, played guessing games as well about the goings-on in the superstar's life. All the secrecy and tight security surrounding Elton led to rumors that he had a new woman in his life—possibly even Billie Jean King, albeit married to someone else—or, alternatively, an unnamed man. There was much speculation that Elton might be homosexual, but the press was unable to discover the identity of any partners.

Closeting himself inside his hotel suite when he was not performing at the Garden, Elton was fed up with not being able to move freely about the streets. He had tried various disguises to no avail and ended up darting back into the hotel. After his concerts he would go off to sleep after watching some television or listening to records. Elton's only night out had been at 12 West, a downtown private gay disco where, according to Elton, everyone left him alone. "They were so into their disco records and passing their poppers," he recounted later on, "if the Queen of England had been standing in the middle of the floor with a tiara on her head, no one would have paid attention."

He was also suffering from a sore throat and some laryngitis. He called singer and Rocket artist Neil Sedaka for advice. Sedaka remembers: "I gave him some of my remedies. Don't go to a disco and shout over the noise. Don't go in smoke-filled rooms. Be careful of iced drinks. Get enough rest and tea and honey."

Elton realized at this point that he also needed to take care of his emotional health. He was full of conflicts and unsure about whether he ever wanted to perform again. Already he had effected an amicable split with his new band to remove any contract obligations on his part and to free them as well to pursue other work. He was also thinking of composing some of his own lyrics, and to this end he encouraged Bernie to write with other people as well.

Five days after the famous radio appearance, Elton broke his silence by granting an interview to *Rolling Stone* which seemed to sum up his confusions. "I might never work again," said Elton. "On the other hand, I might." He was not the least bit remorseful about his diatribe against John Rockwell. As he explained, "After one glass of Dom Pérignon, I was feeling drunk and goosey. I don't remember half the things I said. I doubt if John Rockwell was even at the concert. It was the most piss-elegant review I've seen. 'Performers come and go but we rock critics have to deal with them.' Who the fuck is this John Rockwell?"

Perhaps Rockwell had touched a nerve in Elton. There had been a decline in sales of Elton's last two albums, *Captain Fantastic* and *Rock of the Westies*, though they had entered the charts at Number One. And the live recording *Here and There*, which concluded Elton's DJM contract, was by his own reckoning a "total fuckin' disaster."

In 1976 Elton's popularity was indeed beginning to taper off. *Here and There* was a live recording of songs from Elton's 1974 performances at New York's Madison Square Garden and London's Royal Festival Hall. It was doomed to fail. Live albums, as even Elton knew, were always precarious. Outside of a professional recording studio there was no way to predict the outcome. There were too many variables, both technical and human. Even at the Royal Variety Show the sound system had been primitive, and Elton complained afterward to the press about the amateurish setup there. During his Garden appearance Elton had been understandably both nervous and extremely excited about John Lennon's joining him on stage. As it turned out, the three Lennon duets with Elton were excluded from the album after Dick James decided that the product should be entirely Elton John. Predictably, *Here and There* was panned by the critics.

DJM also released "Benny and the Jets" as a U.K. single, but it did not do anywhere near as well as it had two years before in the States, when it landed Elton on the R&B charts for the first time. During discussions about the final DJM product, James considered mining the company's archives for previously unreleased treasures from Elton's earlier recording sessions. In the end he decided to go with the live recording rather than take such a risk with Elton's future.

Ever since *Captain Fantastic*, Elton had been unmanageable, and James under the circumstances (and in light of the lawsuit Elton would bring against him in the future) behaved with admirable restraint as their contractual agreement drew to a close.

Elton had seemed worried even at the bicoastal launch of *Captain Fantastic* the previous year, Steve James recalls. Elton attended the party at the Universal Studios lot in Los Angeles while Bernie showed up at the festivities at New York's Media Sound Studies. What should have been a night of bright celebration for Elton was instead shaded with melancholy. Steve James and Elton shared a limousine ride after the party, and James relates, "Elton asked me, 'How much longer do you think this is going to go on for?' And I told him, 'Not very much longer, certainly not at this peak. Nothing lasts forever. It'll either stop or slow down or peter out.' Whenever we criticized him, as we had with *Captain Fantastic*, or whenever there was a slide in his popularity, he was always worried that his bubble was going to burst."

Ed Caraeff, a Rocket Records photographer from their Los Angeles office, also attended the West Coast party. He remembers a far less fragile scene. This one involved Elton's manager John Reid during the screening of a slide show of *Captain Fantastic* in Universal's private cinema. When the sound system faltered, according to the photographer, "Reid started screaming, 'The sound's a fucking shambles.' And once the lights went up, he beat up the man responsible for this mishap. He kept screaming and beating him and the man's face was covered in blood. Reid wouldn't stop. He was wild, furious, uncontrollable."

As it turned out *Here and There* proved to be a disaster for DJM too, and it also set off alarms at MCA in America where Elton was their newly minted eight-million-dollar man. Henceforth Elton would record under his own label, Rocket Records, and manager John Reid would assume complete control over Elton's business affairs. MCA in America and EMI in Britain distributed his albums.

Blue Moves marked Elton's LP debut on Rocket. A double album with slow romantic songs and three instrumentals, it was poorly received by the press. Coming on the heels of *Captain Fantastic* and *Rock of the Westies*, it proved by Elton's standards to be a commercial flop as well, reaching only Number Three on both sides of the Atlantic upon its release in November 1976.

Recorded at the Eastern Sound Studios in Toronto, Canada, *Blue Moves* featured some outstanding backup vocal talent, including David Crosby and Toni Tennille, but the album itself was pretentious and full of self-loathing. It was also self-pitying—and this time it was Bernie's turn to cry. He was depressed over his estranged wife, Maxine, who had become involved with a musician. Maxine, blonde and petite, had been the inspiration for the song "Tiny Dancer" early on. Now it was more a story of "Sorry Seems to Be the Hardest Word," a single from the new album which peaked at Number Six on the U.S. charts.

Another track, "Idol," which was about a star on a downhill path and interpreted as a commentary on Elvis, just as aptly described Elton's mounting panic about his own career. Elton had met Elvis for the first time in Washington, D.C., that year, 1976, after a reception at the Capital Center. Sheila who was with her son at the time, remembers, "Elton was so nervous he didn't know what to say." But later on Elton offered another explanation: "By the time I met Elvis, he was completely non compos mentis. It came as no surprise to me when he died. I thought he looked as if he was dead already." Elvis died of a heart attack the following year, at forty-two.

With the apparent downturn in Elton's career with *Blue Moves*, he wanted to avoid, at any cost, ending up as an entertainer at Las Vegas casino hotels like his fallen idol Presley. Such venues were as distasteful to Elton as the cabaret circuit he had so detested in his earlier days with Bluesology. *Blue Moves* would also be the last time for a while that Elton and Bernie collaborated, and Gus Dudgeon was also signing off as producer.

Ironically, at a time when Elton was receding from the limelight, his unsung partner Bernie now wanted to grab a piece of it. For the first four years of their collaboration, Bernie was introduced as "the one who writes the words for Elton John," which used to grate on him. But lately he was getting sacks of fan mail, and now he was comfortable enough with the label pinned on him to use it as the title of his first book, in April 1976. A collection of lyrics from Elton and Bernie's first album through *Goodbye Yellow Brick Road*, Bernie's book included illustrations by rock stars like Alice Cooper and

John Lennon. The book drew its inspiration from Bernie's desire to have everything he had written under one cover.

"I must be the most unrecognizable person," says Bernie. "I don't sing and I don't play anything, yet somehow I get treated like a rock-'n'-roll star. But I couldn't live with the pressures Elton has. I hate going on stage, even when Elton makes me come on and wave. I prefer to stand aside and absorb the excitement."

Success for Elton was a duet with Rocket artist Kiki Dee. It allowed him to fulfill a lifelong ambition to have a Number One hit single in his native Britain. Released in June 1976, it rested at the top of the U.K. charts for six weeks and of the U.S. charts for four. The disco-pop tune, "Don't Go Breaking My Heart," was born of a simple instruction over the phone to Bernie, who was then relaxing in Barbados: "Write a duet."

It was Elton who had come up with the title line, "Don't Go Breaking My Heart," while playing his electric piano in the studio in Canada during the *Blue Moves* recording sessions in March 1976. Bernie, who was accustomed to writing for only one man, was glad for the assist from Elton. For this song they used the pen names of Ann Orson and Carte Blanche.

Both Elton and Kiki drew their inspiration on this duet from Marvin Gaye and Tammi Terrell. Elton initially laid down his track in the Toronto studio. He and Kiki got together later in a London studio, but Elton decided to stick with his Canadian vocal. A video was also produced in the studio and later on Elton would trade Kiki for Miss Piggy for a performance of the song on television's "Muppet Show," declaring afterward in *Rolling Stone*, "I've achieved all my childhood ambitions."

Fortunately, the video age did not yet rule the music business, for in video, looks often seemed to replace talent. Elton, with his bald pate and loud plaid jacket, and Kiki, dressed in a mannish ladies' suit, looked somewhat graceless on the video. Many years later Elton would dismiss Madonna, a sort of video screen goddess, as "all tits and no talent."

Having finally achieved a Number One U.K. hit single, Elton decided to cut back on touring. "This will be the last tour in a long while," Elton told audiences during his American tour. "I feel like stopping for a time. For the last two or three years I've been like a nomad. It's just got so big that it's getting stupid and it's getting to be a bore."

But Elton, a virtual rock-'n'-roll scholar with his famous record collection, was also mindful of impending changes on the musical scene. Mainstream pop, where Elton was king of the charts, was now under siege by punk artists who wanted to make it obsolete and disco divas who might siphon off some of its audience. There was also the sensuous bass-driven reggae—but for the moment it sounded too foreign for most of the audiences. And while disco fans rejected punk's raw frenzy, punk scoffed at disco's throbbing dance grooves; the mainstream public turned its back on both.

Life had become unbearably lonely for Elton. If the blatantly uncommercial *Blue Moves* album signaled a braver Elton, it was also something of a relief, Elton admitted, to relinquish his position at the top of the album charts. So great was Elton's desire to own his life again that five days after his radio appearance he was speaking out again, this time putting his own professional future in jeopardy.

When Cliff Jahr, a writer for *Rolling Stone*, arrived at the corner room of Elton's tenth-floor suite at the Sherry Netherland Hotel, the superstar greeted him with a bone-crushing handshake. The seven-room, faux-Louis XIV suite with a panoramic view of Fifth Avenue and Central Park seemed to engulf Elton, who sat down in the middle of a large white sofa.

To Jahr, who had interviewed him before, Elton cut a shy figure, running his fingers along the edge of a coffee table and staring directly at the tape recorder. Elton, wearing blue-tinted glasses, avoided looking at the reporter. Yet in his remarks he was unusually forthcoming, ranging over many subjects—the lack of privacy and the other side of it, the isolation of the superstar.

This being the day after his last concert at the Garden and of the tour, Elton was also feeling a bit nostalgic. "It was a pretty weird night," Elton reflected. "A very sad occasion, I must say. It came to a point where I sang 'Goodbye Yellow Brick Road' and I thought, 'I don't have to sing this anymore,' and it made me quite happy inside. Yeah, it could be my last gig forever. I'm definitely not retiring, but I want to put my energies elsewhere for a while. Y'know, I feel really strange at this particular time. I always do things by instinct and I just know it's time to cool it; I mean, who wants to be a forty-two-year-old entertainer in Las Vegas like Elvis?"

Whether or not Elton would ever go back on the road remained to be seen. But the pinnacle of his career was now behind him. He had reached a crossroads, he said, and he hoped that he could cross it with the LP *Blue Moves*. But his mind was still tallying his successes as he reeled off album grosses, as if he had to remind himself before it all vanished.

The affection of his fans had sustained Elton for a time. In his suite, on the mantel and tabletops, were handmade gifts, icons, offered up by them: his likeness in oil and tempera, Elton singing in crayons and needlepoint. All this adulation was supposed to make him feel better. Sometimes he felt worse. Elton could not shake off memories of the way his father had belittled him and suffocated his feelings.

Years later Elton would reflect on just how unhappy he had felt at this juncture of his life. "I was almost thirty years old, and I couldn't do anything on my own. I was afraid to walk down the street by myself. I'd always hidden behind my dark glasses, so I decided to get contact lenses and made a point of not hiding behind my glasses."

Elton, the man who cloaked himself in sequins and spectacles, was now trying to locate his authentic self. What was supposed to be a routine magazine interview turned into a confessional. "I go home and fall in love with vinyl," Elton confessed. "I suppose I have a certain amount of love and affection, as far as love and affection go, from friends and stuff. But my sexual life, um, I haven't met anybody I would like to have any big scenes with. It's strange that I haven't. I know everyone should have a certain amount of sex, and I do, but that's it, and I desperately would like to have an affair. I crave to be loved."

It was as if Elton had suddenly discovered the Freudian talking cure as he moved on in the interview to more personal data to reveal a very lonely man. "My life in the last six years has been a Disney film," said Elton, "and now I have to have a person in my life—I have to."

As a measure of just how far his loneliness had gone, Elton had opened his heart not to an intimate friend or close associate, but, incredibly, to a journalist. His life would never be the same again. Elton was ditching his camouflage to bare his shy, confused self. No longer could Elton hide his homosexual longings. Though he knew that he was putting his entire career on the line, being the kind of person he was, he had no other choice but to be honest, instead of continuing to ignore the rumors surrounding his personal life. "Elton is one of the most honest people you could meet," a close friend explains. "He has never been able to take the easy way out."

It was in this vein that Elton began to talk about the real life of his emotions. "Let me be brutally honest," Elton said to Jahr. "I get depressed very easily, very bad moods. I don't think anyone knows the real me. I don't even think *I* do. I don't know what I want to be exactly. I'm just going through a stage where any sign of affection would be welcome on a sexual level."

Elton continued, "I'd rather fall in love with a woman eventually because I think a woman probably lasts longer than a man. But I really don't know. I've never talked about this before—ha, ha—but I'm not going to turn off the tape. I haven't met anybody that I would like to settle down with—of either sex."

Jahr, who had managed to pry these thoughts out of Elton by merely listening well, interrupted Elton's monologue with a direct question: "You're bisexual?"

"There's nothing wrong with going to bed with someone of the same sex," Elton replied, adding, "I think everybody's bisexual to a certain degree. I don't think it's just me. It's not a bad thing to be. I think you're bisexual. I think everybody is."

But for all his liberated talk, as Jahr reminded him, Elton had never said it in print before. "Probably not," said Elton, with a chuckle in his voice. "It's going to be terrible with my football club. It's so hetero it's unbelievable. But, I mean, who cares! I just think people should be very free with sex—they should draw the line at goats."

And so Elton had finally worn his heart on his sleeve once and for all. On the face of it, Elton's revelation should hardly have come as a shock. This was, after all, the Me Decade, and self-expression was now the highest aggression of the culture. British punks were walking around with safety pins in their noses and coloring their hair siren red and emerald green. And disco, with its large homosexual following, was practically a coming-out party every night at glitter-ball clubs all across America. And so as Elton bade Jahr goodbye at the end of the interview, he appeared to be relieved.

Six weeks later, in the October 7, 1976, issue of *Rolling Stone*, Elton was the cover story with a headline that read, "ELTON'S FRANK TALK ... The Lonely Love Life of a Superstar." Elton believed the interview would finally lay to rest all the rumors surrounding his private life, but it backfired on him. Many of his fans were shocked, and some radio stations in America even stopped playing his records.

The news broke when Elton was already back in England. It was the reaction in the United States, which had been kinder to his career than had his native Britain, that disgusted Elton. "You know, calling me a faggot," he remembers bitterly. "And yet America's supposed to be the great liberated, free-minded society, which, of course, it isn't. . . . And they have said in retrospect, 'Would you have done it again?' and I said, 'Yes, of course I would.' I was just trying to be honest, and it hurt my career. And it coincided with my coming off the road, and I think there was a lot of shock, horror, 'Oh no, he can't be gay,' and I got a lot of women trying to save me."

By contrast, the response in England was much less bruising. Elton received letters from both gays and heterosexuals who praised his courage. A poll conducted in a music magazine showed that Elton's fans were unconcerned about what he did offstage in his personal life. Even the macho football players from Watford, whose reaction Elton had worried about, stood solidly behind him after fans from an opposing club chanted slurs against his manhood at a game. Watford team fans were like Elton John's tailor-made army, drowning out the opposition with songs of their own.

Friends and family also showed their loyalty to Elton. Kiki Dee, for one, considered Elton's disclosure to be sensible. "I'm sure it was a great relief to him once the article was printed," she commented. "It was typical of him to follow his instincts, even if what he said was potentially risky. The climate was right for that kind of honesty."

And Sheila Farebrother was still there supporting her son. "I was upset at first," she said. "But I think it was a brave thing for him to do. I would still like to think he can find some kind of happiness. With a male or a female, I don't care."

Three years later Elton himself was still talking about the article. "I realize that it's not everybody's cup of tea," he told a British journalist. "And I am not trying to dwell on the subject too much. I just decided to get it off my chest. That's the way I am and it's no good hiding it. I suppose it was easier for me to come out than for others."

The confessor was now sounding like the crusader. "I can't understand why people are so antihomosexual, and it's very difficult for homosexuals to come to terms with that in their lives. They go through a lot of pain and I would support anyone who is totally frank, because it's not ever easy."

But Elton, the shy Englishman, was not about to sign up for any marches yet. As he had told *Rolling Stone*, "Nobody's had the balls to ask me about it before. I would have said something about it all along if someone had asked me, but I'm not going to come out and say something just to be— I do think my personal life should be personal. I don't want to shove it over the front pages like some people I could mention. To be on the front of newspapers with my tongue down somebody's throat. That's really appalling. I'd like to have some children, but I don't know if the time is right."

Still, it seemed the whole world knew the private Elton. Could he ever astonish them again? Indeed he could.

17

Father Strikes Back

When Stanley Dwight picked up a copy of the January 1976 *Playboy*, he could not believe what he read. There, in big bold print, for all the world to see, was a vicious attack on him by the son he had fathered twenty-nine years earlier and who had inherited his musical talent and determination. "My father was so stupid with me, it was ridiculous," Elton had lashed out. "I was two years old when he came home from the air force. He'd never seen me. And it got off to a really bad start, 'cause Mother said, 'Do you want to go upstairs and see him?' He said, 'No, I'll wait till morning.' Later, when my parents got divorced, she had to bear all the costs. My father was an ogre to her."

Stanley put down the magazine and, gathering his thoughts, began to wonder whether he had actually gone mad. As he picked up the telephone his hands shook with rage. "I rang my solicitor," Stanley remembers, "and asked him to check whether I really had paid the divorce costs and he looked up the files and said, of course I had. He asked me if I wanted to sue, but I said, no, I don't want to do anything that will alienate Reggie. I just don't understand why he was saying all these awful things."

It seemed that despite the liberating and heady experience of his success, Elton was still a prisoner of his childhood. And no matter how he tried to camouflage his pain beneath layers of costumes, Reggie Dwight continued to inhabit his mind, calling up painful memories of his rejecting father. Even during interviews, Elton mentioned his unhappy childhood, but usually for only a few minutes. In the *Playboy* interview, however, he had gone on and on about his grievances against his father.

Later in the year there would be further attacks in a *Rolling Stone* interview. "I was hurt so much as a kid that I'm afraid of plunging into something that's going to fuck me up," he told the magazine.

Understandably, Stanley and his second wife, Edna, were hurt by Elton's remarks. But Stanley tried not to show it and hid the magazine from his other sons from this second marriage. He also tried to conceal his pain around his office as well. At Unilever, the multinational company where Stanley worked as a supplies comptroller, he did not tell his associates that he was Elton's father. Some knew, however. "They said they knew me well enough to know I wasn't like that," Stanley said of his work mates. "I don't go out of my way to tell people I'm Elton John's father, and I told the children not to talk about it at school. The neighbors may or may not know, but they don't mention it to me."

There was, after all, no apparent reason why anyone would suspect that Stanley Dwight was Elton John's father. And his lifestyle did not give anything away. It was totally different from that of his son. For while Elton was the lord of the manor, Stanley lived modestly in a detached house with a living room full of books and classical music tapes in the pretty Welsh village of Ruthin.

Unlike his inordinately wealthy son, Stanley did not have acres of land. Instead, out back was a garden with apple blossoms and neat rows of vegetables. Stanley was nonetheless proud of his patch of lawn, and had won nine medals for his chrysanthemums. There would be no accolades from Elton, however, for his father's green thumb. As a boy, Elton recalled bitterly, he was not allowed to kick a soccer ball around in the Pinner garden for fear of disturbing his father's rosebushes.

But now Elton had the run of a country estate in Berkshire which he had moved into in January 1976. A few miles away from Windsor Castle and named Woodside, Elton's Queen Anne-style house had cost just under £400,000 (almost $1 million) and was said to have been built for one of the Henry VIII's mistresses. A visitor would find, set back from a quiet country lane known as Crimp Hill, a vineyard on the property, a gatekeeper's house surrounded by gardens, a large ornamental dock, and at the rear a white-columned Greek temple, a "folly," popular on country estates.

Inside the mansion were eight bedrooms, six bathrooms, five reception rooms, a pool room, a squash court, a cinema, a swimming pool with a chandelier overhead, a recording studio, and Elton's personal record archives, which now housed twenty-five thousand singles.

Elton had his own private wing in the house, and his king-sized boudoir featured a bed that was said to be a copy of the one on which the Empress Josephine had once rested her head; a crown was placed at the foot. (It was actually a child's coronet dating from around 1880 and had been given to him as a joke at Christmas by his manager, John Reid.)

By now Reid was no longer Elton's roommate, though the singer reserved a suite for him inside Woodside. After the Auckland fracas that had landed Reid in jail, Elton seemed for a time to break his habit of dependency on Reid. Yet he still needed his manager to accompany him on a visit to his father. Reid, meanwhile, bought himself a luxurious house in the fashionable Montpelier Place, near Harrod's. Multimillionaire that he was, Reid was still the quintessential Scotsman, and held by the motto, "A penny saved is a penny earned." A decade later, one writer recalled that he had an appointment to see Reid at the Plaza Hotel in New York City. "He was in this tiny studio there," the writer sniffed, "the stingy Scotsman." Added the same man, "He opened the door and he was naked. He offered me a glass of scotch from a glass in the bathroom where he kept his toothbrush rather than call room service."

There was a time when Stanley had looked forward to visits, infrequent though they were, from his superstar son. But by the spring of 1976, Stanley was a father in distress, unsure about whether he would ever see Elton again. Their relationship had reached an all-time low, and the only contact Elton appeared to have with his father was via the press.

The returned letter that Stanley kept in his wallet merely acted as another reminder of just how seriously their relationship had deteriorated. Stanley had sent Elton the letter the previous Christmas, 1975. Elton had not bothered to reply, and then came the ultimate rebuke in *Playboy* magazine attacking him. Baffled by Elton's acrimonious outburst, Stanley had waited a few months and then decided to do some talking to the press himself.

As Stanley Dwight talked to *Daily Mail* writer Sally Brompton in the living room of his house, he began producing evidence of his relationship with his son. He showed her a book of children's sayings, *God Bless Love*, by Nanette Newman, Elton's friend and former neighbor. It was a present from Elton for Christmas 1972 and it came with an inscription he had scribbled in the front of the book. "To Dad and Aunt Edna, Robert, Stanley, Geoffrey, Simon," Elton had written. "With love for a happy Xmas (yes, this is my card). Love, Elton." Beneath Elton's name was a row of kisses.

Now, though, it was evident that Elton was no longer sending his father warm, affectionate greetings. "It was fine up until three years ago," Stanley recalled. "Up until then we had kept in touch, exchanged cards and Christmas presents, and Reggie would visit us every so often. Then suddenly it all stopped and we haven't heard a word from him since—except for the things he's been saying about me in the press and on television."

The last time father and son had got together was three years before, in 1973, after Stanley had bought tickets for his family to Elton's concert in a city nearby. Stanley recalled, "Elton rang up and said, 'Why didn't you ask me? I'd have got you tickets.'" And then a few days later Elton, accompanied by his manager Jim Reid, paid a visit to Stanley and his family at their home.

Reflecting on the visit, Stanley remembered that it went well. "We had a lovely day," he said. "Reggie played the piano with the boys and kicked a ball around the garden with them. We talked about ordinary everyday things, mostly about him and what he'd been doing—after all, he knows what I do."

During the course of conversation they had discussed cars in general. At that point Elton asked his father to name his ideal car and Stanley said a Peugeot 504 station wagon because it was big enough to fit his children. "The only embarrassing bit of it was when he insisted on giving me a check for £2,000 ($4,712) to buy a car as a sort of late Christmas and birthday present,' Stanley recalled. "I refused to take the check, but then he slipped it in Edna's cardigan pocket later on when he was giving her and the boys a ride in his Rolls. Edna thought it was a note and passed it on to me. I bought the car because he had been so insistent about it, and then I sent him a photo of the boys beside it so that he would know I had kept my side of the bargain and not just blown the money."

Whether that photo of the car with the three boys beside it hurt Elton, who had felt so unloved by his father as a child, remains unclear. Elton had longed for a brother or sister and believed he was a mistake in his father's eyes. Or perhaps the car was Elton's way of humiliating his father just as his father had done to him as a boy.

Whatever the reason, Stanley would have to settle from now on for souvenirs of his famous son. But photos of Elton scattered about the Dwight home, old letters from his son, postcards and a file box in which his wife Edna had compiled Elton's newspaper clippings seemed little compensation for a father who had struggled during postwar Britain to give his son every possible educational opportunity and, more important, claimed to love him.

Though Elton was incommunicado as far as his father was concerned, Stanley continued to send him Christmas presents, a Welsh spoon and a paperweight, and letters three or four times a year. He also attempted to reach him by telephone at a number Elton had given him. "I didn't realize he has to change his number every two weeks," Stanley said. "And when I got the unlisted number operator to put me through, someone at the other end refused to take my call." Stanley's sons had also written to Elton and enclosed pictures they had drawn of him at the concert. They received no response either.

Yet for all the disappointment Stanley expressed about his son's rebuff, he still sounded at times like the faultfinding father Elton had experienced as a boy. "I think Reggie's trouble to a certain extent is he's never grown up." Stanley said. "He takes after me in that he has tremendous self-assurance and the same self-discipline and a good business sense. But he's still very immature."

But there was still no admission from him that Elton's childhood had been anything but blissful. "He doesn't seem very happy to me," Stanley said, "The last time we saw him I asked him who his friends were and he said Elvis Presley and Billie Jean King. But when he was a child they were his idols. How can someone you've only just met be described as a friend? There are friends and friends, and I think Reggie has to buy his friendships."

And even though he was prepared to accept a car from Elton, Stanley seemed unimpressed by his son's vast wealth. "I don't think Reggie's money is bringing him happiness," he said. "Happiness comes from having someone else to think about. Everybody has to have someone to be emotional about—even if it's just the fellow next door."

Elton had yet to give his *Rolling Stone* interview about his gender preference, and Stanley seemed to abet the rumors about his son's sexuality. "I asked him if he had any girlfriends," Stanley recalled, "and he said, 'Not really'—he didn't have the time."

Stanley was even less discreet about his son's professional life. "I don't think Reggie's all that good even now," he remarked. "Quite frankly, some of his songs are rubbish. But I like 'Daniel' and 'Goodbye Yellow Brick Road.' I think he's very lucky. He's worked hard, but I believe luck plays a big part—the right people, the right opportunities, all coming together at the same time. He told me himself, 'Dad, it's all a big con. But as long as the public lap it up, I'm quite happy to go on giving it to them.'"

Stanley Dwight's comments about his son were both sad and ironic. Elton himself had said that luck had played a big part in his career, though talent, hard work and determination allowed him to seize his opportunity. But Elton had been driven, above all, by Stanley Dwight's rejection.

The pain of his childhood, more than future ambitions, had chased Reggie Dwight out of Pinner and had ultimately won Elton John the roar of approval from fans around the world.

18

The Soccer Fan

Though Stanley was not overly enthusiastic about his son's musical career, the following year Elton achieved an honor which his father could not dismiss. Elton was made chairman of the Watford Football Club. Throughout Elton's formative years soccer had been a passion with the Dwights. Many years before, the family had taken pride in cousin Roy Dwight's achievements as a player.

Now it was Elton's turn, and the once-shy, tentative boy who had accompanied his father to games as a child was now in command of his very own team. Sorrowfully, though, there would be no more stadium outings for the father and son who had tackled each other in the media.

Elton was a hands-on chairman, and he had made it clear a few years earlier, when he became a director, that he was there to provide moral support, not to save the team's sorry bank balance. "I don't intend to miss many matches, either home or away," Elton vowed. "I've reached the stage where I don't need to chase all over the world as I used to."

Initially his appointment as chairman was greeted with mixed feelings from the players, who worried that he might be too much of a prima donna. Forward Keith Mercer remembers, "Firstly we knew him by the high heels and green hair, but from the outset he was very approachable."

If players regarded him as a star, Elton felt similarly about them. It was also widely known that he would have traded in his feathers and boas for a Watford uniform any day of the week, for Elton knew the club's history as well as he knew the lyrics and notes to his songs. And he was as demanding of himself as chairman of the board as he was on the concert stage.

Any worries about the appropriateness of Elton wearing the chairman's pants were quickly dispelled by his earnest and affable demeanor. Forward Mercer remembers one conversation that particularly endeared Elton to him: "I was twenty years old and trying to grow a mustache, without too much success, and Elton said, 'I'll show you.' By the end of the week Elton had a full facial growth, and I said to him, 'When you can grow that on your face, it's a shame you can't do the same on your head.' "

Becoming Watford's chairman, according to Sheila, had been a major goal in Elton's life. "He'd move to Los Angeles tomorrow," she had told a *Time* reporter two years earlier, "but he wants to be chairman."

Sheila, who was immensely pleased about his new role, believed that Watford would bring her starry-eyed son back to earth. As she explained, "He's mixing with ordinary people. He's never been more happy. He's more himself than anywhere else, and he can start to live again. You don't find real, true friends in the entertainment world. They all want to climb up the ladder. They all want to use you. I think Elton knows that."

By now Elton had acquired a heady mix of friends and acquaintances, among them Liz Taylor and Shirley MacLaine. "I go for older women," Elton had said, "and Miss MacLaine would do me fine, but she's already happily set up." With both women the admiration was mutual. Liz had attended his concert at the Philadelphia Spectrum the year before and then flown to New York with Elton on his private 727 *Starship One* for his Madison Square Garden appearances.

Elton had also met the stars he worshiped when he was just plain Reg Dwight. "The best have been Mae West and Groucho Marx," he says. "They just don't make people like that anymore." Of his first meeting with Mae West he remembers, "There were six of us, and she swept into the room, looked us up and down and said, 'Mmmm, wall-to-wall men.' '' Later they had tea together a few times.

Back in 1972, Elton had attended the premiere of *Jesus Christ Superstar* in Los Angeles with Groucho, who, he says, "was wonderfully mischievous. He always called me John Elton. Even though he was in his seventies, on the way to the premiere, he picked up two very beautiful young women. There were no seats, so they had to sit on his lap throughout the show."

Sheila did not begrudge Hollywood. At parties she attended at his house there, she and husband Fred often broke into a spirited jitterbug. Elton's friends adored her. Rarely did she hover or criticize, but nonetheless she was a strong maternal presence, a pivotal source of stability in her son's life. Instinctively, Sheila knew what would give her son both comfort and new challenge.

And she was right. For as Elton's association with the club continued, it seemed to bring him great joy. "When I came into the club I was so tired," Elton says. "I didn't want to do anything but rest for a couple of years. But I can't sit around the house doing nothing, and Watford gave me the opportunity to do something different. It has been a fantastic experience."

In early 1977 Elton had decided to suspend any live appearances for the immediate future and to reduce his recording output to one album every eighteen months. Bernie, battling a drinking problem, was nowhere around. He and Elton also agreed they needed time away from each other. "If I'd come off the road and had nothing to do," Elton said, "God knows what would have happened to me. But I had the club to plunge into. I went in with full steam as if I was having a new band."

The concert touring had become stale, and the Rocket Man had begun to wonder if he was living on another planet from other mortals. The wealth and celebrity that had attended his amazing career had lifted him to dangerous heights of unreality. He explains, "I couldn't do anything for myself and I became chairman of the club, where I had to hire people, fire people, go to the bank, do things that normal people do and people like me should be able to do."

Just as he had done with his musical allies, Elton now made the team a kind of surrogate family. Once a year at his Berkshire mansion about twenty miles outside of London, he gave a party for the players and their wives, girlfriends and children. While the adults enjoyed the champagne and caviar, the children splashed around in Elton's swimming pool. A player need only mention that he wanted to see a particular concert and Elton produced the tickets. Similarly, the superstar's chauffeured Rolls-Royce arrived at the gates of the Vicarage Road grounds of the Watford team with boxes of records for the players.

But at the same time, despite his often idiosyncratic, impulsive shopping, Elton was not trying to buy their affections with designer cars and yachts, gifts reserved for close friends and associates. The team, in turn, valued his leadership and presence above all else.

Over the course of his involvement with the team, Elton had infused their coffers with £1.2 million. He did not consider this a handout, but when the club was in a position, after the sale of star players, to repay the interest-free loan, Elton forgave it. By then Watford had reached the first division, and Elton claimed great pride in the team and its future.

Earlier financial advisers had recommended that Elton put his money into real estate. But the soccer fan in him balked at this advice, declaring, "What possible pleasure can you get from looking at a block of flats or a row of houses? I'm getting all the pleasure in the world from what has been constructed here."

Watford was in Elton's blood, and being a die-hard fan, he did not take the team's losses lightly. Nor was he slow to criticize. "They don't train hard enough," Elton confided to a sports journalist. "To get to the top in my profession I've worked hard. I still start at nine A.M. and work till eight P.M. When I play football for charity, I take it seriously and train. In the morning I'm there with the first team. But come lunchtime they all pack up and go home or go off to the golf club. I go back in the afternoon and train. In my experience, tennis players, golfers, athletes, gymnasts, all train harder than footballers."

But Elton also championed larger salaries for the players. "These men the fans go and watch, and who draw the crowds of 40,000-plus every week, are grossly underpaid," he argued on their behalf. "When I go on tour I may play in front of two hundred thousand fans during the course of twelve concerts, but my earnings make footballers' pay look like pocket money. I know a lot of clubs are in financial trouble, but the structure must change."

Elton was determined to push Watford all the way to the top—

just what he had demanded of himself as a performer. To this end he made a decision to hire one of Britain's top soccer managers, Graham Taylor, to take Watford out of the fourth division.

But Taylor would not come cheap. Elton had to fork over £25,000 ($42,500), making Taylor one of the highest-paid managers in British soccer. Elton's decision to hire Graham also had its drawbacks. It hiked up the prices when Watford wanted to bid for players from other teams. However, the money would prove well spent as the Watford team moved quickly up from the fourth to the third division and, within five years, to the first.

In the case of Watford, Elton was merely buying talent, not friendships. In addition to the loan he would later forgive, Elton gave concerts and played soccer at charity matches to raise funds. But around the team's Vicarage Road headquarters he would not cast himself in the role of Santa Claus.

Taylor, Watford's manager, encouraged a more rigorous and formal approach to handling the team. One change, in fact, dictated that the players call Elton "Mr. Chairman" instead of by his first name. And the new boss had also imposed some sartorial rules, too, that Elton heeded in deference to both Taylor and the sport.

Elton himself respected the game enough to alter his wardrobe. "I'd never wear anything casual to a soccer match," said the king of glitz. "I always wear a formal suit and tie. I wouldn't want to let them down. I'd hate anyone to say: 'There he goes, just another sloppy pop star, never wears a civilized suit.' I do it for tradition's sake."

His "costumes" included suits in chalk-striped or plain-gray flannel or bird's-eye tweed. But one tabloid photo spread described one of Elton's getups as "gangster-style." As the caption read, the suit was "ink blue kid mohair, cut with a pronounced drape, long, lean lapels and narrower trousers and a Fedora . . . vintage Edward G. Robinson."

Still, by the time anyone sniffed out the ladies' perfume Elton sometimes wore, it was already too late to do anything about it. In the wake of Elton's bisexuality announcement, Sheila, ever protective of her son, encouraged him to adhere to a conservative dress code, namely suits. To further enhance his new image, Elton took one of the secretaries from Rocket Records to a football awards dinner.

No one quarreled, however, with Elton's performance as chairman. When the team won the fourth division, a highly excited Elton promised to reward it with a preseason tour of Australia. But after Taylor, who also carefully guarded Elton's purse strings, asked the superstar what he would do if Watford won the third or even second divisions, Elton reconsidered his promise. "I think," remembers forward Keith Mercer, "we ended up going to Scotland."

Despite Elton's immersion in the game, the music was not entirely sidelined. He produced "The Goaldigger Song" for a charity event for the sport and later in 1977 a single, the rocker "Bite Your Lip (Get Up & Dance"), which rose no higher than Number Twenty-eight on the U.K. singles charts.

However, Elton's *Greatest Hits, Volume II* became a predictable million-seller. With memorable tunes like "Philadelphia Freedom," "The Bitch Is Back," "Levon," "Island Girl," "Don't Go Breaking My Heart" (with Kiki Dee), and "Sorry Seems to Be the Hardest Word," the album's release filled a creative gap for the artist-cum-football chairman. It also marked the last act of cooperation between DJM and John Reid Enterprises. DJM did not own the masters to two of the singles, and, much to their astonishment, Reid actually agreed to let DJM use them.

The second volume of *Greatest Hits* demonstrated, above all, the talent of one of the decade's most prolific musical craftsmen. Fittingly, the album sleeve showed Elton in athletic gear, albeit as a cricketer, save for his pink shoes and cap. For it was in the sports arena that Elton had derived his greatest satisfaction during that year, 1977.

The professional relationship between chairman Elton and his soccer manager Graham Taylor had proved to be as productive and successful as his musical collaboration with Bernie Taupin. Together they would ultimately take Watford to the top. Their professional association lasted a decade.

Taylor was a steadying force in Elton's life at a time when he had split up with Bernie and was uncertain about his next move. Elton respected and valued the unpretentious Graham for his salutary influence. Elton remembers that at a period when he was drinking excessively, "Graham took one look at me and said, 'Come round to my house tomorrow morning.' I did, and he immediately took out a bottle of brandy and put it on the table in front of me. He said, 'Go on, open it, that's what you really want, isn't it?' In that second I saw what I was doing to myself and pulled myself together.' "

But the man who had introduced Elton to the sport in the first place would not be anywhere around to witness his rock-star son's feats in this arena. Elton had now won at both his music and his favorite sport, and even now there was no relationship with Stanley Dwight.

If Stanley did not celebrate his son's remarkable achievements in the interview the previous year, Elton's fellow countrymen paid appropriate homage to this twenty-nine-year-old overachiever. Elton John was immortalized on March 7, 1976, in wax in the Heroes section of Madame Tussaud's in London, the first rock star since the Beatles to be so honored.

19

A Drinking Partner

Rolling around in the back of a limousine, Bernie Taupin finally realized that he, too, was in a bad way. The gallon jug full of vodka and orange juice was just another reminder that his drinking had gotten completely out of control. Of late he had even been turning up at Elton's business lunches at posh New York restaurants with bottles of vodka in his pocket. At his insistence, too, it was written into his tour contract that Coors beer be provided at every hotel and gig. At the time, the Colorado brand Coors was legally sold only on the West Coast of America, so it had to be smuggled in when Bernie was in the East. "That was the kind of thing you'd do," says Bernie, "just to be a bastard."

Bernie was now no longer in denial about his drinking, and he was determined to do something about it. In truth, he had little choice in the matter. During a routine medical exam a doctor discovered that his liver was in terrible shape and warned Bernie that he had better take care of himself before it was too late. Bernie made a decision to dry out for a few months in Acapulco, Mexico.

Bernie's plans did not seem to interfere with Elton, who was heading for a period of professional single-mindedness. "I rarely see Bernie these days," Elton said. Despite rumors of a tiff, they were still on speaking terms. But they also conceded that they needed a breather from each other. The trouble was, they had spent too much time in the last two years working in tandem. The *Captain Fantastic* album, for example, had been a fusion of their early experiences in the music business, and now each of them wanted time alone to pursue his own separate ideas.

Bernie cited "burnout" around the time of the *Blue Moves* album the previous year as a major catalyst for their taking time off from each other: "We seemed to have done it all. Three albums had gone to Number One on the Billboard chart. We'd filled every stadium and hall it was possible to fill. You literally couldn't fart without hearing Elton John."

But now all that was changing. Elton's new band was suspended and producer Gus Dudgeon had walked out during a dispute over shares in Rocket, saying, "That's it, I'm off." In his place came sound engineer Clive Franks, whom Elton had first met during his earliest days at DJM and who had gone on tour with him in more recent years. At the Hollywood Bowl back in 1973 Franks had been the one to provide the visuals for *Crocodile Rock* by dressing up as a crocodile.

Guitarist Davey Johnstone and Kiki Dee kept up their friendship with Elton and were supportive throughout this period. Rocket Records itself was sort of at loose ends. By the following year Phonogram became its U.K. distributor instead of EMI.

Rocket also lost Neil Sedaka, who had two hugely successful albums, *Sedaka's Back* and *The Hungry Years*, and an enormous hit single, "Laughter in the Rain," on the label. The parting was on the friendliest of terms. In fact, Sedaka had enjoyed a most cordial professional relationship with Rocket and would have continued with them, but his lawyers advised him to sign instead with Elektra because Rocket was not offering cash advances against royalties.

"We always got along very well," remembers Sedaka. "When I moved with my family to London in the early seventies, my career was down the tubes, and Elton played a large role in reviving it. He was very caring. When we recorded the single 'Bad Blood,' which Elton sang on, he was willing to do take after take on it."

Only John Reid, it seemed, would stand the test of time in Elton's life, and he was involved in every aspect of it, even Watford. The team found Reid friendly and shy, an opinion that was in sharp contrast to how those in the music industry perceived him.

Reid in fact told Elton that he wanted to be on the board of the Watford Club. To make room for Reid, another member was forced to resign. That person was Elton's old ally, Vic Edwards, who had booked the singer into the Troubadour, arranged his earliest tours and, incredibly, forged Elton's association with the club in the first place. "The worst blow I ever received," Edwards said of being booted off the Watford board.

Though Reid earned the respect of colleagues for his business acumen and brilliant orchestration of Elton's career, he was not generally regarded with affection on account of his volatile personality. Reid himself told reporters that he adhered to the principle of first exploding and then conducting the inquest. Says Reid, "I yell and scream and say, 'The lot of you get out.' And then I come back and talk about it and it's all okay. I can't understand it if people don't do their work."

One former employee remembers a morning when Reid stormed into the office, ripped out a fire extinguisher and hurled it across the room for no apparent reason. "I was terrified," he says. "Reid was like a deranged man when he lost his temper. He was crazy. He was lucky he didn't hit anybody."

There was also Reid's headline-making altercation in Auckland that landed him in jail. And in later years he would also be charged with whacking a San Francisco hotel doorman over the head with a cane because, he said, his victim had nearly caused him to miss a flight to London.

Starting out life as the son of a welder in Paisley, a depressed town near Glasgow, Reid did not strive to please, only to win. As a businessman, he tended to view the world in black and white, devoid of any artistic shadings or intonations. Either a person won or lost—and Reid was a man who wanted to make sure that he did the former. Because of this he could not tolerate laziness and made enormous demands on himself.

Elton respected and trusted Reid—and with good reason, because such a loyal and protective manager was a rare commodity in this industry. Nor was Reid a quick-buck operator. He kept his eye on the long haul. He was, effectively, on call twenty-four hours a day anywhere in the world. Reid was a powerful ally, going with his hunches as much as his punches, approaching deals with a combination of business genius and brute force.

In under five years Reid had amassed a £40 million ($80 million) fortune, not only as a by-product of managing Elton, but by masterminding several international ventures with offices in London, Beverly Hills, New York and Sydney. Some journalists would later dub him "the J.R. of the music business," a reference to the ruthless oil baron J. R. Ewing (whose initials, ironically, he shared) from the television series "Dallas." Reid's tenacity had served Elton well, and without him, Elton maintained, he might still be earning twenty dollars a week.

Reid himself lived like a rock superstar, with palatial homes in Beverly Hills, England, and his native Scotland. His English country estate sat on fifteen wooded acres in Hertfordshire, with a tennis court and swimming pool, and was often the setting for parties attended by politicians, artists and even royalty. Princess Margaret, in fact, was a guest at Reid's house, and in later years he managed her son, Viscount Lindley, who owned a furniture-design company.

Being bachelors, Elton and Reid were also friends and seldom seen apart from each other. Reid, the recipient of a Rolls-Royce and a yacht from his client and friend, had been generous in return, proffering Elton a £20,000 ($34,000) watch and many other trinkets. It was Reid, in fact, who had encouraged Elton to adopt the trappings of success. Remembers Elton, "I had a Ford Escort and I was very happy with it. But John, who had just become my manager, said, 'You can't drive around in a bloody Ford Escort.' So I went out and bought an Aston Martin, and he had a heart attack."

Even though Elton and his manager spent so much time in each other's company, they also came to blows. Admits Reid, "We've ended up knocking each other around. I've given him more than one black eye." Sometimes Sheila was called in to mediate their disputes. Over the years their arguments often centered on differing opinions of what to title an album.

Upon the release of the "Ego" single the following year, 1978, both Elton and Reid were ready for battle. "Ego" was about stars with inflated notions about themselves. "It's dedicated to the Jaggers and Bowies of the world—and especially to Mr. McCartney," Elton said. "I like most of the stuff the Stones have done, but they're one of the worst live bands I've ever seen. David Bowie is a pseudointellectual, and I can't bear pseudointellectuals. And McCartney's music has gone so far down the tubes, I can't believe it. . . . They all just annoy me."

Judging from Elton's own behavior around this time, he might well have added his own name to this list of large and difficult egos. When the single failed to chart well, Reid fired two Rocket executives. Elton meanwhile launched an attack on the respected British Market Research Bureau, the compiler of the charts used by the BBC, on the grounds that "Ego" was moving up faster in the trade-paper charts.

While Elton had gone along with this system, he was now behaving like a spoiled child used to having his way. "Ego" did no better, of course, on the *Billboard* charts. In fact, of his twenty-two previous singles, only "Border Song," released before Elton was really known in the States, did worse.

This was an uncharacteristic public outburst from a man, quick with a quip and thoughtful with a gesture, who appeared to have mastered the art of civility. In an attempt to increase the sales of "Ego," a video promotional short was made of the single. Of course, it was also a tribute to Reid's foresight that there was any video at all. The age of MTV had not yet dawned and Reid had already figured out how a video could enhance a record even at a cost of the £50,000 ($90,000) that Rocket reportedly plowed into it.

Understandably, with Bernie no longer supplying the lyrics, Elton became increasingly nervous about his musical future. Initially Elton had looked forward to experimenting with various writers and producers. But his first major disappointment during this period of exploration came from working with a man he greatly admired, Thom Bell, the Philadelphia-based writer and producer of the Stylistics and Detroit Spinners. "I'm a big soul fan," Elton said, "and that led me to Thom Bell. I just loved the way his records sounded. Very dry-sounding records."

Elton first invited Bell to his Los Angeles home for a musical confab. Out of this meeting came the idea for sessions divided between Philadelphia at the famed Sigma Studios and another facility in Seattle, Washington. Elton returned from these sessions feeling buoyant and hopeful, convinced that they would yield another chart-topping LP.

But once Bell finished producing the tracks, Elton's high spirits plummeted. He complained they were too instrumental and over-produced to the point of sounding almost saccharine. Bell, however, disagreed. Elton then wanted to discard the LP altogether. Ultimately, after a great deal of reworking, they compromised with a three-track maxi-single in England and a mini-LP, with only six tracks, in America. In the end Elton managed to salvage something of this project. "Thom Bell taught me a lot," he says, "how to breathe properly and to use my voice in a lower register."

Elton had also formed another working partnership with percussionist Ray Cooper. What Elton, without his band, was lacking in terms of bodies on stage was more than compensated for by Cooper's energetic style. When both men appeared at London's Rainbow Theater, however, it would be a Royal faux pas involving Elton, and not his new act, that would make the front pages.

The concerts held for the Queen's Silver Jubilee Trust, a Royal Charity, also provided yet another time to take stock. Elton explains: "I had to look at the situation and think about where I was going. Maybe things were running away a bit. But I just fancied having a go on my own."

And so he did, giving a performance that was fit for a Queen. Meeting royalty had never caused Elton any discomfort or attack of nerves. He was already a good friend of the Windsor family and a favorite entertainer at their public and private functions. Having dined with Princess Margaret on numerous occasions and played concerts before the Queen Mother, the idea of performing in front of Princess Alexandra, a cousin of the Queen, at the Rainbow Theater in Finsbury Park, North London, did not seem especially daunting to Elton.

Indeed, Elton seemed at perfect ease with himself as the curtain went up on the evening of May 3, 1977. He was relaxed enough, in fact, to joke with the audience at the start of his performance. "Your Royal Highness, ladies and gentlemen, and Moss Brothers," said Elton, referring to a famous company that rents evening wear. "I hope you've brought your choices with you. It's going to be a long program."

It was, as Elton trotted out hit songs from almost seven years as a recording artist that, by at least one accounting, comprised two percent of worldwide sales. But the goodwill at the event, which included a standing ovation, evaporated at show's end.

Backstage at the end of the concert Elton experienced one of the

THE MANY FACES OF ELTON JOHN

Early Elton. (Terry O'Neil. Globe Photos)

Pensive Elton. (Terence Spencer, Globe Photos)

A star is born. (Globe Photos)

Football crazy. (Bob Noble,
Globe Photos)

Elton the Raver. (Mark Anderson, Globe Photos)

A bouquet from fans. (Norman Parkinson, Globe Photos)

A married man. (G. Dalla Pozza, Globe Photos)

"Mad Hatter," with wife on
Bastille Day. (Alpha/Globe)

most embarrassing moments of his career. The Princess posed a question to him, "Do you take cocaine?"

Elton was shocked and stunned by her inquiry. He remembers, "I was astonished. It was one of the first questions out of her mouth. Of course, when I recovered I told her I did not take cocaine before I go on stage, which is the truth."

In fairness, the Princess had just witnessed a frenzied performance and must have wondered if Elton needed any chemical props. Elton later reflected, "I don't think she quite understood that anybody could work so hard onstage for so long without taking some sort of stimulant."

What bothered Elton more than her remark, however, was his own lack of discretion in discussing this incident with the press. "I hope very much," he stated publicly, "that the Princess isn't embarrassed that I repeated her remarks."

Just as Elton had surmised, Princess Alexandra was ashamed about it and dashed off a personal letter apologizing for her "unfortunate" question and assuring him that she had not meant it as a personal slur. In turn, Elton willingly accepted this Royal apology.

Something of a grudge collector in general, Elton often was not so quick to forgive. A few months later, at London's Heathrow Airport, in fact, it was hard to recognize the man who had been so mild-mannered and acquiescent with a member of the Royal Family. "I'm in an absolutely filthy mood," Elton screamed as he stormed through the terminal building.

His temper had taken off just minutes before when he had arrived at the TWA desk to find that he had been the victim of an innocent mistake. "Your reservation has been canceled," a check-in clerk informed him. "There are no more seats in first class."

Elton could not believe what he was hearing. Standing there, with enough baggage to stockpile for a nuclear attack, he fumed at the clerk. Was it possible that the king of seventies pop music, who made transatlantic flights the way other people rode commuter trains, had been bumped from his seat?

The airline staff tried to placate Elton by offering him a seat in economy. "No," Elton snapped. "I will not accept that." A standoff ensued for a few minutes as clerks scrambled to figure out a solution, with Elton raging at the counter.

Realizing, however, that it would be an economy seat or nothing,

Elton eventually conceded, but not without a vociferous protest. "It's one big fuckup," he seethed. "Everyone seemed to know it was canceled apart from me. I'm so furious. I think I'll stay away until 1981."

And with that a livid Elton, the man who could be charming and ingratiating when it suited him to be, boarded his flight to Los Angeles like anybody else.

20

Saying Good-bye to the Road

Elton was screaming and yelling backstage at Empire Pool, Wembley. He was furious because some berets and caps he had ordered for a charity concert on this night in November 1977 had not turned up. As he festered over the missing headgear, he wondered how much more he could take of touring.

But when Elton took the stage, he was once again the consummate performer, betraying none of the despair he had felt moments before. The audience was mesmerized for more than two hours by fourteen classic Elton John songs. For part of the show Elton performed solo. Later he was joined by the Rocket group China, which featured Elton's guitarist Davey Johnstone. At one point Stevie Wonder, whom Elton had spotlighted in the audience and praised effusively, came on stage to play piano for the rocker "Bite Your Lip."

Even those fans accustomed to Elton's extravagant showmanship could not have anticipated the high drama that would unfold on this stage that night. Nor did Elton's cronies backstage have a clue about it either. The histrionic moment would come just prior to the finale in the form of an announcement.

"It's been a painful decision whether to come back on the road," Elton John told the audience. "I've really enjoyed tonight. But I've made a decision. This is the last one I'm going to do. There's a lot more to me than being on the road."

Fans reacted by weeping and shouting down his announcement. "No, no, no!" they chanted. Elton tried to soothe them, confessing, "It's been a painful decision." Then, as if tugging at their hearts some more, he followed up with "Don't Let the Sun Go Down on Me." And, finally, he brought on Kiki Dee to sing their chart-topping duet, "Don't Go Breaking My Heart."

Backstage, meanwhile, his entourage was flabbergasted. Manager John Reid, Elton's closest ally, paced the floor stuttering. He appeared to be talking to himself: "He's really gone and done it. I've got to discuss this whole thing with him tomorrow. I don't know anything about it.' "

Reid's assistant, Alex Foster, who had organized this event, stood openmouthed. Stevie Wonder, who came backstage after the concert, was not convinced that Elton meant what he said. "You may think you mean it," he cautioned Elton, "but it's hard to retire in this game."

Wonder was right. Within eighteen months Elton would return to the stage. But for the moment at least he seemed to be enjoying the shock waves he had created.

Around the Vicarage Road stadium, however, Elton's announcement came as no surprise. Soccer, after all, had become his consuming passion in the last year. The next day, when Elton turned up there, reporters were swarming. He declined all interviews about his startling announcement. Privately he confessed to the Watford players that his decision had not been a spontaneous outburst, but something he had given thought to before appearing on the Wembley stage. In later years, Elton reflected, "I suddenly realized that I was once again doing a concert with trunk after trunk of equipment. I was doing things that I promised myself that I would never do again. I was angry with myself."

At thirty, Elton believed it was time for some major revisions in his life. For all his wealth and celebrity, he felt cheated out of living. Just as he had missed out on his adolescence, he had watched his twenties come and go, as if he had been living a movie, not real life. His success in the seventies could be compared to that of the Beatles in the sixties. There seemed very little left for Elton John to achieve. In the last seven years he had toured America ten times. There had been no pause for thought. It was time now, Elton believed, to give himself a break. As Andrew Hill, his personal assistant, put it, "Elton wanted to concentrate on enjoying himself."

In fact, when Elton interviewed Hill for the job, he asked, "Do you play tennis?" In addition to customary duties like arranging Elton's press events and itinerary, Hill was required to stand in as tennis partner at his employer's home courts in Berkshire and Benedict Canyon. After their first match, Elton even paid for lessons for Hill and provided him and other guests with the best rackets.

"We spent a lot of time in Los Angeles," Hill remembers. "Tennis was very much in vogue, and Elton wanted to concentrate on improving his game. Many stars—Rod Stewart, Billie Jean King, Bryan Ferry—used to come over to play."

The hiring of Hill had come about through their mutual love of soccer. Andrew was the son of George Hill, the proprietor of Northwood Hills Pub, who had given Elton his first break as a saloon singer. Father and son attended weekly matches at Watford, and it was there that Elton suggested that Andrew become his personal assistant.

Andrew, having just completed his school-leaving exams, had planned to start university as an engineering major. Hill recalls, "Looking back on his own early years, Elton felt it was an unwise choice to go straight into university after finishing my exams. He said it would be more beneficial for me to take a year out."

During this year Andrew saw a man of many faces: extremely generous, but rarely foolish with his money; needy for companionship, but craving solitude; highly accomplished, but constantly looking for confirmation that he was any good.

Hill remembers accompanying Elton on forays through Tower Records in Los Angeles and New York, where he would fill a shopping cart with records and tapes. "Elton had hundreds of thousands of records," Hill remembers. "His library took up as much space as the ground floor of a normal-sized house." On a whim Elton would tell Andrew to pick out whatever music he liked for himself.

Even so, the man who never forgot a friend or close associate's birthday and rewarded them with jewelry, furs and, in the case of his manager, a yacht and Rolls-Royce, also knew how to say no. "I think I can vaguely recall when Elton's true father asked him for money and Elton flatly refused," Hill says. "I believe he asked for it in a letter and Elton said he was not going to give it."

Interestingly, Hill's recollection seems to give more credence to Elton's version of events regarding his father. In Stanley Dwight's *Daily Mail* interview a year earlier, though acknowledging that he had received money from Elton to buy a Peugeot station wagon, Stanley Dwight said he felt some reluctance about writing to Elton for fear that his son might misinterpret his letters as a request for money.

Though Hill accompanied Elton to Philadelphia and Seattle for the Thom Bell sessions, he remembers his boss devoting much of this year to having fun. There was a stop in Rio for Carnival in 1976, when Elton came dressed as a sailor, and a visit to New York for an Andy Warhol party at the Xenon disco. Even while on tour with the band in Hawaii he spent two weeks encamped in a beach bungalow in La Haina on the island of Maui, and a most relaxed Elton gave an impromptu recital at a beach bar.

On this Hawaiian trip everyone in Elton's party took tennis lessons, and Elton became friendly with the pro whom he dubbed Dirty Dick. On the last day of their stay, Elton, Hill and their entourage went by Dirty Dick's ground-floor bungalow down the road from the tennis ranch to say good-bye. Dirty Dick was not in.

Hill recounts, "Elton decided to move every bit of furniture in his place into the garden. We put the whole house in the garden. It took three or four hours to do. And Elton left a note saying we were all sorry Dirty Dick was not home when we came along to say good-bye."

Rock stars were famous, of course, for trashing hotel rooms, sometimes dumping their entire contents in a swimming pool. Elton's prank, however, was different. It was neither mean-spirited nor drug-induced, but merely an act of good-natured mischief. Almost like a dutiful schoolboy, Elton made sure that every piece of furniture from the tennis pro's house was not only intact, but also perfectly arranged in the garden.

One minute Elton coveted company and in the next he would barricade himself away from civilization in a room for days on end. "After a concert Elton was always high," Hill remembers, "but then you knew when to expect the depression." The mood shifts were dramatic. During Elton's self-imposed solitudes he would stay up half the night listening to music on the stereo equipment he carried with him everywhere or reading voraciously. One of his favorite books that year was *The Amityville Horror*, a bestseller about a haunted house where a deranged son had murdered his parents and siblings. "After Elton finished the book," Hills says, "he begged me for a whole month to read it."

Elton, according to Hill, was a lonely man who longed for a partner. "If Elton met someone he liked, he wanted to spend as much time as possible with that person. He really wanted companionship more than a romantic relationship."

To this day, Hill maintains, "Had Elton not found stardom, he would have been an ordinary married man with kids. I could never understand why he made those statements about his preferences because I believed that he still had it in him to get married."

Despite hit after hit, Elton needed constant reassurance that he was good at his music. The death a few months earlier of Elvis Presley, whom Elton had worshiped as a boy, haunted him. They had met a year earlier and Elvis's face had looked almost embalmed. Worse, according to Elton, his idol had become a parody of himself.

Now, when Elton turned on the television, he saw the punkers, a decade younger than he, and he was starting to feel, he said half-jokingly, like an old-age pensioner. With their leather-studded jackets, Doc Marten boots, Mohawk hairdos and safety pins in ears and noses, Elton's feather and boas were starting to look, by comparison, almost frumpy.

A reminder of the aging process had come in the form of his own hair loss. Having always been self-conscious about his appearance, going bald worried Elton a great deal. "He was concerned with his overall physical appearance," Hill says. "He just didn't think he was attractive. It was not just his overweight, but his general appearance—his face, his stocky physique, the balding."

Initially Elton tried to explain his baldness as the cumulative effects of a hairdressing dye. But as each threadlike strand fell out, he finally gave up on that explanation, and was devastated by the realization that soon he might have no hair left on his head.

Others, however, did not take his loss of hair so seriously. When Elton's "Girl Friday," Alex Foster, was asked to make arrangements for Elton's hair transplant, she roared with laughter, but quickly realized that this was not a joke. Indeed, Elton's hair loss was a very sensitive issue with him, and so Alex tracked down a business contact of Dr. Pierre Pouteaux, the French surgeon regarded by many as the world's leader in hair transplants.

And so in 1977 Elton headed for Paris to begin a series of transplants. Hair was removed from the back of Elton's scalp to be replanted in squares in the front. It was a painful process and after the first session, according to Andrew Hill, Elton had to have the plugs redone the same day. "As he went to get into the car," Hill explains, "he hit his head on the top of the door, knocking half of the squares out."

Elton was now donning all kinds of hats to conceal his bald head. There were straw hats, Stetsons, berets, top hats, cloth caps—a collection that would soon rival his enormous eyeglass selection. But it would take another year before Elton would take his hat off for photographers. Alex Foster, however, could not wait that long and begged Elton to show her the results of his treatments. When he did, she was horrified. "It looked so funny," Alex said, "more like a lawn that's been reseeded."

But Elton was happy with the results. In all he would make five trips to Paris, at a cost of around $5,000, but from his point of view it would mean a solution to at least one problem in his life. In the meantime, too, as the music press seemed to pay more attention to new acts, Elton continued to make headlines.

21

Mr. Hypochondriac

Driving along in her car on a November day in 1978, Alex Foster, who was also personal assistant to manager John Reid, turned up the volume on the radio when she heard the words, "News bulletin— Pop star Elton John has been rushed to hospital after suffering a heart attack."

Alex could not believe it. Over the last few months she had dismissed Elton's aches and pains as largely imaginary. Frequently she had heard Elton turn a pain in his arm into a stroke and a twitching of the leg into a blood clot. But at this moment, hearing the announcement on the radio, she began to have second thoughts. Maybe Elton had been seriously ill all along.

In the past Elton had certainly burned the candles at both ends. But over the last few months there had been no respite from work. In fact, Elton had been working six days a week, until two or three in the morning, without eating. His diet had consisted of sequential cups of coffee. Elton was totally obsessed with the making of a new LP, *A Single Man*, which, he hoped, would restore his position at the top of the charts.

To this end Elton had locked himself away at the Mill Studios in

Maidenhead, just outside of London and close to his Berkshire home. "I'll show those bastards," Elton muttered to himself as a challenge to critics who proclaimed him to be a washout and finished. Elton was now on a mission to record his best work yet. His only indulgence, it seemed, was watching his cherished Watford Football Club play on Saturday afternoons.

Elton's incredible workload, combined with an unhealthy diet, appeared to have caught up with him. He gobbled up vitamins like M&M candies while going on wild diet swings—a period of fasting followed by a feasting on a huge meal; cutting sugar out of his diet only to consume a pint of ice cream later; disregarding his carrot juice for a champagne and brandy binge. His habits of living were as erratic as his diet regimen. Even when he was supposed to be relaxing, Elton could not take it easy. He had to win at everything he did. Whether it was a game of squash, tennis or backgammon, Elton John aimed to be the best.

Now, though, as Alex Foster turned her car around to rush to the hospital, she reflected on Elton's internal conflicts. She told one London journalist, "I found early on that despite Elton's love of the bright lights and the adulation of his fans, he often wants to be completely alone."

Over several months she had come to know the shy, introspective man who sometimes needed to shut out the world. Elton had once got so fed up with people calling him that he had two phones altered by the telephone company so they could not accept incoming calls. The only way anyone could contact him at Woodside was via the telex Elton had installed there. In fact, if he chose, Elton could ignore all communications from the outside world for weeks on end.

Alex herself had tried for two weeks to contact Elton about papers which needed to be signed immediately. It had been to no avail. Eventually John Reid dispatched her to Woodside with these instructions: "Don't come back without Elton's signature on all these papers." Even to this day Alex Foster cannot understand why Elton failed to respond to her letters. She even sent a telegram begging him to reply. It was worded, "Please, please, please get in touch." But still she heard nothing.

As she approached Woodside with papers in hand, Alex was very nervous. Trembling, she stood on the doorstep and worried how Elton might react to her visit. Suddenly, he appeared and did a complete about-face, welcoming and ushering her inside the house. Elton seemed delighted to see her. "Hi, sweetheart," Elton chirped, "fancy seeing you here."

It was almost like Dr. Jekyll and Mr. Hyde. The man who had refused to even acknowledge her barrage of telegrams now behaved like a long-lost friend. Alex was flabbergasted. "I could have strangled him," she remembers thinking. "But instead I calmly handed him the stack of papers, and he signed each one without hesitation and then invited me to stay for lunch." Alex could not believe this drastic change of mood. She asked Elton why he had shut out all communications over the last fourteen days. "I just didn't feel like it," Elton explained. "I've been too busy playing tennis and backgammon." But that was Elton John, the most mercurial person Alex Foster had ever met. "Lovable one minute," she remarks, "infuriating the next."

Now, driving toward the exclusive private hospital where Elton lay in intensive care, Alex reflected on the aspects of Elton's personality that endeared him to her. Her employer was capable of great hospitality. He was also the man who had once confided to her that he did not know how many real friends he had. Indeed, it sometimes seemed like Elton had found a trusted confidante in Alex. In turn, Elton would become quite protective of her. One time she turned up at Woodside to find a group of gay men lounging around the swimming pool, and one of them sniped, "But Elton, she's a chick." Elton, quickly coming to her defense, declared, "Alex is my friend. She's cool, and she can do what she wants."

While Alex was well aware of Elton's sexual preference, she never saw any evidence of promiscuity. Unlike a lot of pop stars, Alex says, "he doesn't indulge in orgies or take drugs. And though his sexual preference is predominantly gay, Elton has been to bed with women and found it pleasant."

Alex was also sure that one day Elton would settle down with a wife and family of his own. Talking to a London paper, she said that Elton had once confided that was all that was missing from his life.

During her time with him, Alex witnessed a lot of females making advances to Elton. "Women adore him," she says. "Often at parties and receptions I've seen girls move in on him with only one thing in mind. But Elton is wise to their antics. He knows that in most cases these women want to get him into bed so they can later boast that they have converted him."

But at this moment, Elton's future, romantic or otherwise, was uncertain as he lay in his hospital bed at the Harley Street Clinic. The medical drama had started when Elton collapsed at his home just minutes before leaving for the airport to fly to Paris for another hair-transplant session. Sitting in a chair and talking on the phone, Elton had felt fine. Then he stood up and, suddenly, just keeled over on the floor.

He was in agony. Staggering, he made his way to his live-in assistant's room in another part of the house. Bob Halley took one look at Elton and knew he was ill. He called an ambulance immediately, and within minutes Elton was being whisked to London's Harley Street Clinic. Though conscious upon arrival, he was admitted to the coronary care unit. After a series of intensive tests, a spokesman for the hospital assured the press, now camped outside, that Elton John had not suffered a heart attack, but would remain, nonetheless, in the clinic for further observation.

When Alex Foster walked into Elton's room, a feeling of relief came over her. She threw her arms around him. "I thought you were on the way out," she said. To which Elton responded, "Sorry to disappoint you, but there's no way I'm leaving this earth before Watford have gone the first division."

Despite his good humor, Elton was clearly suffering from exhaustion, and many of his friends were not surprised by his collapse. Over the past few months his schedule had been grueling. The new album, A Single Man, was Elton's first original LP in two years. And there was the uncertainty of working with a new cast. Only producer Clive Franks, who doubled up on bass, remained from the early days. The new lineup consisted of Steve Holly, Kiki Dee's former drummer, and Tim Renwick on guitar.

The biggest change of all had been Bernie Taupin's replacement, Gary Osborne. Gary had known right from the beginning that Bernie Taupin was a hard act to follow. An experienced jingle-maker, Osborne was viewed by some critics as an odd fit with the Elton John music machine. Osborne, too, realized that he was in a no-win situation. "I know I won't get the credit if the album is a success," Osborne said at the time. "I will only get the blame if it fails."

To his credit, Osborne had already written Kiki Dee's chart-topping single "Amoreuse," her debut on Rocket. But, above all, he was Elton's friend. He had never been a fan of his music until one day when Elton, visiting Osborne at his home, sat down and played a tune that appealed to him. And when he told Elton that he liked it, Elton suggested that he write some words for it.

Osborne was a totally different personality from Taupin. Flamboyant and gregarious, he had wayward blond curls and was given to wearing oversized coats. He was there at a time when Elton most needed a friend he could trust to fill a void in his professional life. Their method of working was totally opposite to the John-Taupin collaboration; now Elton supplied the melodies first and Osborne put the words to them.

Elton had also included the dubious musical talents of the Watford Football Club as backup vocalists on two tracks, the bluesy "Big Dipper" and the gospel-like "Georgia." Remarkably, out of a chorus of twenty-five, who had all been transported to the studio by bus, there was only one truly atrocious voice, and that player was edged out of the front lines.

Ironically, Elton's passion for soccer had contributed to his hospitalization. On the previous Sunday he had played a strenuous game of soccer in a five-a-side match for charity. The following day he had a rigorous workout on his home tennis court with friend and champion Billie Jean King, and on Tuesday he collapsed. On the work front, he had staked a great deal on *A Single Man*, and some weeks earlier had given a preview of the album for executives from his American label, MCA.

At the MCA gig Elton had felt intense pressure to prove that he was still capable of topping the charts. Just before the show, he had to take headache pills to calm himself down. "I'm so nervous," he told the Westside Room audience in Los Angeles, on the night of October 16, 1978. "I just hope I can remember all the words." This was his first U.S. concert in more than two years. But as he sipped champagne and the lights went down, the roar from the crowd was overwhelming. The purpose of the concert was to thank the people at MCA Records for their support and, more important, to get them enthused about *A Single Man*.

By evening's end, although he hit a few wrong piano notes and forgot some of the words early in the show, the crowd was impressed. "Part-Time Love," that's a Number One record," said one promotions man. Another disagreed: " 'I Don't Care,' that's the single my people want." Elton did not mind which track they gleaned from the album as a single. He was just glad that they were behind the album and that he had managed to make a success of this solo performance.

It had been a risk. "When you do a big show," Elton said, "you can hide behind everybody else. It becomes too cozy. The audience doesn't even notice it when you make a mistake. Even if they do, you can always blame it on someone else. But this way I feel completely naked out here. If I make a mistake, it is noticed, and I have no one else to blame. It forces you to concentrate. It's more of a challenge. Tonight it was more like it should be out there. The adrenaline was really pumping. I was really nervous. When I sat down at the piano, my knee was shaking, so I had to put it on the pedal, but it just kept shaking. If I do come back, that's what I want to do, just me and the piano."

Now, sitting up in his hospital bed, Elton wondered if he would ever perform again. But he knew that for as long as he continued to breathe, soccer would be a part of his life. Elton even arranged for a telephone line in his hospital room to keep him up to date on a Watford game against Exeter. In return for his devotion to the team, Chairman Elton was rewarded with a 2–0 win.

But on a more serious note, Elton's collapse had served as a reminder that he was not invincible. "This has really shaken me," he admitted. "When you are used to nonstop tours across the States and so on, you start to think you are superhuman. Then something like this happens and you realize you've got to slow down like everyone else."

During his three-day hospital stay every possible test was done on Elton and he was given a clean bill of health. But he knew that from now on, even at the age of thirty-one, he would have to slow down.

While the medical experts were blaming Elton's collapse on exhaustion, singer-songwriter Tom Robinson offered another diagnosis: "Chinese food," he thought at first. Robinson, who had achieved some notoriety that year after his single "Glad to Be Gay" was banned from play by BBC radio, had recently met Elton at a Guiness Book of Pop Records photo session and they subsequently had dinner together. Later on they would collaborate on an album and make a controversial video together.

But on the day of the photo shoot, both men, Robinson on a motorcycle and Elton in a vintage car, were cruising the block for a parking space. "Down came the smoky windows of Elton's car and he asked me where I was going," Robinson recalls. "It turned out we were both going to the same place. Elton and I had never met, and I hadn't supposed we would like each other." But during the photography session they talked, and Robinson got an invitation to dinner at Elton's place in Berkshire.

Remembers Robinson, "I took my boyfriend there, and Elton had no food in the house and asked Bob Halley to go out and get Chinese takeaway. So we had Chinese takeaway at Elton's mansion. The next day the headline in the *Evening Standard* said Elton collapsed and was rushed to the hospital. I thought it was the Chinese food."

When he came out of the hospital, many people began to speculate that Elton was now a has-been. But within a short time he was able to prove them wrong when the single "Part-Time Love" bounced straight into the Top Ten.

Inadvertently, his hospital stay may have worked to Elton's advantage. Not only did it remind him of his mortality, but it also proved there was life after Bernie. "I went in there and 'Part-Time Love' was out and doing three thousand a day," he admits. "As soon as I went into hospital it was doing twenty thousand."

Changing Faces

22

Elton's Glasnost

Elton was missing the applause, and as the new year, 1979, approached, he had already made up his mind to come out of semiretirement. But he also knew that if he continued to tour only the Britain-Australia-North America axis, he would end up feeling the same boredom and staleness that had led him to quit in the first place. Elton wanted to stretch further afield.

In discussions with his manager about his plans, John Reid had come up with a novel suggestion: "Why not tour Russia?" Elton was excited by the idea, and since he was already scheduled to perform in Europe and Israel, he gave Reid the go-ahead to add Russia to his itinerary for the coming year.

Arranging a tour of the U.S.S.R. was, of course, easier said than done. No Western pop star had ever toured there. Bob Dylan, Paul McCartney and Fleetwood Mac, among others, had tried and failed to get permission to do so. In fact, only a year before, a Leningrad concert featuring the Beach Boys, Joan Baez and Santana had been canceled at the last minute by Soviet authorities without any explanation. Western pop music was still regarded as an instrument of capitalist decadence.

Remarkably, though, the negotiations for Elton's U.S.S.R. tour seemed to go smoothly. Reid enlisted the help of British concert promoter Harvey Goldsmith, and together they flew to Moscow to conduct meetings with Gosconcert, the Soviet state promotion monopoly. Literally hundreds of hours were spent completing the necessary paperwork. All of Elton's songs for the concerts had to be cleared by censors, and much to his delight not a single one was banned.

Initially Reid asked the Soviets for permission to stage two Moscow shows, and they came back with a request for ten in both Moscow and Leningrad. Eventually the parties agreed on four shows in each city, with Leningrad the first stop. Reid and Goldsmith also managed to talk the Soviets into allowing a live broadcast of one concert to Britain on BBC Radio One as well as a television film of the tour. Meanwhile, Melodiya, the Soviet record label, jumped on the Elton John bandwagon. They requested and got Reid's permission to release a live album of the tour.

For each concert Elton would be paid $1,000. Not since his Troubadour days nine years before had he received so little remuneration. But Elton believed that the chance to play Russia was worth every penny of the $25,000 the tour would cost *him*. Besides, the television film of the tour would allow him to recoup the moneys down the line.

In May 1979, five months after the start of these negotiations, Elton finally headed east with an entourage of twenty-seven people. Thirteen tons of equipment, including sound props, pianos, lights and wardrobe, were trucked in. He also brought with him a new, sparser show that earlier in the year had won over Israeli and European audiences.

Opening night for Elton was May 21, at Leningrad's Bolshoi Oktyabrsky Hall, which had been built in 1967 to commemorate the fiftieth anniversary of the Bolshevik Revolution. History was once again in the making as Elton John, first Western pop music star to perform in the U.S.S.R., arrived on stage in the thirty-five-hundred-seat hall. The standing ovation that greeted him went on and on.

Bathed in flashing multicolored spotlights, Elton, a lone figure crouched over a Steinway grand piano, opened with "Your Song," appropriately, for this concert was Elton's gift of song to the Soviets. However, in his stained blue trousers and green shirt, and with cloth cap hiding his hair transplant, Elton was something of a fashion disappointment to the fans, who had come expecting the noise, the clowning, the glitter and the showmanship of an Elton John spectacle. The mood of the audience was somewhat subdued as Elton ranged over ballads, both slow and up-tempo, like "Daniel" and "Don't Let the Sun Go Down on Me," but during "Goodbye Yellow Brick Road," as red and yellow dots swirled around Elton, they clapped along.

Midway through the two-and-a-half-hour show, percussionist Ray Cooper materialized on stage in a puff of smoke. Despite his undertaker looks, his pale and somewhat dour visage and dark pin-striped suit, Cooper managed to enliven things on stage as he leapt and cavorted about while hammering on a huge gong and beating drums.

With Elton punching out chords on his electric Yamaha piano and Ray banging on his drums and cymbals, they kept up a nonstop half hour of hard rock. That sent the Russians into a frenzy of swaying, singing, clapping, dancing and bopping in the aisles to "Crocodile Rock" and the Motown hit "Heard It Through the Grapevine."

"Elton, Elton, Elton," they chanted, bringing him back for an encore. He gave them a Beatles song, "Back in the U.S.S.R." Elton remembers, "I just thought of doing it that moment. But I realized after a few notes that I didn't know the words, so I just kept repeating, 'Back in the U.S.S.R.'"

The audience did not seem to care, and in a scene reminiscent of Beatlemania they threw clenched fists and victory salutes his way. Elton, in turn, tossed back into the crowd carnations and tulips the fans had placed on the stage for him.

By the time Elton returned to his dressing room the tumultuous applause had overflowed onto the streets. Opening the louvered windows, Elton saw two thousand Russians standing there, blocking the tram lines, and wildly cheering him. A teary-eyed Elton responded by throwing red carnations their way.

"This was like starting all over," Elton reflected at the time. "One of the reasons I wanted to come here is that I didn't know what to expect, so it makes you play harder."

Indeed, not a single one of his records had ever been on sale in the state music shops. For Soviet youth the only exposure to pop music came via the Voice of America, the BBC World Service or West Berlin radio broadcasts—unless, of course, someone was lucky enough to have a friend who traveled abroad and smuggled in some records. Somehow they managed, though, to keep up with the latest trends and chart hits, and in their view Elton John was definitely the Rock Superczar of the seventies.

Elton had arrived in Leningrad the day before the concert by first-class overnight train from Moscow. Fans had awaited him at the Moscow station, and two middle-aged women even succeeded in pushing past security to get Elton's autograph and give him a present, a guide book to Leningrad's Hermitage Museum.

Some fans were even prepared to spend as much as $150 on the black market for tickets. At the official price of nine dollars (six rubles) each, two tickets would have cost more than the average Soviet worker earned in a month. Many young Russians protested that the event had been sold out long before the concert was announced on the radio. "Only important people can go," moaned one disappointed fan, while another reported that only a small number of tickets had ever gone on sale in the first place. In fact, about ten percent of the tickets had been reserved for Communist Party members, city bureaucrats, their sons and daughters and the Youth League. Joining them in the first ten rows at each concert were members of Elton's entourage.

Elton liked Leningrad and particularly appreciated the classical beauty of the city, which, astonishingly, he compared to Manchester and Birmingham in the north of England. It is questionable, though, just how much he actually saw of this majestic city, with its Venetian-style canals, and the sumptuous Summer Palace, just outside the city, with hilly lawns and gardens and ornate statuary. For one thing Elton skipped out on touring the Hermitage Museum, the largest in the world, with seven major sections housing some of the world's greatest art treasures. Five minutes into a tour that included the museum, Elton said he felt ill and returned immediately to his room at the Europeiskaya Hotel in downtown Leningrad.

Elton managed to see more of Moscow. And despite its heavy, drab, Brobdingnagian buildings, he found it beautiful. But what most appealed to him, as he meandered through Red Square, home of the Kremlin, was that tourists paid more attention to the changing of the guard at Lenin's Tomb than to the superstar from the West. In his magenta trousers, high-heeled boots and floppy cloth cap, he was virtually ignored.

Here Elton put in a pitch for Paul McCartney, who had once expressed a desire to give a concert in Red Square. The response from Elton's guide was a firm *nyet*. Furthermore, said the representative of Soviet authority, he could not think of a more inappropriate venue. Elton said he hoped that his own appearance in the Soviet Union would open the way for other rock stars to perform in the U.S.S.R.

Why the Russians had permitted Elton to give concerts there remains a mystery. But one theory, suggested by a British journalist covering the tour, was that it was Elton's association with the Watford team, not his music, that had ingratiated him with Russian authorities. Soccer was, after all, a favorite proletarian pastime in Russia. In fact, while in Moscow, Elton watched the Red Army team play Minsk and praised some of the players.

But when asked at a press conference about the boycott by several nations of the forthcoming Moscow Olympics, Elton let down his diplomatic guard. "They thought they had problems in Montreal. . . ." he cracked, adding that he would not go anywhere near the event.

Elton was also constantly mindful that he was in a country where homosexuality carried a five-year jail term, so consequently he did not go around making any declarations. When asked his opinion of apartheid in sports, Elton said he opposed all forms of discrimination—whether on the basis of sexual preference, race or religion. In their translation, the Russians, quick to censor, deleted "sexual preference" from his answer.

At his opening-night concert in Moscow, Elton sensed a kind of heavy, if not oppressive, atmosphere in the giant hall of the Rossiya Hotel. Later on he would point out that Party members and city bureaucrats were out in full force. But one teenage girl nevertheless managed to rush by security to give Elton a carnation. Enormously touched, Elton bent down to kiss her on the cheek. At his other Moscow concerts, attended by a larger contingent of teenagers than authorities, the mood was much more joyful.

Privately, Elton said that he was not happy with Moscow's hotels. The city was in the middle of a heat wave, unprecedented for May, and there was no air conditioning in the rooms. But at a British embassy reception, Elton did not voice any discomfort as he munched the ham-and-chicken sandwiches. Instead, he told the other guests that he had been overwhelmed by the reception given him by the Russians.

Elton's mother and stepfather had come along on the trip too, and attended all four concerts. Though delighted by Elton's triumphant reception, Sheila Farebrother had other concerns on her mind. For her, the first Western pop star to tour the U.S.S.R. was, above all else, her son—and she was becoming increasingly worried about his personal happiness.

During a walk through Red Square, she confided to a British journalist: "Loneliness, that's the one thing I worry about for him more than anything else." Sheila told David Wigg of the *Daily Express*, "I would like to see him settle down and have a family. At the moment I feel that he's got everything, but nothing. I don't think he's ever had complete happiness anytime in his life."

In recent times, Sheila confessed, she had found it hard to talk to Elton, a situation made worse by Elton's cutting off his phone lines. "He can make outgoing calls—but you can't ring him," she said. "One day he said, 'Get those phones out of the house—they drive me mad.' He's very good to me and he obviously loves me. He shows that in his generosity. But for all the generosity, I would like to have just ten minutes of his time to sit and talk like we used to years ago. We were very close then. It was like a brother-and-sister relationship."

Sheila also voiced her belief that Elton's lifestyle cut him off from the world. Eight years had passed since Elton, then twenty-four, had confided in his mother about his sexual preferences. In fact, Sheila blamed her son's homosexuality on show business, saying, "I don't think he'd ever have been, if he hadn't gone into show business." While publicly she seemed to accept it, privately she continued to hope that Elton, having reached thirty-two, would settle down and have a family.

Elton, yet to resolve his personal torments, left Russia as a man happy in his professional life. As the former Captain Fantastic later put it: "I don't have to do handstands on the piano anymore. I can concentrate on my music."

Many memories of the tour would remain with him, and in a few years, one of the wishes Elton's mother expressed in Red Square would be answered, in part, in another foreign land thousands of miles away.

23

Part-time Partner

Despite the triumphant Russian tour, the name Elton John might well have disappeared from the headlines as the seventies drew to a close. But Elton managed to keep himself in the news by virtue of his involvement with the Watford Football Club and his Parisian hair transplant. "People come and go," he remarked philosophically about the rock music scene. "Right now I'm just happy to have survived."

Even so, Elton still needed to open the eighties with a bang—and he did so by reminding the public of his prolific output during his glory days, in the mid-seventies, with the release of the *21 at 33* album. The "21" connoted the number of his recordings, a figure arrived at by counting the double albums as two records each, and the "33" was his age. The message was that Elton was not yet ready to consign himself to rock-'n'-roll memorabilia.

Elton was once again "Chasing the Crown" of pop music, as the album's lead track was titled, however much it may have eluded him in recent times in America and England, despite his triumphant reception in Russia.

Of his recent albums, the 1978 LP *A Single Man*, his first without Bernie or producer Gus Dudgeon, was at best uneven. Only the instrumental "Song for Guy" seemed to be of any enduring value. A memorial to Rocket messenger Guy Burchett, who died in a motorcycle accident, it was Elton's first self-penned U.K. Top Ten single since "Crocodile Rock" seven years earlier. "Song for Guy" also earned Elton a music industry Ivor Novello Award. "Part-Time Love," a bouncy, likable tune, was the album's other memorable offering.

Then came *The Thom Bell Sessions*, an ill-fated mini-LP released in 1979 but recorded two years before. Elton sang on only three tracks, including the single "Mama Can't Buy You Love," which, though not his own composition, gave him his first hit single in the United States in recent years. Some months later the disco-pop album *Victim of Love* fared no better. Not even the participation of Pete Bellote, Donna Summer's coproducer, the strong backup vocals of the Doobie Brothers' Michael MacDonald, or Elton's fiercely rhythmic piano managed to pump up sales.

Disco simply did not appeal to his fans. Elton himself recognized his own limitations in this genre, too. He admits, "I'm not very good at writing disco music, so I just sang on the album." That market was virtually owned in the late seventies by disco diva Donna Summer (with hits like "Love to Love You Baby" and "Last Dance") and Elton's fellow Britons the Bee Gees, who spun hit after disco hit, including "Staying Alive" from the sound track for the wildly popular movie *Saturday Night Fever*.

"I've learned to be much more patient than I used to be, and I'm much more tolerant," Elton said in June of 1980. "And I've learned to be a good loser. I used to be the worst loser in the world, but when I took over the soccer team, we lost so many games my attitude had to change. I grew up a lot."

But now there were signs of change in the other direction, and it appeared that Elton might even be headed for a winning streak. "Little Jeannie," an Elton John-Gary Osborne single from the *21 at 33* album, rose quickly into the Top Ten in America, peaking in June 1980 at Number Three. It was Elton's first hit in the United States since his superstar days, when he had reeled off more than a dozen, including six Number Ones. The album itself reached Number Twelve in the United States and Thirteen in Britain.

21 at 33 marked Elton's return to a style that had pushed him to the top of the charts before. The up-tempo ballad "Little Jeannie" was as sweet as "Daniel" and reminiscent of its style with its caressing electric piano and sing-along choruses. "Oh, Little Jeannie, I'm so in love with you," sang Elton, now reclaiming what he did best.

Most significant of all was that Bernie was back, though Elton was now maintaining that his alter ego had never left. "A lot of people think Bernie and I had a parting of the ways," Elton said, "but we never really did, really. . . . But there was a time when I didn't come to America for a year and Bernie lived in America, so there was no way to do much."

By now Bernie had sorted out his personal life back in Los Angeles. In 1979, he hired a new manager to put his finances in order, and he remarried the next year. His new wife was Toni Russo, the sister of the top American fashion model, Renée Russo, and it was she who helped him repair both his self-esteem and his partnership with Elton. More than a decade later, in 1991, other artists would celebrate Elton and Bernie's body of work in an LP titled *Two Rooms.*

Bernie contributed three songs to the new album. They were "Chasing the Crown," which suggested the hard edge of "Saturday's Alright for Fighting"; "Two Rooms at the End of the World," chronicling his isolation during their split; and "White Lady White Powder," about the fascination with cocaine. Remarkably, "White Lady White Powder" eluded the BBC Radio censors, just as "Rocket Man" and "All the Girls Love Alice" had done before.

Bernie also had his own album, *He Who Rides the Tiger,* on the Asylum Records label. It was his solo debut. Since their split after the 1976 *Blue Moves* LP, the album was Bernie's only musical venture, aside from a collaboration with Alice Cooper on the forgettable *From the Inside.*

On *Tiger,* Bernie was up to his introspective musings again. One track, "Approaching Armageddon," covered his writer's block, alcoholism and lack of self-esteem. Another autobiographical offering was "Lover's Cross," about a romantic betrayal that seemed to parallel the demise of his first marriage: "I don't want to hang on no lover's cross for you," Bernie wailed. "I won't be your crucifix or savior to bruise." But without Elton's melodies, Bernie's imagery, religious or otherwise, did not hold much sway with the record-buying public. Nor could Bernie's eager voice lift the LP onto the charts.

In addition to Taupin and Osborne on Elton's *21 at 33,* there was lyricist Tom Robinson, who contributed two songs, the archly titled yet striking ballad, "Sartorial Eloquence," as well as "Never Gonna Fall in Love Again." Their friendship had started the evening of the Chinese take-out dinner at Elton's mansion two years previously. A few days after that, Robinson sent Elton some spare lyrics that were lying around.

"I always found it easier to write the lyrics than the music," Robinson relates, "so I decided to give them to Elton. One of the legends that I'd heard about him was that he could sit at the piano and spontaneously compose and sing any set of words. He could write melodies from the phone directory." In fact, it is true that Elton had once even composed a song—both the lyrics and the music—about his Polaroid camera while at the house he rented the summer of 1979 in the south of France (during the recording of *21 at 33* at the Superbear Studios in Nice). A campy number, it remains unpublished to this day. The lyrics, Robinson remembers, were "Sylvania Flashbar, King of the Casbah, Polaroid Swinger and Older Than Bill." "Bill" was a reference to Old Bills, British slang for the police.

Robinson remembers Elton's generosity as much as his genius: When a song they wrote together, "Reach Out to Me," became a Number One hit in France in 1981 (sung in French as "Les Aveux" by a popular French chanteuse, France Gall), "Elton generously suggested that we split the royalties equally, and he lowered his share to make this possible."

The public was far less generous to them in its reaction to a video the two men made for "Elton's Song," a single from *The Fox* album. According to Robinson, the video's theme was based on the 1969 movie *If . . .* with Malcolm McDowell. It was about rebels in an exclusive boys' boarding school with its hierarchical, savage, ruling-class environment. However, the way Elton and Robinson improvised on this theme was to show unrequited love between a younger boy and an older one. "In the cotton candy world of pop music," Robinson explains, "we showed the younger boy gazing longingly at the older boy and the older one going off with a girl. In 'Elton's Song' it was not at all specific about whether we were talking about a boy or a girl except that the song's speaker loves him for being 'cynical and lean,' which was not a female description."

Nonetheless, the final sequence showed the handsome older boy walking through the dormitory with his shirt off while the younger one, in pajamas, closes his eyes: Elton sings, "Crying for the moon, they think I'm mad. / I would give my life for a single night beside you."

The two schoolboys were played by professional actors. However, thirty Boy Scouts, aged fourteen to nineteen, were recruited to play schoolboys in the video. And a famous boys' school was hired for the shoot. The Scouts and the school were told only that it was to be an Elton John video. According to writers Angus Mayer and Frank Murphy in the British tabloid *News of the World,* school officials were shown a watered-down video script. But once the video was screened for them by these reporters, the school authorities and the Scouts' parents were outraged. As it turned out, Elton knew nothing about the deception. It was the work of filmmakers Russell Mulcahy and Keith Williams. Said Mulcahy, who admitted in the same article that he had deliberately misled the school:"If they had heard the song, we would have been thrown out on our arses."

If Elton's *21 at 33* album hinted at a throwback to an earlier style, so did his lineup at a major event this year, an outdoor concert in New York's Central Park. Joining him were original band members, bass player Dee Murray and guitarist Nigel Olsson, along with keyboard player James Newton-Howard and guitarists Richy Zito and Tim Renwick.

What a difference a year had made. It was just the previous October that Elton, accompanied only by percussionist Ray Cooper, had played an eight-night run at the thirty-five-hundred-seat Palladium in New York. Insecurities about whether he could fill huge stadiums, as well as worry about slumping concert sales in general, had caused him to choose smaller venues. During that tour, which amounted to almost nightly concerts, Elton showed some signs of exhaustion when he collapsed from the flu on stage at the Hollywood Universal Amphitheater. But after resting for ten minutes he returned to finish the three-hour show.

"Yeah, it did go through my mind at first that people might have forgotten me," Elton admitted at the time. "But I've kept my name pretty much alive in Europe during the last couple of years with my soccer team, and I'm not as obsessed about success as I used to be. Well, not obsessed, but when you're used to having hits and Number One albums, you want the next thing you do to go to Number One, too."

Rocket Records, too, was enjoying a brief resurgence with two hits, a Number Seven in Britain from the Lambrettas (of a cover version of the Coasters' "Poison Ivy") and a Number Six from an unlikely country and western singer, Fred Wedlock, with "The Oldest Swinger in Town." The title just about described his ageing appeal. Their other big artist was Judy Tzuke, who had a moderate hit that was reminiscent of Kiki Dee's torch song, "Amoreuse."

In large measure the label owed its success to its new managing director John Hall, a young entrepreneur who had previously run his own label and would later on amass a fortune with still another venture. Somehow Hall managed to circumvent John Reid's often difficult behavior. He was also fond of Elton and was particularly touched when Elton, alighting from a helicopter later that year in Central Park, spotted Hall's children and rushed over to chat with them.

From the beginning at Rocket Records, the personnel situation was like a game of musical chairs, with employees coming and going on Reid's whims. One day, however, Reid arrived at Rocket's offices on Wardour Street in Soho to find that there was no one left to answer the phones. Apparently he had fired everyone the previous day in a fit of anger.

Even Steve Brown, Elton's closest ally, after Caleb Quaye, from his DJM days, had quit for a time to go into farming; he returned eventually, however. One of Dick James's closest associates, Geoffrey Ellis, had also gone over to Rocket for a while, but ultimately he, too, would flee the raging Scotsman. In the end Rocket was largely Elton John himself.

Elton's decision during that period to perform in more intimate settings mirrored his desire to get to know himself again. "Even though I've had a lot of press coverage," he said, "I don't think people really know that much about me. I'm just beginning to find myself out, really. I'm a very deep person. . . . I'm a loner, really. There's a side of me that can be very, very quiet. Very deep and thoughtful."

In keeping with this mood, Elton exchanged his glasses for contact lenses, and the glittery costumes stayed in the closet. "I think people still think of me as wearing huge high-heeled shoes and sparkly glasses and flashy clothes, which I haven't done since 1975 or 1976," Elton said. "In fact, when I look at some of the things I used to wear, I really have to chuckle."

But on this, the afternoon of September 13, 1980, with a blanket of humanity stretched before him on the Great Lawn of New York's

Central Park, the "Single Man" was now doing a complete about-face. Instead of an audience of three to four thousand people, a highly energized Elton was entertaining a crowd estimated at 350,000, his largest single audience ever.

Sartorially speaking, Elton momentarily reasserted the flamboyance of his superstar days, materializing on stage in a Donald Duck costume that had taken weeks to construct. This thrilled his fans. By comparison, the pink jumpsuits and cowboy togs which he also donned later in the performance looked as conservative as three-piece suits.

Jointly sponsored by Calvin Klein Jeans, the New York City Department of Parks and WNEW-FM radio, the concert was a charity event, with $75,000 in proceeds from souvenirs and buttons going to revitalize the park. Elton, a regular on the charity circuit back in Britain, felt an affection for New York and was glad to pitch in. He had broken house attendance records in New York, and now he wanted to do something in return for this city.

For nearly three hours, Elton gave them mostly gold. While he did showcase new hits like "Little Jeannie," he delighted in reprising classics like "Goodbye Yellow Brick Road," "Saturday Night's Alright for Fighting," "Sorry Seems to Be the Hardest Word" and "Your Song." On stage at the Great Lawn, framed by tall oak trees and the famous skyline, Elton appeared to own New York. The resounding cheer of his fans drowned out the dissonant city sounds, the banshee ambulance sirens, and the honking taxis and roaring trucks.

"A song I wrote for Miss Billie Jean King," said Elton, breaking into a manic rendition of "Philadelphia Freedom." And there was another tribute as well, "a song written by a friend of mine." With that, Elton segued into John Lennon's "Imagine."

No one, least of all Elton, could have imagined that after a career drought of nearly four years he would be dazzling these multitudes. All these fans, swaying, singing and clapping, looked like some vast ant colony swarming across the Great Lawn. It was a Woodstock-like celebration, with his fans camped out on an array of colorful blankets, mellowing out on marijuana, and keeping cool in the Indian summer afternoon by sipping water and beer.

But by the year's end, Elton's celebratory mood would be broken by the news of the death of a friend and rock music icon.

24

Death of a Hero

John Lennon was tired. He and Yoko had planned to go out for dinner that evening in New York, but after a busy day in the recording studio, they decided to return directly to their home. Why their rented limousine did not drive through the archway of their co-op apartment building remains a mystery to this day. Instead, it stopped at the corner of Seventy-second Street and Central Park West. Yoko got out of the car first, and John followed. Quickly he was underneath the Gothic arch of the Dakota.

As he headed toward the building's interior courtyard, he heard a voice call out from behind, "Mr. Lennon." A man gripping a .38 special with both hands started to open fire, pumping one bullet after another into him. The man would later be identified as Mark Chapman. "I'm shot!" Lennon screamed, as he crawled to the guard booth with a trail of his own blood following him. Seconds later he collapsed.

As Yoko held her husband in her arms, Chapman dropped the gun and looked on. Kicking the gun away from the crazed man, the doorman asked, "Do you know what you did?" From Chapman came this reply: "I just shot John Lennon."

Within minutes police were on the scene; the madman stood

214

around waiting for them, thumbing through a copy of J. D. Salinger's classic novel of adolescent rebellion, *The Catcher in the Rye.* As two officers frisked and handcuffed him, two others rushed to help the bleeding Lennon. "I turned him over," recalled patrolman Anthony Palma. "Red is all I saw." Turning to a rookie cop, who looked like he was going to throw up, Palma said, "This guy is dying. Let's get him out of here."

Bleeding profusely and semiconscious, John Lennon was placed into the backseat of Officer James Moran's patrol car. "Do you know who you are?" Moran asked Lennon, who moaned and nodded, "Yes."

As Moran rushed Lennon fifteen blocks to Roosevelt Hospital, Palma followed in another car with Yoko. Throughout the brief journey she kept up the same plea: "Tell me it isn't true, tell me he's all right."

But her husband was not all right. In fact, John Lennon was pronounced dead on arrival at the hospital. Even so, a team of seven surgeons tried desperately to resuscitate him. But his wounds proved too severe. There were three holes in his chest, two in his back and two in his left shoulder. Lennon may have lost four quarts of blood from gun wounds, nearly eighty percent of his total blood volume. After working on him for half an hour, the doctors gave up.

Meanwhile word of the shooting began to reach the public. Outside the Dakota apartment building, fans held a spontaneous vigil. By one in the morning, a crowd of nearly one thousand people had gathered there. As more details emerged about Lennon's death, this outpouring of grief was accompanied by rage.

President Jimmy Carter spoke of the irony of John Lennon's death. "[He] died by violence," Carter said, "though he had long campaigned for peace." Meanwhile President-elect Ronald Reagan pronounced Lennon's murder "a great tragedy."

Back in England, where Lennon's life had begun, a portrait of the Beatles was placed at the entrance to the Tate Gallery in London, along with floral tributes. "We usually do this [only] when a British artist whose work is represented in the Tate dies," a museum spokesman said, "but we thought John Lennon was a special case."

In Lennon's hometown of Liverpool, the lord mayor announced plans to hold a memorial service for him in the city's giant cathedral;

and local teenagers placed flowers on the parking lot that was once the site of the Cavern Club, where the Beatles had had their start.

Meanwhile, thousands of miles away, Elton John was traveling in a plane over the skies of Australia when he first learned that Lennon had been murdered. He was devastated. "When John died," Elton remembers, "I couldn't believe it. I was close to him for a year—let's put it on the record—and I hung out with him and I loved him. I never met anybody who impressed me so much as that man."

Though never a particularly religious man, Elton was so moved by Lennon's death that he went the next day to the cathedral in Sydney to have ten minutes of silence as Yoko had asked fans to do around the world. Elton says, "I was just lucky enough to know John Lennon for a year and, God, that was one of the happiest years of my life."

Even if Elton had never met Lennon, he was part of the generation that seemed most affected by the former Beatle's death. They were the Baby Boomers, who were now in their twenties and thirties. Lennon's death represented the last nail in the coffin of the sixties and the end of childhood for this generation.

For Elton, at thirty-three, the loss of Lennon was particularly significant. It was, after all, the Beatles who had inspired the lonely, lumpy Reg Dwight to make a life out of his music. Their success had convinced him there was a future in rock 'n' roll.

So it was in his music that Elton felt that he could best pay tribute to John Lennon. Initially he wrote an instrumental called "The Man Who Never Died," but it was not released. "That song made me upset when I wrote it," Elton says. "That was my tribute to John. Then Bernie came up with the lyric to 'Empty Garden,' which I thought said it all. It was very hard to say in a lyric, and a lot easier in an instrumental."

"Empty Garden (Hey Hey Johnnie)" likened the slain Beatle to "a gardener weeding out tears" and went on to muse, "It's funny how one insect can damage so much grain," in a reference to the apparent killer, Mark Chapman. "A richly textured ballad," wrote Paul Grein in the Los Angeles Times, "with the dramatic sweep of John's old hit, 'Don't Let the Sun Go Down on Me.'" Unlike Paul McCartney's delicate, subtle "Here Today," "Empty Garden" spoke directly about the tragedy.

On the other hand, Stephen Holden, a New York Times music critic, pronounced "Empty Garden" quite dreadful. "This strained, mawkish eulogy is typical of Mr. John and Mr. Taupin's sloppy, pretentious writing. . . . They've never taken the time to refine their craft. That's why, except for a dozen memorable singles, their work isn't likely to be remembered for long."

The track would reach only Number Thirteen on the American charts and fail to make the Top Fifty in Britain. "Empty Garden" was part of the *Jump Up!* album, released in May 1982. It was a mixture of high-energy rockers like "Where Have All the Good Times Gone," a shameless reprise of Elton's 1976 hit "Philadelphia Freedom," and ballads, including the torchy "Blue Eyes." Early signs indicated *Jump Up!* might crack the Top Ten, his first album to do so since *Blue Moves.*

Fittingly, the *Jump Up!* LP was released on Geffen Records in America, the same company that was producing Lennon's new album. Elton had signed with Geffen in September 1980, and *Jump Up!* was his first LP with the label. The LP only made Number Seventeen in the U.S. and Number Thirteen in the U.K. It was the failure of MCA to promote "Song for Guy," an instrumental that was also a eulogy, that had led in part to Elton's split with them. Disc jockeys like New York's Scott Muni played "Song for Guy" to mourn the death of Lennon.

But Elton did not exactly arrive on the Geffen label by choice. It was more an eleventh-hour move after John Reid threw a tantrum at the MCA offices in Los Angeles. Reid had gone there believing that he could pull off a deal as big as the 1974 contract that made Elton the eight-million-dollar man. In fact, he had blabbed it all around town that he could get Elton something like $25 million for five years.

However, it was now 1980, the decade of Michael Jackson and Madonna and George Michael; Elton was no longer the megastar he had been in the seventies. MCA said that they would consider Reid's asking price only if they got world rights. Reid stormed out of the meeting and tore one of the gold discs off a wall in the secretarial area. "I made this fucking company," he screamed. "They can stick their fucking records . . ." Reid effectively closed the door on himself, at least for the time being.

At that point David Geffen, who had recently started his own label and had tried to sign Elton to it months before, was the only logical choice. Reid had already blocked off channels with larger recording companies, the only ones who could offer the kind of money Reid was seeking. In the end, Geffen paid about $1 million an album, about the same as MCA had under the 1974 contract Reid had negotiated so brilliantly. Elton explained it publicly by saying that he was glad to be on the same label as John Lennon.

Although Elton's latest album did little to revive his own career, he was absolutely determined to keep the legend of John Lennon alive. As further homage to his hero, in March 1981 Elton released a long-playing duet of "I Saw Her Standing There," which they had recorded back in 1974 on stage at Madison Square Garden on Thanksgiving night. The record was only available in the United Kingdom, and though it barely made it out of the Top Fifty, to Elton it was a way of preserving this magical moment.

The lives of Elton and his hero Lennon would be inextricably linked in the memory of fans. Lennon had joined Elton on stage that night for three numbers. Neither man, of course, could have known then that this would be the last public appearance of John Lennon's life.

The tragedy of Lennon's death would haunt Elton for many years and in some ways taint his view of America, the country that had embraced him from the very beginning. "I wouldn't live in America if they paid me one hundred pounds a minute," Elton announced months after the murder. "Thank God, guns aren't on sale openly in Britain. If young people could buy guns in supermarkets like they do in the States, we'd have fans dead at soccer matches."

Elton, like so many other people, had just come to terms with the fact that the bullets from only one gun could kill a little bit of all of us.

25

The Odd Couple

When Elton met German-born Renate Blauel, it was a bit like the chairman of the board of a corporation picking an anonymous female employee out of the steno pool. The place was the AIR studios in London, where Elton was finishing work on the *Too Low for Zero* album, in 1982. Renate was working there as a second recording engineer, a job that also entailed making coffee and taking phone messages. In her customary outfit, jeans and a T-shirt, she looked like an ordinary working woman, except for the fact that her job was normally filled by a man.

Yet Elton John, chairman emeritus of the record charts, noticed the shy, quiet Renate, and he looked again. After a few days, whenever Elton arrived at the studio, he would go over and say something to her. Renate, in turn, would chuckle. No one in the studio, meanwhile, suspected that romance was in the equation. But, much to their amazement, when the album was released there was a tribute reading, "Special thanks to Renate Blauel."

There was more intrigue to follow. On the eve of recording the next album, *Breaking Hearts*, in November 1983 Elton balked at traveling to AIR-Montserrat studios in the Caribbean unless Renate came along. By now, a year later, Renate had become a fixture in the studio, yet no one there was aware of any socializing outside the studio. "I'm not going," Elton told Rocket managing director John Hall, "unless Renate goes out there too." Again, Renate, still in jeans and T-shirts, seemed to be just one of the recording gang. Elton and his touring party remained on the island through Christmas 1983. Shortly after the New Year, Elton was preparing to fly to Australia and New Zealand to begin another tour. Once again, Elton stipulated that Renate had to come along.

On the night of February 10, 1984, Elton and Renate went out to dinner alone and returned after midnight to the Sebel Town House hotel in Sydney, Australia, where the tour party was staying. Hand in hand they entered the bar, where Dee Murray and other band members were having a late-night drink. "Guess what?" Elton announced to Murray and the others. "We're engaged." Over an Indian dinner of tandoori chicken and beef Elton had proposed to Renate and she had accepted.

Within days, as news of their impending marriage made headlines around the world, Elton revealed that he had asked Renate to marry him once before. More astonishing still was that Elton and Renate planned to be married on Valentine's Day, February 14, four days later. The hasty manner in which the marriage was announced immediatley cast suspicion on Elton's romance. Had the prospective groom been anyone other than Elton John, of course, there might have been rumors of a shotgun wedding. And the bride-to-be dispelled any farfetched notion that she might be expecting a child. "We are being old-fashioned and waiting for the wedding day," Renate remarked to the press. "It really will be a white wedding." At the hotel they maintained separate suites.

Elton and Renate broke the news to an exuberant chorus of congratulations from band members and others in the entourage. Then the champagne flowed until dawn. Between sips, Elton spent most of the wee hours of the morning on the phone to family and friends. Among the first to get word were Watford manager Graham Taylor and record producer Clive Franks. The latter, awakened by Elton's call, initially dismissed the news of the impending wedding as a prank.

Elton's mother and stepfather, meanwhile, were thrilled. They received the news at the West Sussex home Elton had bought for them.

Sheila, believing her only son was finally going to make her a grand-mother, told the press that her wedding present would be a baby stroller.

"He's sensible and likes a home life, and most of all he loves children," she said. "And I don't think he'll waste any time making sure he gets some." Fiercely protective, Sheila once again blamed Elton's dubious sexuality on the show business environment, saying, "I'm sure Renate must understand Elton's lifestyle and what goes on in the entertainment world."

Confident that her son would keep his promise about a second ceremony upon his return to England in April, Sheila and her husband decided to forgo the journey to Sydney. Renate's parents also did not attend, but from a suburb of Munich her father, Joachim Blauel, a publisher, commented, "I did not know anything about the love affair but we are very happy." Four days was too short notice for them to make the journey to Sydney.

Two members of Elton's inner sanctum, however, were not exactly celebrating. Bob Halley, his personal assistant and live-in companion, feared that he might soon find an eviction notice from the bride-to-be at Woodside. Halley had started out as Elton's chauffeur over a decade before, and with his increasing duties, his own marriage had collapsed under the strain of his devotion to Elton. So bonded were the two men that they even sported matched earrings as a symbol of their tie. Renate did not oust Halley after all, but one tabloid news-paper reporter in England described Halley as "mute with shock" when he heard the news.

Manager John Reid meanwhile conducted business as usual, hag-gling over a prenuptial agreement that he wanted Renate to sign in order to preserve Elton's many millions should the marriage fail. "It's the real thing. That's for sure," said Reid, shrugging off reports that it was a publicity stunt.

The state attorney in Sydney considered the marriage application and waived a thirty-day waiting period intended to restrain couples from acting impetuously in order to let the thirty-six-year-old singer and the thirty-year-old recording engineer walk down the aisle on Valentine's Day, 1984.

Back in England, meanwhile, when Elton's octogenarian grand-mother, Ivy Harris, heard that her grandson was getting married, she had to take a pill to calm herself. Her reaction, although exaggerated by her advanced age, was echoed throughout the world. One of the hundreds of telegrams that greeted Elton's wedding announcement seemed to say it all: "You may still be standing," it read, "but we're on the floor."

From the general public, who perceived Elton as more gay than straight, reaction to his marriage was one of amusement. But in his tell-all *Rolling Stone* interview Elton had, in fact, declared himself a bisexual and also expressed a desire to father children. Now he was sticking by his story. "Bisexuality's not a solo proposition," Elton explained. "Everyone does some experimenting. I'm not denying anything I've said. But I have a right to make a choice."

Elton's bisexuality was not a problem for the five-foot-seven, leggy, blue-eyed Renate. "I've heard all sorts of stories about Elton and that he's supposed to be bisexual, but that doesn't bother me," she maintained. "He's the nicest guy I've ever met. He's got a great sense of humor, he makes me laugh and he is considerate. I'm just feeling fabulous." Renate, too, it seemed, shared his desire for children, and at thirty, she was worried about her biological clock ticking away.

The future Mrs. Elton John could not have imagined a more lavish ceremony. Elton's celebrity friends, including Rod Stewart, tennis star John McEnroe, and Michael Parkinson, one of the best-known television personalities in England and Australia, jetted in from America and England for the occasion. Aussie stars in the wedding party included singer Olivia Newton-John and comedian Barry Humphries, known to the British public as Dame Edna Everage, a character he created in drag. Celebrity well-wishers from afar included Michael Jackson, who contributed probably the most original telegram: "I had to set my hair on fire to make news," he wired. "You only had to get married." Elton was especially touched by a phone call from his godson, Sean Lennon, in New York congratulating him.

At the ceremony, Elton looked more dapper than dandy. He was dressed in black trousers, a white silk tailcoat made by his friend and tailor Tommy Nutter, a lilac-striped shirt and matching bow tie, spats and a straw boater with a lilac ribbon round it. Renate wore a floor-length white silk wedding dress with a froth of Swiss lace she bought in Sydney's exclusive Double Bay for a reported $1,000 Australian ($930). Elton, who had never seen Renate in anything but T-shirts and jeans before, would later say that the sight of her took his breath away.

Never one to tone down his act, Elton ordered the bridesmaids to wear hot-pink dresses. One of them was Bernie Taupin's second wife, Toni, whose jewels, worth $47,000, would be stolen a few weeks later in Perth, Australia, from a hotel where Elton's tour was staying. John Reid acted as best man. Up until the last second he had tried to get the recalcitrant Elton to sign a prenuptial agreement, but to no avail. Elton refused to even countenance such an agreement, believing that it would not bode well for the marriage to start off with an implicit lack of trust.

As the wedding party approached St. Mark's Church in the Darling Point suburb of Sydney, hundreds of spectators lined the streets. From a nearby house, Elton's "Kiss the Bride" blared forth. There were some jeers, too, from the crowd. "Oh, the poof's finally got married," one man taunted. To which a jaunty Elton retorted, much to the delight of the guests in the wedding party, "It just goes to show how wrong you all were."

The pretty Anglican church was festooned with orchids and roses flown in from New Zealand. The groom arrived seventeen minutes early and the bride three minutes late. The last time he had been engaged, back in 1968, he had faked a suicide to get out of the wedding. But this time Elton did not get cold feet. He and Renate exchanged vows and rings, and he bestowed on his bride a heart-shaped necklace with twenty-six diamonds. An odd touch, however, was provided by the church choir: at the groom's request, they sang the Twenty-third Psalm ("The Lord is my shepherd . . ."), more appropriate for a funeral than a wedding. But Elton had always been a master at mixing up the melodic and the mawkish. Characteristically, the wedding reception held at the Sebel Town House hotel, where the newlyweds spent their first night as a couple in two adjoining suites, turned into an Elton John extravaganza said to cost over $100,000 Australian ($93,000).

The one hundred-plus guests feasted on oysters, lobsters, crab, roasts and ham, washed down with Cristal champagne at £60 a bottle ($125). Elton, currently in rehearsals for a world tour, took the day off and let an old-time Palm Court orchestra provide the music. The five-tiered square fruitcake, with giant letters "E" and "R" carved out of ice, had taken twenty-four hours to make. Only the most tactless remarked on the choice of cake.

Not even the heavy rains could dampen his spirits on his wedding day as he doted on his bride. "I never said I didn't want to get married," he insisted to members of the press. "I knew Renate was very sincere. She's also intelligent and not the clinging sort, which is important."

Indeed, it was. For as Renate was to discover the very next day, when Elton went off to rehearsals, she had become the wife of an unregenerate workaholic. On the first day of wedlock, Elton gave Renate a rose-pink-tinted diamond bracelet with a huge emerald. At that moment Elton, by his own description, saw himself going through a "renaissance" in his life as a man.

Similarly, Elton was experiencing a resurgence in popularity with the hit singles "I Guess That's Why They Call It the Blues" and "I'm Still Standing." The latter was also nominated for an MTV music video award. Both singles had come from *Too Low for Zero*, the album which was responsible for his meeting Renate.

There was even more good news on the career front. From Elton's latest LP, *Breaking Hearts*, came the Top Five single "Sad Songs (Say So Much)." And with another track, "Whose Shoes Are These," about a man working out his jealousy for a woman who left him, Elton had made an outstanding talking, singing, dancing music video.

The old gang was back, and in the coming year they would see more of Elton than his new bride would. Olsson, Murray, Johnstone and keyboardist Fred Mandell all looked forward to this up-tempo, exuberant Breaking Hearts tour. Bernie and his wife Toni were also traveling with the Elton John party. Five days after the wedding, Elton was off to New Zealand, where he and Renate honeymooned between concerts. A month later they returned to London for a brief spell.

But no sooner had Elton unpacked his bags than he was off again, rocking around the world as Renate padded around Woodside thinking up decorating ideas when she was not working in the recording studio. "Just because I'm married to a famous superstar," she said, "doesn't mean I'm going to give up my job."

Though Elton said this was his last tour, everyone had heard that before. And at the end of the tour he went straight back to the studio again. Yet the absentee husband talked about home and hearth as if he could hardly stand to be away.

Elton also toured China with his beloved Watford team during the first year of his marriage to Renate. There the team played two exhibition matches in Beijing and a third in Shanghai. They won them all. But as Elton stood on the Great Wall of China, he had a most sobering experience. For the first time in thirteen years, no one recognized him in the streets.

Elton was delighted. "I used my status wrongly in the past," he told reporters covering him in China. "But the club has done so much for me because nobody there will put up with all that. In my business it was all luxury jets, the best hotels and shows before twenty thousand people. Then I'd walk into Watford and the washing-up lady would toddle up and say, 'I don't like your new record.' "

"It's nice to come home and actually share things," Elton said. "I've no regrets about actually giving up my bachelorhood. I could see myself ending up an eccentric and incredibly fussy," he added as he praised his wife for the feminine touches, including flowers, that she put in the house.

Many fans wondered whether Elton's marriage was serious. Some still could not decide whether, as *People* magazine put it, the new Mrs. Elton John was "a lover or a cover."

26

The Blond Bombshell

Los Angeles, December 1990

The marriage of Elton John was very much on the mind of twenty-nine-year-old Tommy Williams, a would-be Hollywood set designer, as he went to keep an appointment at the Hamburger Hamlet restaurant on Beverly Boulevard in Los Angeles.

As he approached the hamburger restaurant on this dry, sunny day, Tommy focused on the palimony letter he had sent to Elton just days before the superstar's wedding to Renate.

Tommy had grown up in Anaheim, the home of Disneyland, about fifty miles south of Los Angeles. The product of a middle-class family, Tommy had migrated to Hollywood to try his hand at set design in his late teens.

Yet when Tommy sat down in a booth with another man, he did not want to talk about his background; instead he focused on Elton John, the man whom he had once depended on like family. Inside the dark-wood restaurant, the other man listened and occasionally jotted down notes while his tape recorder picked up everything.

Their meeting had been arranged the previous week when,

through two intermediaries, Tommy had contacted the man, Paul Francis, a reporter for a supermarket tabloid, the *Globe,* at the paper's Los Angeles office. Francis remembers his first impression of Tommy Williams: "He seemed very straightforward and honest and not at all embarrassed by what he had to tell me. His main concern was that we did not oversensationalize the story."

Now, as Francis sat hunched over a table with Tommy at the Hamburger Hamlet for the second of five interview sessions, he listened to stories of wild orgies and cocaine abuse that, despite Tommy's concerns, had all the earmarks of a major tabloid exposé. "I'm telling this story not maliciously to hurt him," Tommy said, "but to help him remember the promises he made to me and didn't keep."

Tommy, who claimed that he was still an Elton John fan, faulted him for reneging on a promise to put him through college. He was still upset about this and believed that dredging up details of his affair with Elton might be worth at least the price of tuition. At this moment in his life Tommy Williams had not yet established himself as a Hollywood set designer.

Francis, a former Fleet Street journalist, listened and believed him. As a result, he began compiling a thick file on Elton and Tommy's whereabouts on the days the latter alleged they were together. Among the documents were copies of Tommy's passport stamped with the Caribbean island of Montserrat and Nice, France, places where Tommy said Elton had taken him. Of course, the fact that both men were in the same country at the same time would not prove conclusively that they were there together. However, Francis and his editors at the *Globe* found the details Tommy provided impressive and strong enough to justify printing the stories Tommy told them. Further, Tommy supplied photos of Elton and himself; he also took and passed a lie detector test.

The result was a three-part series in the *Globe* in January 1991. "He was thirty-five, heavy, and out of shape," barked part one of what the tabloid billed as an "exclusive bombshell report." "And I was twenty-one and looked sixteen." Elton's marriage, which preyed on Tommy's mind, he would save for the last installment.

The tale Tommy told the *Globe* began in a West Hollywood gay bar, the Rose Tattoo. According to Tommy, one night in August 1982 he and a friend approached the club, where he was a regular, and noticed a white Rolls-Royce parked outside. "I'm going to marry the man who owns that car," Tommy joked to his companion.

Inside, the club was abuzz with news that Elton John was there. Tommy, who had been an Elton fan since childhood, was delighted. But on this night Tommy was not on the lookout for just an autograph. Instead, the boy, who made his living as a male prostitute to support himself as he tried to become a set designer, was on the prowl.

Elton turned out to be a likely prospect. In fact, within moments of Tommy's arrival, Elton sent a member of his entourage over to invite the blond, baby-faced twenty-one-year-old to his table. "I'm sorry," Tommy responded, "I'm with someone else." Though flattered, Tommy wanted to gather his thoughts before meeting his hero.

Minutes later he plucked up the courage to join Elton and five other men, all of whom called each other by girls' names. Elton, a.k.a. Sharon, conferred the name "Lady Woodside," after his mansion in England, on Tommy. They sat around and talked for a while and, according to Tommy, Elton made a pass at him.

"I wasn't surprised when he put his hand on my leg," Tommy explained, "because when gays are attracted to you they do things like that." Within an hour or so of their meeting, Elton asked Tommy, "Can you get rid of your friend and come back to the hotel with me?"

Tommy did just that. But it was not any special attraction for Elton, but rather the hypnotic effect of superstardom, he admitted, that moved him to accept Elton's invitation to Bungalow Ten at the Beverly Hills Hotel. There Elton was encamped in the four-bedroom, four-bathroom suite with a whole room reserved for all his matching and monogrammed luggage. Elton had sold his mansion in Benedict Canyon, preferring to use a hotel when he was here. The two men arrived in Elton's white Rolls, the very same car Tommy had observed earlier in the evening outside the club.

Inside Bungalow Ten Elton fixed Tommy a drink and showed him his bizarre glasses, even letting him try some of them on. He also showed off several of his costumes. Tommy stayed the night, and he and Elton made love. Tommy remembered that Elton's eyes were "beautiful, blue, with long thick lashes" and "the gap between his front teeth made him look even cuter." He also found Elton extremely hairy. "It was everywhere," Tommy said, "except his head."

Admittedly, Tommy, who had heard stories about how some stars were kinky and demanding, was nervous about having sex with Elton.

But it ended up being warm and cuddly, much as Linda Woodrow, Elton's ex-fiancée, had described fifteen years before. "Elton seemed rather innocent—almost pleasant and friendly," Tommy revealed to the *Globe*. "He was not a petty demanding love machine. We had sex, but it was pretty basic and simple, and we went to sleep right away. What struck me was that he went to sleep with his arms cuddled around me. When we woke up in the morning, we were in exactly the same position."

Thus began an affair between Tommy and Elton that was to take place in various countries over the next eighteen months. The first stop on their itinerary was Las Vegas. They arrived in the gambling capital the following day by Lear jet for a concert Elton was giving. Returning late that night to Los Angeles and Bungalow Ten at the Beverly Hills Hotel, Tommy got his first glimpse of a darker side of Elton John. He was astonished by how open Elton and his friends were about their drug use. "Cocaine, pot, you name it," Tommy said. "This turned out to be standard procedure after each concert."

In the days that followed, Elton gave three Los Angeles concerts. On the last night, he asked Tommy to pick up some boys to bring back to the hotel. Eager to please him, Tommy recruited a friend whom he trusted, and two other boys. "The drugs flowed again," Tommy recalled. "Elton could sometimes do eight or nine grams of coke a night and drink a whole bottle of Johnnie Walker scotch. He was insatiable."

According to Tommy, Elton was more a voyeur than a participant in the orgy. By his young lover's accounting, Elton had a vast collection of porno videos as well as Polaroid photos of nude boys that he had taken all over the world; there was also one of Elton posing nude for the camera.

While Tommy observed many details of Elton's life, the singer appeared totally in the dark about his new boyfriend. Tommy chose Kansas City to break some news about himself. "He admitted to Elton that he was a male prostitute," the *Globe*'s Francis reported. "Tommy said that he hoped that he would not get dumped for admitting this to Elton. They agreed that Tommy should go back to Los Angeles and sever his connection with the call-boy service, which he did, with the help of an influential producer and lawyer who apparently put pressure on the man who ran the service." All along, Francis added, Elton's management company had been paying off the service.

America was not the only place where Elton and Tommy met. On October 5, 1982, Tommy flew to Montserrat in the West Indies to spend a week with Elton. For Elton, the recording studio there, owned by former Beatles producer George Martin, evoked happier days at Château d'Hérouville in France almost a decade before. It was to this tiny volcanic island, with its black sandy beaches and green hills, that Elton had come to record *Too Low for Zero*.

It was the first album since *Blue Moves* of 1976 on which all the songs were cowritten by Bernie Taupin. It also marked a reunion with his old band, Davey Johnstone, Dee Murray and Nigel Olsson. The producer was Chris Thomas. The LP produced two big hits, "I'm Still Standing," inspired in part by Elton's problems with Rocket Records, where he was by now the only artist left on the label, and "I Guess That's Why They Call It the Blues," a playful ballad about homesickness. There was also the Caribbean-flavored "Cold as Christmas (in the Middle of the Year)" about the isolation of a marriage in tatters.

Elton was in a jubilant mood, believing that once again he might have a megahit on his hands and, above all, feeling confident about his music, much as he had been back in 1973 with "Goodbye Yellow Brick Road." "We were just as excited as we were in the early days," Elton remembers. "We really were."

Upon the album's release, in June 1983, Elton would chirp to *Los Angeles Times* music critic Robert Hilburn, "When [David] Geffen called the other day to tell me how well it was starting off, I was jumping up and down—literally jumping up and down like a twelve-year-old kid."

Tommy Williams remembered Elton's upbeat mood during the recording of the LP. Elton's office had made all the arrangements for Tommy to spend time with Elton. They had arranged a passport for him, booked and paid for his airfare and provided three thousand dollars in spending money. Tommy received an effusive greeting: "Elton gave me a very torrid, passionate kiss in front of everyone," Tommy remembered. "He didn't care who saw." Among the spectators, according to Tommy, was recording engineer Renate Blauel, whom Elton would later marry.

On their first night together on the island, according to Tommy, Elton was in a particularly intimate mood and confessed to Tommy that he had once been in love with Bernie Taupin but that, when he told his writing partner, he was completely rebuffed. Whether Elton ever told Tommy this is unclear. But what was indisputably wrong about Tommy's account was that he said the two men had met in music school when, in fact, they did not get together until later on. Bernie never even studied music.

On the last night of the weeklong stay, which Tommy described as a "second honeymoon," he and Elton danced the night away with close friends at a reggae bar, the Agotee. Then it was off to New York City for rest and relaxation, which Tommy recalled less fondly, "if you could call staying up all night, snorting cocaine, and shopping nonstop by day relaxing."

They checked into the penthouse suite at the Helmsley Palace Hotel, which would become the scene, once again, of another group sex session, this one with a young man Tommy said Elton met at the Calvin Klein boutique while shopping in Bloomingdale's. Nonetheless, Elton proclaimed his devotion to Tommy on their last night in the Big Apple. "I want you to move into Woodside with me," Tommy quoted Elton as saying. "I love you. I'll always take care of you, Tommy, no matter what. You can have anything you want. Even if we break up, I'll look after you. I'll pay for you to go back to school."

This was the first time that Elton had actually said the words "I love you." Tommy reciprocated. But what Elton's young lover thought then was a "dream come true" would turn ugly in a matter of weeks. While Elton spent lavishly on himself and close friends, charging up almost one million dollars on his American Express card during the period of their involvement, at home, according to his new mansion-mate, he was "a mean-spirited tightwad who pinched every penny."

"No matter how many clothes he owned," Tommy recounted to the *Globe*, "he would never let me borrow anything. Not even a T-shirt or a pair of socks, even if I hadn't done my laundry and ran out of clothes." Perhaps Elton's attitude was more territorial than penurious.

As one of Elton's friends, Tony King, a former Rocket executive, had explained a few years earlier in an interview with Lewis Grossberger in the *Washington Post* of November 4, 1979, "Elton's so funny about little things. For instance, if I said to him that I needed anything, I'd get it. But try sipping his drink. He pulls such a face when I do it sometimes. And yet if I said I wanted a glass of champagne, he'd buy me a case of Dom Pérignon. He's very quirky that way."

Tommy moved into Woodside on October 25, 1982, and the grandeur of the mansion, he said, was matched only by Elton's morning ritual of descending the stairs of his private suite to a tape of a Royal march turned up to the highest decibel. But they spent night after night at what Tommy said were Elton's favorite pastimes—"snorting coke and watching porn videos."

Elton, normally a shy, guarded person, rarely opened up to anyone about his life. But during one of their rare moments of intimacy, Tommy said that Elton admitted having slept with two women—one a gypsy whose name he could not remember, and the other . . . Part two of the *Globe*'s exposé screamed, "Elton Boasted: I Slept With Shirley MacLaine."

Perhaps Tommy just embellished on earlier interviews, in this case the infamous 1976 *Rolling Stone* interview in which Elton confessed his bisexuality. In it Elton had said that Shirley MacLaine was the type of woman he found attractive, but he also stated categorically that she was quite unavailable, already taken.

From the outset, Elton never made any attempt to conceal his relationship with Tommy, even turning up with him at football games in England and introducing him to show-biz pals in Hollywood. After each concert Tommy waited in the limousine, where he would dry Elton off after a sweat-producing performance. But by November 1982, four months into their relationship, Elton was starting to treat his live-in lover, in Tommy's words, "like a tiresome hanger-on."

Surprisingly, according to Tommy, just as the relationship started to show some cracks, Elton invited Tommy to meet his mother and stepfather. It was just before Christmas 1982. Talking about this visit, Tommy "revealed" some already well-known facts of Elton's life, namely that Sheila said her son detested the name Reginald Dwight. On the other hand Tommy was privy to the fact that Elton referred to his stepfather as Derf—Fred backwards—which was a joke British kids often played. Yet Tommy seemed a bit vague about where exactly Sheila and Derf lived. He told the *Globe* he visited them in Wales, when it was Elton's natural father and his stepmother who lived there.

Christmas Day itself, which Elton and Tommy passed at Woodside, was an unhappy experience for Tommy. "Elton became like a modern-day Scrooge," he said. "Cold and uncaring." Not even a surprise gift of a gold bracelet could lift Tommy's spirits. He discovered that Elton's assistant had picked it out.

A change of scene after the holidays did not alter Elton's behavior. A hotel suite in Sydney, Australia, from Tommy's point of view, might just as well have been Woodside back in England. Elton was up to his usual pursuits, staying up all night snorting coke, and when Tommy refused to go along with it, Elton began spending his evening with some of Brett's Boys, a call-boy service in that city. "When he ordered a call boy for himself," Tommy said, "he always ordered one for me, but I wasn't interested."

The two lovers began to argue incessantly, usually over something as petty as the use of bureau drawers where Tommy liked to store his socks and underwear. "Elton went berserk," Tommy recalled. "There was an unwritten rule that all the drawers were for his things. He threw my clothes all over the room and screamed, 'I won't have my territory invaded by somebody like you.' "

At that point Tommy decided to leave and told Elton's assistant to book him a flight back to Los Angeles. But a remorseful Elton begged his wounded boyfriend not to go, and Tommy relented. The next day Elton chartered a 180-foot yacht in Sydney Harbor for a tryst with Tommy and another man, but before the boat reached open seas it was forced back to shore after the jealous lover of the other man on board found out and radioed the captain.

By Valentine's Day, 1983, the romance appeared to Tommy to be getting back on course. Elton presented him with an $8,000 watch. But within days that very same watch would become a weapon. During a fracas, Elton hit Tommy's wrist, causing the new watch to dig into his skin. Tommy, in turn, removed the watch and hurled it across the room at the wall.

Another watch would figure in yet another blowup once they returned to England. It was a $23,000 Cartier watch and Elton accused Tommy of stealing it along with a twenty-one-carat sapphire ring valued at $100,000. He even reported Tommy to Scotland Yard. Tommy retorted that it had to be others in the house—because on the night of the theft, he was with Elton in the video room at Woodside snorting coke and watching videos until five in the morning.

What infuriated Tommy most was that Elton had felt a need to hide from the police the fact that they had been together all night.

Eventually, though, Elton withdrew the charges against Tommy. But the ordeal damaged whatever was left of their relationship. "Right then," Tommy declared, "I realized how untrustworthy and disloyal Elton could be."

The end of their affair would come in April 1983, during the making of Elton's "I'm Still Standing" video in Cannes. The first five days went off well enough, and during breaks in the shooting Tommy and Elton strolled the Croisette, shopping and having drinks with Elton's friends. The two men were staying in a luxurious suite at the Negresco overlooking the Mediterranean. The Negresco, where all the major stars and movie bigwigs stay during the Cannes Film Festival, would become the scene of a violent encounter between Elton and Tommy.

"I'm still standing" was not at all Tommy's experience in Cannes. First, Elton took a fancy to one of the dancers in the video, Tommy said, and brought him back to the room for sex à trois. But Tommy refused to participate, and this irked Elton, who began spending more time with the other man.

But the crisis point of their affair would not come until the sixth day. According to Tommy, that was when the director fell off a pier with all the footage that had been shot so far. With only one day left, the video had to be shot in twenty-four hours. But there was still more turmoil when a member of the crew accidentally spilled water on Elton's all-white suit, which he had just changed into. Already feeling enormous pressure, Elton snapped and started screaming and shouting, his rage fueled in part by excessive drinking (six vodka martinis by the end of the shoot).

Staggering into his suite, Elton flung open the door and began smashing everything in sight—vases, chairs, tables—while hurling all his clothes around the room. Terrified, Tommy tried to calm him. Next, Elton attacked Tommy, pushing him to the floor and threatening to smash his face with a vase. Then Elton broke down, sobbing.

Elton's assistant rushed into the room, tried to soothe Tommy, then told him to wait in the hall. The tirade continued. Then someone else chased the assistant out and shut the door, only to dash out to administer a beating to Tommy, who remembers, "He leapt out into the hallway and, without warning, smashed me in the face. I felt my head hitting the marble wall. I didn't know what was going on. He started kicking me in the stomach and face and screaming obscenities."

Once Tommy's attacker (a member of Elton's entourage whom he did not name to the *Globe*) fled, the assistant returned to give him some Valium and carry him to another room, where he passed out. When Tommy woke up, he tried to call Elton, but getting no answer he dragged himself up to the room. There was no trace of the superstar, only the wreckage he had left behind. Most of Elton's colleagues and friends, it seemed, had also checked out, and over the next few days an ailing Tommy visited a local doctor, who patched him up while he waited for a substitute passport and some money to get home.

Home, quite unfortuitously, was by now Woodside, and it was here, incredibly, considering the circumstances, that Tommy returned to collect his belongings and announce his intention to go back to America. Elton agreed it would be for the best. Elton's going-away present to Tommy was a Volkswagon Golf car and $2,000 in cash, which was mailed to him in the States.

But Tommy was not satisfied with this mere handout. Ten months later, after Elton had long since stopped taking his calls, Tommy enlisted a lawyer to draft a letter stating his intention to sue Elton under California's palimony law for $500,000 for physical abuse and broken promises. The letter, written on February 8, 1984, was sent to Elton at Woodside, though he was in Australia at the time.

The real shocker was, as the *Globe* headlined its final installment of the exposé, "Elton Wed Renate Four Days After I Hit Him for Palimony." Tommy also claimed that the palimony letter produced threats from some of Elton's powerful friends: "If I didn't drop this and leave him alone, I'd be taken care of. . . . I didn't know if that meant I would be killed or beaten up. But I didn't want either one. I knew they meant business." Wanting to spare his family any negative publicity from a lawsuit, Tommy eventually decided to drop it and went into hiding for a while. And as a coda to this whole sordid affair, his lawyer, disbarred for possession and sale of drugs, also ultimately vanished.

Initially Tommy believed that a palimony suit would expose Elton's gay lifestyle and drug use. But by the time he came forth with his tell-all story for the *Globe* it seemed, in view of developments in the Elton John marriage, a bit anticlimactic.

27

Trials and Tribulations

Minutes after hearing of the judgment in May 1982 in the case of British singer Gilbert O'Sullivan against his former manager, Dick James called his son Steve into his office and made a prediction. "We'll get a copy-cat lawsuit from Elton," he said. "You can bet your bottom dollar."

James was right. Three months later Elton filed suit against DJM, the company that had discovered him. The case would take three years to come to trial. "The claim was word for word from the O'Sullivan case," Steve James remembers. "The fact that the case was nowhere similar didn't seem to matter to them. [John] Reid wanted to pin the same thing on us [in order] to get the copyrights and masters awarded to Elton."

O'Sullivan, a British singer whose entry onto the charts had preceded Elton's by a few weeks, had contended in his suit that he had not got his due share of revenues from his songs and recordings from his manager, Gordon Mills, and his company, Management Agency and Music Ltd. He had only received £500,000 out of £14.5 million grossed by the recordings. In its decision, the High Court in London awarded O'Sullivan the copyrights, master tapes of his records and £100,000.

In a move to preempt a suit, during the three-month period between the O'Sullivan judgment and the serving of papers on DJM, James had offered to sell the copyrights and masters to Elton, but manager John Reid flatly rejected this proposal. "He didn't want to discuss it," Steve James maintains, "because he knew we would want market price and he thought he could get them for Elton in return for legal costs alone. The court case cost £500,000 but he saw that he could end up with copyrights and masters worth probably £20 million."

The ruling in Gilbert O'Sullivan's favor provided ammunition for Elton and Bernie Taupin to try to retrieve the copyrights to 144 songs. Also at issue were previously unreleased John-Taupin songs still retained by DJM, but which Elton felt might be future money-spinners.

They also wanted a larger share of the £200 million generated during their prolific DJM period. James claimed, however, that he had only made a £1.5 million profit while Elton had received £13.4 million from his recording contract and a million plus from the publishing agreements.

The emotional cost of the lawsuit for Dick James, the man who had been a kindly and concerned father figure to Elton, would be enormous. "My father felt very betrayed," says his son Steve. "He treated Elton like a son, and neither of us could believe that Elton was prepared to go through a trial without discussing it with us."

Dick James was by this time chairman of DJM, having stepped down as managing director to let his son run the company in 1982, after undergoing a quadruple bypass. Eight years earlier Dick James had suffered a mild heart attack that forced him to quit smoking. But he appeared to be in relatively good health through moderating his diet and relaxing with his wife at their St. John's Wood penthouse and at their flat in the south of France.

Elton himself had told *Rolling Stone* back in June 1971, "Dick is a straight, right-down-the middle, Jewish publisher. To me he's been like a father. If there's any problem, Dick will sort it out for me. On the other hand, Dick's sort of, you know, Dick's very . . . very aware of money. But I'd rather have Dick on my side than anybody else, because Dick is honest."

Now, fourteen years later in the High Court, James felt that his reputation and honor were impugned by Elton in the eight-week-long trial, which took place during the summer of 1985. At the heart of the case was the notion that James had seized on the naïveté of both Elton and Bernie, twenty and seventeen, respectively, when he signed them in 1967, at £25 ($67) a week and a combined weekly salary of £50 ($134).

Many people who remembered Elton's days at DJM now believed him something of an ingrate, considering the opportunity James had provided him and the money which DJM plowed into making this songwriting team a success. However, Elton and Reid's real motive was to recoup past royalties at a higher percentage. Disputing the contract on grounds of naïveté was just a legal ploy.

Elton's first boss, Cyril Gee, former managing director of Mills Music, was disgusted with Elton's suit. Bluesology's John Baldry and Elton Dean, from whom Elton took his name, regarded the DJM association as a big break for any musician and pointed out, further, that publishing contracts with a fifty-fifty split were standard back then.

On the other hand, Ray Williams, the man who put Elton and Bernie together and delivered them, albeit indirectly, to DJM, gave written testimony against Dick James. The songwriting team, he claimed, evidenced no special understanding or sophistication about the music business and thus James had taken advantage of them. Of course, Williams believed all these years later that Dick James had fired him as Elton's comanager in order to reap all the profits for himself. But, according to Steve James, it was Elton who demanded that his father get rid of Williams.

Even a week into the trial James still believed his differences with Elton could be resolved out of court. To this end, through an intermediary, he arranged a secret meeting with Elton at the Westmoreland Hotel, now called the Lord's Hilton, in St. John's Wood near Regent's Park in central London. It was set for two o'clock in the afternoon. But as Dick James prepared to leave his office, forty-five minutes earlier, the phone rang. Someone from John Reid's office was calling to cancel. "I'm really sorry," a dejected James told his son. "I think I could have worked it out."

All along, the Jameses believed that John Reid, whom they had never trusted, was behind the suit. At one point, during Elton's four

days in the witness box, the singer said that he was very fond of Dick
James and had only brought the suit because he had no alternative,
since James had refused to sell the copyrights and masters to him.
"Elton never knew that we had made an offer to do just that," Steve
James claims, "because John Reid never told him."

Bernie, meanwhile, was a hopeless witness, frustrating his cross-
examiner by a total amnesia about dates. Perhaps the most damaging
testimony against James came from Sheila Dwight, who had been
present at the signing of her son's first publishing contracts. While
acknowledging that Dick James had told her to feel free to have a
third party look them over, he had not pressed her to hire a lawyer.

"Her testimony was extremely unhelpful to us," Steve James explains, "because that was the one thing the judge wanted to hear.
He felt that the onus was on us to insist that she saw a solicitor
[lawyer]."

But the younger James felt no rancor against Sheila, whom he
describes as a "very nice woman" who had been given the contracts
to look over and had kept them for a week. He added, "My father
told her that if there was anything she was unhappy about or did not
understand to please come back and discuss it with him. My impression of her at the time was that she was quite happy for Elton to do
whatever would make him happy. She would never make him do
this or that . . . but maybe he needed a bit more guidance from her
than she gave him."

On November 29, 1985, when Mr. Justice Nicholls ruled in a four-
and-a-half-hour judgment in the High Court that Elton and Bernie,
young and awestruck by this giant of the music publishing industry,
had been led to rely on James alone to assure them the agreements
were fair and reasonable, it was clear that Sheila had made her point.
The judge also described the publishing contract, with no provision
for increasing royalties, as an "unreasonably hard bargain." Further,
Nicholls ruled, Elton and Bernie were entitled to moneys from ir-
regular royalties paid them by DJM's overseas subpublishing companies as well as excessive fees charged by the company for making,
producing and distributing Elton John's records. Reporters estimated
the figure owed Elton and Bernie, including interest from 1967, to
be around £5 million ($7,198,000). The sum was never disclosed, and
to this day Steve James claims it was nowhere near that amount.

John Reid, who had testified in detail about how he had persevered

over eight years, enlisting two accounting firms to pinpoint irregularities in the royalty payments, even got a mention from the judge.
"A young man both astute and tenacious," the judge said of Reid,
who, of course, stood to receive an enormous payout if Elton won
the suit.

In James's favor, the judge stated that the defendant had not con-
sciously sought to take advantage and, above all, as James had given
the songwriting team their start with no guarantee that they would
ever become so successful, he could hold on to the copyrights. Too
much time had elapsed, said the judge, for Elton and Bernie to try
to take over the copyrights and masters.

Both sides claimed they won, Bernie calling the decision "a moral
victory" and Elton remarking, "It's a pity about the copyrights, but
I think the judge handled it fairly." Elton also advised other music
industry neophytes, "Get a really good lawyer."

Steve James disagreed, explaining that back in 1967 lawyers were
not swarming all over the place and that the judge could not transport
himself back to then. "No one used lawyers," he says. "Brian Epstein
[the Beatles' manager] *never* used one. The judge's perspective was
limited to 1985."

In the end, though, no one probably won, and Elton himself had
to wonder if the trial had been worth the effort. James retained the
copyrights and masters, valued at about £20 million ($28,792,000).
Elton's lawyers estimated the trial cost at £500,000 ($719,800).

Elton's legal team, meanwhile, calculated the financial settlement
of back royalties ordered by the judge to be worth as much as £5
million ($7 million), but as his annual income exceeded this figure
and legal costs amounted to £1.5 million (over $2 million), the net
gain seemed dubious. And Elton could never measure the sorrow
that ensued from this chapter in his career.

On February 1, 1986, less than three months after the judgment
was handed down, Dick James died of a heart attack. He was sixty-
five. To this day his son, Steve, now in his forties and running DJM,
believes that the trial was the major contributory factor. "The whole
case was an extreme strain on him," Steve says bitterly. "He couldn't
come to terms with some of the things the judge said because my
father was one hundred percent honest and fair in all his dealings.
He couldn't understand how the lawyers could build a case against
him."

In his full, productive lifetime James had served as chairman of the Music Publishers Association and also received, among other honors, the Ivor Novello Award for service to the entertainment industry as well as the prestigious Queen's Award for Industry for DJM's export record. James was especially humiliated that Elton had sued him personally along with DJM and This Record Company. Before the trial he was dealt another blow when it was discovered his long-time accountant, who had been involved in drawing up Elton's publishing contracts and was expected to testify on James's behalf, had inoperable cancer. The accountant died a few weeks later.

The greatest sorrow for Dick James, while he went through the trial, was that he felt horribly betrayed. At the very least, he believed, Elton owed him the respect to meet and discuss the suit, and he was convinced they could patch it up. In a direct reference to John Reid, whom he describes as "an animal only out for himself," Steve James says, "One felt that Elton allowed certain people around him to have too strong an influence and maybe he should have stood up himself and said, 'I don't see anything wrong with meeting with Dick, and I insist on doing it.'"

But that, adds James, was Elton—"always getting people to do his dirty work for him. I remember when someone had to be fired from the band or the road crew, he'd always get John Reid or my father to do it."

Only a few months earlier, drummer Nigel Olsson and bassist Dee Murray were dumped for the second time. Once again Murray was on vacation, this time in Florida. The first firing, a decade before, in 1975, had come while he was in Barbados. "We'd just finished the *Breaking Hearts* album and the tour, and I figured I would take some time off knowing we were going to record again," he recalls. "I was supposed to call the office in L.A. to find out when I was supposed to turn up. I got a call back saying we [Dee and drummer Nigel Olsson] wouldn't be needed—and that was it."

Characteristically, Elton, upon hearing about Dick James's sudden and unexpected death, sent condolences via a third party. But Elton did, as a gesture of respect, absorb the James's legal costs of the trial.

28

Royal Intervention

Even before they tied the knot, Elton had leveled with Renate about the demands of his career. "I told her, 'Listen, I'm going off on tour for a year, so it's not the right thing to get married and leave you alone,'" Elton recalled. "And she said, 'It's like a dentist appointment—you're trying to put me off.' So I did it and I had no qualms. I knew it was the right thing to do."

Clearly Elton had not duped his wife into thinking they would live like a couple, strolling arm-in-arm together through life. In fact, the two of them seemed to behave more like long-lost cousins. "Elton Comes Back in a Flash" read the headlines in August 1986, but they were talking about Elton tending the fires of his creative life, not home and hearth. Two and a half years into the marriage, Renate was growing restless, itching to return full time to the recording studio as Elton roamed the globe.

Elton at this stage was behaving like the "Single Man" of yesteryear, off on a five-month, eight-country tour. He was camping it up onstage in a bright Mohawk cockscomb headdress and black-and-silver Bob Mackie cape. Elton also worked on his next album, *Leather Jackets*, in Holland, and he remained there for much of the year, ostensibly to avoid Britain's stiff income tax by spending fewer than 120 days annually in England.

By summer 1986, with Elton now appearing more like a runaway than absentee husband, it seemed that it would take a royal miracle to mute the talk of trouble in the marriage. This time it arrived courtesy of the Queen's second son, Prince Andrew, and his fiancée, Sarah Ferguson. Elton was the Prince's favorite pop star, and it was left to Andrew and Fergie to bring Elton and Renate closer together. Having dined with Andrew's aunt, Princess Margaret, and accompanied her to the cinema, as well as performing at private royal events, Elton had by this time become a virtual court musician.

Elton, in fact, had even commissioned a coat of arms for himself. It would depict the two major areas of his life, music and football. Missing were his signature glasses, which, according to coat-of-arms design supervisor Patrick Dickenson, Elton had felt was too common and gimmicky. "Elton treated this very seriously," Dickenson said. The Spanish phrase on the singer's coat of arms was "The music is good."

An invitation to perform at the Prince's bachelor party was the first step in smoothing the way for Elton and Renate to make a rapprochement. For one thing it was a big enough event to recall Elton to England, something Renate had yet to achieve on her own. But if anyone thought Renate was twiddling her bejeweled fingers at home on the night of the party, July 15, 1986, as Elton pounded the piano late into the night, they were wrong.

Rescuing Renate from one more solitary evening at the mansion, Fergie drafted her as a party crasher, along with Princess Diana and Pamela Stephenson, the wife of comedian Billy Connolly. It would become a hen night to remember, when Fergie, dressed as a policeman, with her trio of accomplices wearing policewomen's uniforms, hit the night spots of London after they crashed the bachelor party. Annabelle's, the fashionable London club, had never seen anything like it as Princess Diana kept the joke alive by sitting at the bar in her police constable's costume.

Eight days later, on July 23, Mr. and Mrs. Elton John were granted front-row seats, displaying their position in the young Royals' inner circle, at Sarah and Andrew's Royal Wedding in Westminster Abbey. They had also attended the prewedding ball at the Guard's Polo Club in Windsor.

At the request of the newly created Duke and Duchess of York, BBC Radio Two played Elton's songs on the morning of the wedding. Two of them, "Nikita" and "Wrap Her Up," a duet with George Michael, both from the new *Ice on Fire* LP were hits on both sides of the Atlantic. "Nikita" was said to be about a lonely Russian girl, but actually it was a boy's name.

By way of thanks to Andy and Fergie (the latter having had long talks with Renate to still her doubts about the marriage), Elton invited them to a party at the Vicarage Road home of his beloved Watford Football Club. Ever the opportunist, he staged the romantic event in October 1986 to showcase the newly built West Stadium there. Now, with Renate at his side and flanked by the Duke and Duchess of York, all the torments of Elton's bisexuality announcement finally vanished. No one, he vowed to himself, would ever again chant, as twenty thousand people had once done in the stadium at the time of the famous interview, "Elton John's a homosexual, tra-la-la." The sight of Mr. and Mrs. Elton John, in the company of Royals, erased any memories of the Watford Club chairman of the early days prancing around the field in platform heels.

Watford was as much a stage for Elton as Madison Square Garden or the Hollywood Bowl. At Vicarage Road his personal assistant would drive him out onto the field in a Range Rover. For away games in places like the Midlands, Elton sometimes alighted from a helicopter in the car park of a hotel, whereupon the cooks, waiters and chambermaids all came running out to meet him. At the matches themselves, Elton always signed autographs and then positioned himself on the side of the grandstand to watch the game.

The new West Stadium had cost £2.5 million ($4.5 million) to build, with £1 million ($1.8 million) of it coming from the pocket of the man who had insisted only a few years earlier that he was not going to become the team's personal banker or favorite philanthropist. That was, of course, Elton John.

Despite his unwavering devotion to the Watford Football Club, Elton was still a mercurial man and a man in conflict. Nowhere was this more visible than in his marriage. The previous December, Elton, then thirty-eight, had told the *Daily Express*, "We are trying for children. It hasn't happened yet. I'd just like to have children. I don't mind whether it's a boy or a girl. I simply want to be a family man — and I'm not getting any younger. I was an only child and I didn't like that very much. Ideally I'd like to have two—but you never know. Please God that we can have one. It would be nice to have another talent." Then the married man disappeared for most of the year.

For the moment, with Andrew and Fergie's help, the couple were together again. But whether Elton would actually ever get to experience the tender emotions of the "Greatest Discovery," the ode to a newborn baby he so poignantly sang on his first album, *Elton John*, back in 1970, remained a big question mark.

In the meantime, sixteen years and twenty-five albums later, Elton John, at thirty-nine, had filled tens of millions of concert hall seats. But he had yet to make possibly the "greatest discovery" of all. Himself.

29

Mozart Manqué

With his Live in Australia With the Melbourne Symphony tour in November–December 1986 Elton was trying to achieve a fusion of pop and orchestral sounds. A decade before, on the *Here and There* LP, he had attempted the same thing, but the results had been disastrous. Then, the musicians had not belonged to a symphony orchestra; they were, Elton sniffed, mere session players. This time there would be cohesion among the eighty-eight-member Melbourne Symphony Orchestra and, further, special microphones on each musician would ensure that they would not be drowned out by the singer's own thirteen-piece band.

The former Royal Academy of Music pupil particularly liked the notion of being the first pop star to tour with a full orchestra. In over six weeks of touring they would play an ambitious twenty-seven dates. Whether it was with his position on the record charts or the results of a Watford football match, Elton was always keeping score. He always had the need to surpass himself. On this six-week, sold-out tour he saw himself as not just a pop star, but a concertmeister and piano virtuoso as well.

Elton dressed the part, in stage costumes designed by Bob Mackie.

For the orchestral section of the program he cloned a Wolfgang Amadeus Mozart look right down to the pompadour wig and designer patch, eighteenth-century style. As if to drive home the difference between his roles as a pop musician and concertmeister, when his band held sway Elton wore a glitter tailcoat, chandelier earrings and a pink punk-style wig that looked as if it had been electrocuted.

Bathed in lights that airbrushed his white Steinway concert grand piano pastel pink, blue and purple, Elton orchestrated a spectrum of moods, from full-tilt rockers to lushly orchestrated ballads. For ninety minutes he dazzled his fans Down Under with signature pieces like "Candle in the Wind," "Goodbye Yellow Brick Road," "Daniel," "Sixty Years On" and "Your Song." Mince-stepping, jumping, shimmying, dashing across the stage, down on his knees, atop his piano, feigning sleep, then startling himself awake, Elton did an extended twelve-and-a-half-minute version of the already manic "Bennie and the Jets." Musically, he strutted his versatile talent, traversing gospel, blues, hard rock, soft rock and ballads, wistful and despairing.

But on this night, December 9, 1986, as Elton neared the end of the tour, it was becoming all too apparent that, even dressed up as Mozart, he was no kid anymore. Yet no one, not Dick James, not John Reid, not even his own mother, had ever succeeded in persuading Elton to slow down.

Only a crisis situation, like the altercation in Auckland or his bogus heart attack (which turned out to be exhaustion), made Elton curtail his punishing schedule. The minute the scare had vanished, Elton was back on the treadmill—in his case another gargantuan tour. In the decade of the eighties, music videos allowed some stars, like Madonna and Michael Jackson, to sell millions of records before they ever went out on the road. But in this music video culture, where image now sometimes superseded talent, the bald, squat singer figured that the best way for him to give his albums an initial boost was to hit the tour circuit.

During a recent five-month tour that had included two hundred concerts, Elton's throat had been bothering him. Over the last year he had consulted several specialists, but none of them seemed to be able to figure out what was wrong. The pain returned in Sydney, and as Elton sang "Don't Let the Sun Go Down on Me," he began to cry. "It was me falling to bits," he remembers. "I couldn't sing, but

I sang, but I don't know how I sang." Minutes later Elton collapsed on stage.

Elton was rushed to St. Vincent's Hospital as rumors spread that he had throat cancer. As he lay in bed, Elton feared the worst. In the past when he had landed in the hospital, he resumed working after a few days' rest. This time, though, he knew it was more serious. Now his whole career was in jeopardy and he might never sing again.

Noticeably absent from his bedside was Renate, and Elton was reportedly greatly irked by her failure to fly to Australia to be with him. Now, three years into the marriage, Renate, having resumed her career, preferred to go about recording in Los Angeles. Elton felt let down.

As exploratory surgery got under way in early January 1987, throat cancer was ruled out. "Elton John has a nonmalignant lesion," Dr. John Tonkin announced to the press. "He is expected to make a full recovery." On January 6, 1987, the lesions were removed by laser surgery, and the greatly relieved singer promptly canceled a concert in Perth as well as all 1987 performances, including a thirty-two-concert United States tour scheduled to start the following month.

By year's end, the *Live in Australia With the Melbourne Symphony* album met Elton's own expectations by becoming a collector's item for many fans. The two-record set spun off a hit, the new live version of "Candle in the Wind," in America. It was enhanced by a music video that cut between Elton's live appearance and striking footage of Marilyn Monroe. Until now the single, originally on *Goodbye Yellow Brick Road*, had only been released in England. A third TV special in eight years, after those of the Russian and Breaking Hearts tours, was made of one of the concerts. "Live in Australia" was aired over America's Showtime cable channel and also available as a video.

Back in England, Elton's former piano professor, Helen Piena, received a copy of the TV special from one of her pupils. "He sits well," she remarked, "like a classically trained pianist." But Elton John, in her view, was no Mozart. "I couldn't bear to listen to the music," she said. "It was dreadful."

Elton, meanwhile, under doctor's orders, sat out the year. But he continued to make headlines. During a previous hiatus, in 1978, Elton's hair transplants had been the fodder for the tabloids. This time, however, the stories were enough to make the superstar pull out whatever hair he had.

Coming Around

30

Poison Pens

"They can say I'm a fat old sod, they can say I'm an untalented bastard, they can call me a poof," Elton declared. "But they mustn't ever lie about me, because then I'm going to fight. And I'm determined to be a winner."

Frequently Elton had felt violated by stories about his personal life. He never expected, for example, the brouhaha that had surrounded his bisexuality confession over a decade before. Much as he was hurt and angered by it, however, there was no denying that he had made the statement to the reporter. Similarly, Elton was upset about the teasing he got in the tabloids over his hair transplants. But here again, these were factual accounts, and in the end he even posed for photographers with his new thatch of hair. The snide innuendos about his marriage also produced resentment. Still, he had yet to unleash his wrath against their poison pens.

That would all change in February 1987, when a young male prostitute named Stephen Hardy walked into the *Sun* newspaper offices in London to tell all about "Orgies With Elton," as the bold headlines said. The same day the story appeared, Elton hit back with a £5 million ($7,640,000) libel suit against the tabloid.

The prostitute, code-named Graham X in the articles, claimed that the previous year he had provided Elton and his friend Billy Gaff, a record company owner and former manager of Rod Stewart, with at least ten "rent boys," as male hustlers are colloquially known in England, for drug-filled homosexual orgies. Each of the rent boys, according to Graham X, was paid $100 per session and all the cocaine he could snort in return for sexual favors.

The prostitute said that he was telling his story because he was "ashamed of what I have done" and also to warn other gullible young boys "to steer clear of people like these." Initially the *Sun*'s lawyers had counseled caution by the editor, Kelvin McKenzie, who put his brother Craig and another reporter on what promised to be the hottest show-biz exposé on Fleet Street. In return for the titillating stories, the tabloid reportedly paid Hardy $4,000, a handsome sum of money for a young man who was having trouble making ends meet.

As these fabrications about Elton dominated the headlines back in England, Elton, recovering from throat surgery in Sydney, felt deeply angry and humiliated. There were descriptions of Elton "wearing only skimpy leather shorts and looking like Cleopatra" in the Pink Room of Billy Gaff's Finchampstead, Berks, mansion just outside of London. The Pink Room was so named because everything in it, including pajamas, was pink. The prostitute also said he witnessed Elton "cutting cocaine with a Gold American Express card."

Elton's health became a paramount concern to those around him. One friend lashed out at the tabloid: "I don't know why the *Sun* just don't deliver him a rope and tell him to get on with it," he said. "It can only be a matter of time before this kind of media muckraking pushes someone over the edge. What he gets up to in his private life harms no one, while he himself is being driven to the very end of his tether by this public trial of his morals."

While many of Elton's friends launched a counterattack in the press, Mick Jagger advised him to lie low for a while. The Rolling Stone, who over the years had endured his fair share of negative publicity, figured that the story would be forgotten in two or three days if Elton ignored it.

Elton rejected Jagger's advice. He felt that he was being persecuted for no apparent reason. He had never deliberately hurt anyone, Elton reasoned, so why should he allow the tabloid to attack him in this unmerciful way.

Despite his hard-hitting approach, Elton was clearly beginning to feel the strain of it all. As he remembers: "I cracked in private. I had a nervous breakdown. But I fought them. If anything is wrong, I'll fight it."

Deferring to his lawyers, Elton issued a brief statement: "There is no truth to the *Sun*'s allegations," he said, "and I'm happy to leave this whole matter in the hands of my lawyers."

Next day, the *Sun* followed up with "The Story They're All Suing Over" under the headline "Elton's Kinky Kicks." This earned the tabloid another suit. Then came "Elton's Drug Capers" a few days later, and the next day, "You're a Liar, Elton." Elton sued again. And again. In fact, before the affair ended, he sued seventeen times. Gaff, however, decided not to sue to protect his family, he said, from more tabloid assaults.

Some of the articles were accompanied by graphic details of Elton begging one boy to tell him about his sexual fantasies while the singer produced a bondage bag of handcuffs and whips. "I knew Billy and Elton wanted to do weird things," the male prostitute said. "They had a bondage bag which they called their bag of tricks."

Elton managed some levity, though, when asked about another headline, "Lust for Bondage." "Oh," Elton said. "Bondage—that's a beach in Sydney." He was referring to the famous Bondi surfing beach which he often used.

For the most part, though, Elton was hardly amused. He was furious. Stephen Hardy, meanwhile, apparently oblivious of the tremendous pain he was causing the singer, seemed unable to contain himself during his "fifteen minutes of fame."

He recalled for the British public via the tabloid how he had first met Elton. After a briefing by Billy Gaff about someone important waiting in an upstairs bedroom, Hardy said he entered the Pink Room and saw Elton lying on the bed. "He didn't have his glasses on," Hardy recalled, "but I recognized him immediately." Then Hardy took another swipe at the superstar: "He asked me what I did for a living and if I wanted to be a millionaire. He then turned the conversation around to himself, asking if I found him attractive. Well, to be frank, he wasn't. He had a big fat stomach and didn't look fit at all. Still, he was so stoned on cocaine that he didn't care. All he wanted to do was talk about himself and he needed me to be an audience."

Within a short time of rendering his services as a prostitute, Hardy said that he was "promoted" to pimp by Billy Gaff and asked to provide other boys for Gaff and Elton. According to the prostitute turned pimp, they liked them "no older than nineteen" and "rough trade . . . skinheads with tattoos and spiky-haired punks." Indeed, Elton had been heard to remark following a one-night stand years before in Liverpool, "He had so many tattoos it was like sleeping with the Sistine Chapel."

Whether or not Elton actually ever made that remark, Hardy's claims were far more shocking because they had serious implications. By suggesting that Elton had engaged in sexual relations with boys under twenty-one years of age, Hardy was accusing the star of breaking the law under the Sexual Offenses Act of 1967. The law states that an adult male cannot engage in sex with males under the age of twenty-one.

The allegations against Elton that the *Sun* printed engaged the interest of Scotland Yard, too. For many years young male prostitutes had been a major problem for police in Britain. Few of these rent boys were actually homosexual, but they had been driven into male prostitution by circumstance. Many of them had run away or been kicked out of their homes, and they believed they could find better chances in big cities like London. Some were as young as thirteen and saw the life of the streets as their only means of support. Their stomping ground in London was the Piccadilly Circus area, where they hung out on the street or in gay male porno clubs.

According to Chief Superintendent Bill Carnie of the Club Squad at the West End Central Police Station, "The *Sun's* exposé made our investigation more difficult because the rent boys fled." He asked the newspaper to supply details of its sex and drug allegations against Elton, and for further information on Graham X." Carnie also made an appointment to interview Elton John himself.

The *Sun* exposé had financial repercussions as well. Elton was dropped from a £3 million ($4.5 million) advertising campaign by the giant chocolate manufacturer Cadbury, which had paid him an undisclosed amount to appear in their television commercials. While his public image seemed to crumble around him, Elton, although glad that his voice was mending, found that the *Sun's* articles were once again putting his future in jeopardy.

While Elton exuded confidence in a legal repudiation of the *Sun's* allegations publicly, privately he was mortified, confessing to his assistant Bob Halley, "I give up. How can they get away with printing stuff like this?"

There was still more to come. The tabloid now seemed more determined than ever to nail the superstar. No less than six reporters were assigned full time to the story. The paper also retained the services of a convicted pimp and con man, John Boyce, to track down other rent boys who might have been involved with Elton. In return for signed affidavits of their involvement with the superstar each boy was to receive $3,000. Later Boyce confessed in a television interview, "We used to bring people to a hotel room and they would tell us they had had an affair with Elton John and you knew it was all pure crap."

When Elton turned up in Los Angeles, the *Sun* staked him out in his hotel lobby and, Elton claimed, even planted a bug in his room. But despite their extra manpower, all the *Sun* managed to come up with were three snapshots of the singer in the nude with another adult male at his side.

"Elton Porn Photo Shame" barked the headline in April 1987, and this time the paper said the two Polaroid snapshots they printed had been taken during a five-day orgy at Elton's Berkshire mansion in the early eighties. Two more suits were filed against the *Sun* for this latest assault.

However, these new allegations bore no relevance to the rent boys scandal. None of the men in the three photos was underage, and therefore no offense had been committed. A third young man, mentioned by the *Sun* as appearing in a photo they did not publish, was around twenty-five.

John Reid issued a statement at the time. "While Elton believes this photograph, like the others, to be genuine, it is thought to have been taken about ten years ago," Reid said. "Elton has long since admitted to being bisexual. In that he is not alone. He feels, however, that the treatment of his private life and that of his family by certain elements of the tabloid press has now become unique in its disregard for truth and decency." But Reid vehemently denied that there had been a five-day orgy back then at Elton's home.

While the *Sun*'s saga continued, Elton flew home, declaring, "I'm coming back to England for my wife, my future career and my fans." Once back in Berkshire, Elton, who would spend the bulk of his time over the next few months in seclusion at his mansion, gave a television interview to talk-show host Michael Parkinson, a friend and neighbor, about the terrible strain the publicity had put on his marriage. After a year and a half of marriage, he said, Renate had left him, though she remained supportive throughout the ordeal, even volunteering to make a court appearance on his behalf. "I still love Renate very much and she loves me," Elton said. "The marriage isn't over as such—we've just temporarily separated for a while."

By now it was becoming clear that the snapshots of Elton were a last desperate attempt by the newspaper to back up a story that was, in fact, fast losing credibility and public interest. Moreover, in a country where other rock stars like Eric Clapton, Keith Richards and Boy George had become heroin addicts and drummer Keith Moon had drunk himself to death, Elton John in the buff in a seven-year-old photograph was hardly a lurid story.

At the offices of the rival *Daily Mirror*, journalists had already begun unraveling the *Sun* scandal. Their research yielded, among other details, a shocking portrait of Stephen Hardy as a master storyteller who used various aliases and even pretended on one occasion that he was an American.

When Hardy was not operating in the twilight world of male prostitution, he eked out a living as a presser in a laundry by day. Once his name and identity were revealed, Hardy was fired from his job. It also came to light that he had a live-in girlfriend who knew nothing about his other sordid life, and had a four-month-old baby with her.

The only specific dates provided by the *Sun* were April 30 and May 1, 1986. Here again, the rival *Daily Mirror* had done its homework. Reporters had gotten in touch with Elton to ask about his whereabouts on those particular dates. Elton had little trouble providing this information. After all, as an international superstar with a demanding schedule, he kept a carefully documented diary. As his diary revealed, Elton had been in New York being fitted for stage clothes during that weekend when, according to Hardy, he was supposedly in a state of undress in the Pink Room of Billy Gaff's mansion.

Elton, along with his assistant Bob Halley, had stayed at the Carlyle Hotel on the night of April 30, when the rent boys romp at Gaff's mansion was allegedly in progress. The following morning, May 1, Elton and Halley were collected at their hotel at seven A.M. by a New Jersey-based limousine company, Music Express, and driven to

Kennedy Airport, where they boarded the British Airways Concorde Flight 192 to London. Both the limousine company and British Airways confirmed Elton's itinerary.

The manifest for the British Airways flight showed a Mr. E. John and Mr. B. Halley listed as passengers, and next to Elton's name was a special notation, "Famous Singer." Elton's alibi was rock solid. Now it was the *Sun* that was cast in a humiliating light.

But the final blow to the tabloid came when a front-page story headlined "My Sex Lies Over Elton" appeared in the *Daily Mirror*. Again, Stephen Hardy was the subject of a major tabloid exclusive. Only this time he was denying everything he had told the *Sun*. "It's all a pack of lies," Hardy told the *Daily Mirror*. "I made it up. I only did it for the money, and the *Sun* was easy to con. I've never met Elton John." Then, adding insult to injury, Hardy said, "In fact, I hate his music."

Further exoneration came after Scotland Yard interviewed the singer. Club Squad Chief Carnie, a tight-lipped, beefy man, and two other senior officers met with Elton early one evening in the office of Elton's lawyer, Frank Presland, in Lincoln's Inn Fields, in London. The interview was set for a time when the building emptied out to give the impression that everyone had gone home. But the tabloid press managed to find out about the meeting and camped outside the building.

For three hours Carnie and his deputies grilled Elton. Said Carnie in his best police monotone, "Mr. John wore a trilby hat to the interview. And I found him to be courteous. I knew what I wanted to ask him and I remember I was in the middle of putting a question to him and his legal adviser interrupted, telling him that he did not have to answer the question. But Mr. John said quite firmly, 'Let me answer the officer's questions.' "

Carnie says that he was satisfied with Elton's answers and that on the dates alleged in the *Sun* exposé Elton John was certainly not with Stephen Hardy or other rent boys. Now Elton had a clean bill of behavior from metropolitan police. Meanwhile, letters from Elton's fans, outraged by the stories, poured into the tabloid's offices.

The libel trial had been set to begin on December 12, 1988, in the High Court. But Elton's attorney managed to pull off a brilliant legal coup, arranging for the seventeenth, and last, suit against the *Sun* to be heard first. It had to do with an allegation made in a September installment that Elton had the larnyxes ripped out of two watchdogs prowling his estate to keep them from barking.

The story was patently and unequivocably false. In fact, all that a *Sun* photographer dispatched to the scene found when he went to Berkshire to take pictures of the allegedly tortured dogs were two German shepherds who appeared to be in perfect barking order. The story did provoke howls of laughter, though, up and down Fleet Street.

Ultimately, the *Sun* had to concede, "Sorry, Elton!" which it did on the front page of the December 12 paper, almost two years after they had printed the first scandalous story. Announcing a £1 million ($1.5 million) out-of-court settlement—the largest libel payment in British history—the *Sun* also apologized publicly. "We are delighted that the *Sun* and Elton John have become friends again," the article stated, "and we are sorry that we were lied to by a teenager living in a world of fantasy." When the editor wanted to drop the exclamation point in "Sorry, Elton" from later editions of the paper, he provided clear proof of how Elton's legal team had pummeled the *Sun*: he had first to clear the change with the singer's attorney.

It was on this uncommonly mild December day in 1988 that Elton, wearing a dapper gray suit, emerged from his lawyer's office and held an impromptu press conference on the front steps of the building. "This is the best Christmas present I could wish for," Elton said. "I don't bear any malice toward the *Sun*."

From there, Elton went straight to his friend and tailor Tommy Nutter, on Saville Row, who makes all of the superstar's day suits and regular clothes. Elton's favorite classic tailcoats, including the white one in moiré silk from his 1984 tour that had served as his wedding outfit, were also Nutter creations. "Elton was absolutely thrilled," Nutter remembers. "We had a sherry to celebrate. Elton then bought practically everything I had hanging in the store."

But despite Elton's momentary jubilation and satisfaction, some time would pass before he would feel whole and intact again. Months would pass, too, before Elton could even talk about the effect the ordeal had had on him. "I wasn't suicidal," Elton reflected. "I tried that once before in my life, and that wasn't the answer. But what was happening to me did depress me. I did not want to become a hateful person out of it. There was a danger of becoming bitter, but in the end it's not worth it. My true personality isn't like that, anyway. I didn't like what I'd become. I just sat there and thought everybody was horrible."

The fact that the scandal was smeared across British papers was particularly upsetting to Elton: "It was my pride that was hurt over those false accusations, and in my own country too," he explained. "I just couldn't understand why now."

A brigade of his tabloid accusers had even turned up outside his manager's house on the occasion of Elton's fortieth birthday party on the night of March 25, 1987. One of the guests, singer and lyricist Tom Robinson, remembers: "The tabloid press were picketing outside. They chanted, 'Happy Birthday, Elton,' and carried placards with slurs against him."

A horrified Robinson remembers trying to figure out why Elton was a target of the tabloids. "It's almost Jungian," he says. "For some reason, the flamboyance, combined with Elton's perceived lifestyle, triggers something in them. Someone once said that pop stars are similar to inkblot tests where people project their fantasies on them, and I think something about the particular shape of Elton's inkblot dredges up these kind of lurid monsters out of the collective unconscious of some journalists."

Renate was a no-show at the event. The party was attended by 350 guests at the ten-bedroom Georgian mansion, Lockwood House, which John Reid had recently bought himself in Rickmansworth, Middlesex. Reid, whose relationship with Elton often resembled a kiss-and-make-up ritual after their frequent blowups, presented Elton with an £80,000 ($127,384) Ferrari Testarossa sports car decorated with ribbons.

By now Elton's mother and stepfather had relocated to the sunny Spanish island of Minorca. While Sheila frequently mediated their fights in the past, now Elton had to fend for himself. For the moment, though, his relationship with his friend and manager was on an upbeat note, in contrast to the dissonance in his marriage to Renate.

Indeed, in the middle of the whole scandal, the Duke and Duchess of York proudly attended the party. "Nothing was ever mentioned," Elton says. "One wouldn't want to embarrass anyone and I wasn't suddenly dropped from any list. I think people are intelligent enough to see through that."

Yet for all of Elton's many friends, there were the betrayers among them, including one man to whom the singer had lent a substantial sum of money to buy a house. "There's nothing you can do about it," Elton reflects. "You are just very disappointed and wonder how they can sleep at night. I know who they are and they are not happy people. They are so miserable inside that they have to do these sort of things. So that's punishment enough. These kind of people are so rotten they are full of maggots anyway. Their own destiny is sealed by their attitude. Fortunately, I've got many other friends. I don't resort to violence. I leave that to John Reid. I will get my revenge in my own way."

At forty years of age, despite the adage about life beginning then, everything that was important to Elton seemed to be put in question. During this period he had lost a good friend, Neil Carter, to AIDS, and it was also apparent that his marriage could not be salvaged.

The effects of the *Sun*'s exposé were enormous. Although it eventually produced the largest libel settlement in the country's history, prompting a review of England's law of defamation, it also plunged the superstar into a severe depression.

But for all the pain, Elton also learned how to steel himself for the future. "After all," he remarked, "once you've been exposed naked on the front page of the *Sun* you ought to be able to face anything."

31

Bidding for Lots of Elton

It was an odd way to get rid of a wife, but some people were speculating that the only way to remove Renate from the house was to empty it for renovation. What looked like the biggest garage sale of the century was actually a four-day auction at Sotheby's in London in September 1988.

Two thousand items, including Mario Bugatta furniture, a Picasso aquatint, an art deco diamond-and-onyx pendant, Watford football shirts, a satin outfit with a tropical fruit motif on the shoulder pads, eyeglasses shaped like little grand pianos and a pink hat crowned with the Eiffel Tower, all went under the hammer. Only the singer's fourteen cars and mammoth record collection were exempt.

Elton Hercules John, the Captain Fantastic of Conspicuous Consumerism, was just trying to put his life in order. The burdens of the last eighteen months—the throat operation, the tabloid scandal and his failing marriage—had all made Elton think increasingly of poor old Reg and simpler days.

"All the possessions made me feel like Citizen Kane," he said. "I've enjoyed it, but they had begun to take over. There were boxes around the house that I had never opened. I needed to get rid of things to start over again."

Over the years Elton's passion for collecting art nouveau and art deco, not to mention his piles of baubles and jewelry, glasses, hats and warehouse-sized wardrobe, had gotten out of hand. He was now a prisoner of all these possessions, and it had become increasingly difficult for him to maneuver around his mansion without bumping into some exotic objet d'art. The Rocket Man had simply run out of space.

"When I first went there," said Sotheby's British chairman, Lord Gowrie, "it was an Alladin's cave, a magic toy shop, but hard to find somewhere to sit." It took a team of Sotheby's workers almost two weeks to inventory and then remove all of Elton's possessions.

Elton had also grown bored by his taste, and now he wanted to move into an ultramodern collecting phase. Only two months before, at Sotheby's first-ever auction in the Soviet Union, he had bought two paintings by relatively unknown Soviet artists for £150,000 ($255,000). One was a tempera landscape and the other a portrait in oils. Elton's winning bid by telephone was said to far exceed the estimated value of the paintings. But, of course, with his own Sotheby's auction, he stood to more than recoup any expenditures.

Elton had been ahead of his time when, in the late sixties, he began collecting art nouveau and art deco furniture, glass, paintings, jewelry and sculpture. Then, it had seemed corny. Now it was chic.

Philippe Garner, the man employed to catalog the superstar's art nouveau and art deco collections, thought it was one of the best he had ever seen assembled. He declared, "It's not didactic, the kind of collection that has been built up by poring over historical records and wanting the rarest academic items. It is a collection put together by someone who delights in the extravagant decorative appeal of art nouveau and art deco."

Indeed, just as with his concerts, which were more often festivals, there was an element of fun and whimsy to his collecting mania. "I'm impulsive," said Elton in the preface to the four-volume, £75 ($127) catalog. "If I see something I like, I just buy it." The catalog, a boxed set with Elton in silhouette on the cover, was divided into art nouveau and art deco; stage costumes; and memorabilia, jewelry and diverse collections.

Of course, with Elton's many golden hit records and singles, Elton had plenty of cash to splash on his every fancy. The fact that he had worked hard for his money, he believed, liberated him to spend it as he wished.

Unfettered by the traditions of English-style inherited wealth, Elton was able to indulge his curiosity and playfulness. The middle-class child of suburbia rebelled at doing things by halves—enough to get by, but somehow never enough. Rewards, too, were based on achievement, so Elton felt entitled.

Even from the earliest days of his success, just after the Troubadour debut, Elton went and bought Mickey Mouse ears at Disneyland and also hunted for antiques, all in the same week. This odd mixture of acquiring would be his pattern. At the start of his collecting, he enlisted the help of his Virginia Water neighbor, Bryan Forbes, who represented "breeding" to him. But by and large Elton's taste was instinctive, if not inadvertent, and much like a pack rat's; amidst all the clutter he had items whose real value was unknown to him. And by mere force of habit, his eye became trained and refined over time.

In a way, Elton's collecting was not unlike his music-making. The sheer volume of his acquisitions, like his song output, ensured that there would be material of enduring value along with the dross. Always buying in bulk and surrounding himself with a surfeit of possessions seemed to comfort the shy, lonely side of him that related at times more easily to inanimate objects than to people.

Prior to the auction there was an advance showing in London at the Victoria and Albert Museum, just down the street from the now-defunct Speakeasy, where the former Reg Dwight and his Bluesology band had been signed up to back Long John Baldry more than twenty years before.

The exhibit received a snub from critics, but proved to be a windfall for the museum. With lines around the block, hundreds paid five pounds a head. There were videos of the collection as it was arranged at Elton's home. The Doc Marten skinhead-style boots, for example, that Elton wore in *Tommy* were placed next to the superstar's swimming pool. "Riveting," wrote Claire Clifton in the *Wall Street Journal* of the videos, "because his objects looked so marvelous together, something it was hard to imagine from seeing them in a museum. At the John house, a coffee table full of Lalique glass was set up in front of a ravishing suite of a settee, two armchairs and two side chairs, each covered in different tapestries designed by Raoul Dufy."

Sotheby's had estimated that the hoard of possessions that Elton had spent twenty years accumulating would bring in $5.1 million. But the final tally, helped by wide advance publicity where selections from the Sotheby's Collection were exhibited in New York, Tokyo and Sydney, was $8.2 million. Elton's treasure trove had exceeded all expectations.

The auctions took four days to complete. Even the duration of one of the sessions, five hours and twenty-three minutes, was longer than anticipated, almost causing auctioneer Hilary Kay to lose her voice. No less than six hundred bidders, who had received seats months in advance, filled six halls of the auction house in London's Bond Street. Sheila Farebrother sent a friend in her stead to pick up a part of her son's past before it was gone forever.

During the first hour of the rock memorabilia auction, three pairs of the superstar's glasses fetched £13,940 ($23,698). Elton, meanwhile, on tour in Miami, kept in touch by phone. This part of the auction netted nearly £421,185 ($709,276), double Sotheby's estimate.

One of the more unusual items, the Doc Marten boots from *Tommy*, fetched £12,100 ($20,376). The buyer, ironically, was the man whose firm had made the boots. But he felt they were worth every penny. Similar sentiments were echoed by the buyer of a Wurlitzer jukebox, circa 1940, in domed mahogany veneer, for £17,600 ($29,638), and gold and platinum discs to the tune of £6,160 ($10,373).

More high-brow collectors took part in the auctioning of artworks, jewelry and furniture. One of the top sales was a painting by the surrealist Magritte of a blue fish wrapped in pearls. It went for £70,200 ($118,217). Other acquisitions included a pair of pottery busts of Queen Elizabeth II, a chamber pot and a pair of Cartier silver baskets that Elton used as soap dishes.

In only four shopping days, music fans, art lovers and professional collectors had all but closed out Sotheby's sale. "We have hardly any unsold goods at all," a Sotheby's spokesman reported. But no sooner had the hammer been laid to rest when rumors began to float about the pasha of pop music selling off all his trinkets and treasures to avoid pauperhood.

"Oh, heavens no," said Elton, chuckling over the suggestion. "If I needed money, I'd just go back on the road and do some shows."

But farfetched as the rumors sounded, there were friends and family members who worried about Elton's ability to hold on to his money. All along Sheila had worried about her son's unbridled generosity: "I'd like to know Elton is financially secure for the rest of his life," she had told the *Daily Mail*'s David Wigg back in 1979 on a walk in Moscow's Red Square during the tour of Russia. "People just laugh and say, 'Of course he is.' " But Sheila, who tended to Elton's household bills back then, pointed out, "He doesn't know anything about finance. Everyone else does it for him."

One friend, former Rocket executive Tony King, had also cautioned Elton about his excessive gift giving around the same period. "Elton used to call up and say, 'I'm making all this money—let's go out and spend it.' And they would. Fancy restaurants, Cartier's—I mean, I had something like $12,000 worth of jewelry [that he had given me] in the bank. In the end I thought, 'No, that's not right,' and I had a talk with him about this."

Elton's profligacy dated all the way back to his DJM days. Steve James remembers, "Elton used money a lot on extravagant things and gifts for himself. They always had to be two or three of a thing; he just couldn't buy one. He doesn't watch his expenses. He has a lot of people around him who use him for their own gain and I think probably rip him off."

It was feared initially that Renate would be an extravagant Mrs. John. But she was not. And whatever anyone thought of Elton divesting himself of his possessions, she was clearly not the reason behind it. Elton was, simply, clearing out his life. By November 1988 Rocket Records had virtually wound down its operations and was now a mere outlet for Elton John, while Watford Football Club, once the love of Elton's life, was also put on the block. Elton John was going back to basics. There was only one other area of his life to sort out. He would get to that next.

32

Solo Again

As Elton sat alone and examined the state of his marriage in the fall of 1988, he knew that it was beyond salvaging. And while the cynics from Sydney to London would be quick to remind the world "I told you so," Elton was desperately unhappy about the whole situation.

For while he had not hidden his sexuality from anyone, he knew that his union with Renate was his one real shot at being a father and having the family he so desperately wanted. Now that dream had collapsed, and a split was necessary.

From the beginning there were too many odds against the marriage working. Not least of all was the circumstance of the millionaire superstar—the self-proclaimed bisexual—and the ordinary working woman pairing off. It was hardly a match made in heaven. But as the press and public raised their eyebrows in disbelief, the brave, if not bizarre, couple were undaunted by the ridicule and went ahead with their plans. Sadly, though, there were other factors at work. Shortly after the nuptials in Sydney, Elton felt the irresistible tug of his old lifestyle.

Frequently he could be found in the company of his homosexual friends, whom Renate saw as a bad influence. Despite the fact that Elton could provide her with the material comforts of Woodside, a far cry from the small room she occupied during her days as a single woman in the drab North London section of Kilburn, it was not enough to keep the marriage together.

Although John Reid helped Renate when Elton was off on tour, the couple seemed to grow apart. Not even the Royal intervention by their close friends, the Duke and Duchess of York, who earlier had been credited with saving the Johns' shaky marriage, could do anything this time around. Gone were the days when Elton told the press how much he liked to come home and share things with his wife, and that they were trying to have children. Instead, friends who had defended the marriage and who had loved the EHJ and RJ monograms everywhere, conceded that it was finished.

Elton himself spoke about his heartache to a close friend, the journalist Nina Myskow. "Of course it's sad," he told her. "I gave it my best shot. And it's certainly not Renate's fault. She's done nothing wrong. That's what makes it so hard."

Naturally, though, his decision came with feelings of guilt. In many ways, he reminded friends, Renate had been very helpful to him. She had stood by him, after all, through the whole tabloid scandal. In fact, at a time when Elton locked himself away in his room, alone with his depression, Renate even got a ladder and climbed up to his window, to check on him, despite her fear of heights. It seemed that she really adored him, and they truly had a special bond.

For Elton, the divorce was a painful affair, dredging up the unhappy memories of his own parents' split. And despite his bisexuality, he was also a bit old-fashioned, if not courtly. It could be said that Elton had—at intervals—given the marriage his best.

In March 1988, Elton had thrown Renate a lavish thirty-fifth birthday bash. Held at Convent Garden's trendy nightclub, Brown's, the party was attended by a stellar crowd that included George Harrison and Ringo Starr. The room was festooned with balloons, and a bouquet of white flowers was set in the icing and marzipan of the cake. And on the *Leather Jackets* album, one of whose tracks was written by Renate under the pseudonym Lady Choc Ice (the name being an in-joke about a fledgling band by that name), Elton included a dedication: "Thanks To L. C. Ice for being a continued source of inspiration."

Yet when the press announcement came on November 17, 1988, that the couple were seeking a divorce, nobody was really surprised. It was rumored that Renate's divorce settlement was anywhere from £3 million ($5 million) to £25 million ($42 million). Reportedly, she did not lay claim to his Berkshire mansion or his fleet of cars.

But Elton retained fond memories of his brief marriage, four and a half years in all. He remembered how beautiful his bride had looked when she walked down the aisle of the church in Darling Point, Sydney, and their happiness at that moment. Elton had gone on the road while the new Mrs. John returned to Woodside and a life of luxury she had never known before. But she was a stranger among her servants, and her husband was at the end of a transatlantic telephone line.

In many ways the marriage had proved beneficial to Elton. Rock critics even noted that he seemed calmer. At an appearance at Carnegie Hall in New York, one journalist called the now-married Elton "a much more mature performer." During their public outings, at Watford matches, occasional meetings in foreign cities, or their appearance, arms entwined, at the Royal wedding, Elton relished his image as a married man. Until the very end he had really hoped the marriage would work, resolving the torment he had lived with his whole life concerning his sexuality.

What the marriage did for Renate is not known. She was hurled into a jet-set pop-star world, and then hurried out of this life. Today, her affairs are still handled by John Reid, and she lives in a home Elton provided her, reportedly at a cost of £350,000 ($632,975). It is a pretty seventeenth-century cottage called Cobblers. It has a meadow in the backyard and a garden of thyme in front. The oak-beamed thatched cottage is in a picturesque village in Surrey's "Stockbroker Belt" about forty-five minutes outside of London. Parked outside is an SLX 300 Mercedes-Benz. There Renate lives with an aging cocker spaniel. From her new home she runs her own recording studio and enjoys a life away from the camera and innuendo. Still, she keeps her married name, Renate John.

Much to Bernie Taupin's regret, his book of prose, *A Cradle of Haloes: Sketches of a Childhood*, was published near the time of Elton's divorce. According to his publicist, Belinda Harvey, Taupin had hoped to keep his life as a lyricist separate from this childhood autobiography. "We spent all our time fending off the tabloid press,"

Harvey remembers. "Under the guise of wanting to talk about the book, they asked about Elton's marital split. I think Bernie was pissed off that everyone only wanted to know about Elton and Renate."

Indeed, the book had meant a great deal to Bernie, who had wanted to use a different side of his creativity. Taupin had made the initial approach to the London publisher Aurum Books about a memoir of his English childhood and musical influences dating from the time before he had ever met the future Elton John. Aurum's editor in chief, Michael Alcock, remembers, "He wrote, rewrote, worried, and refined it. He is a remarkably painstaking person and extraordinarily craftsmanlike and artistic. He's a proper poet, so prose is different, more extended, and he said he was not an expert. He was remarkably open."

On the subject of Elton's divorce announcement, however, Taupin was quite taciturn. In the November, 19, 1988, *Daily Express* he told writer David Wigg, "It's sad. I've been aware of their problems and I've seen this coming. But it's none of my business."

33

Reg Returns

Rarely had a man put on such a full-scale production of a midlife crisis as Elton did during five sellout concerts in October 1988 at New York City's Madison Square Garden. He appeared in a relatively subdued blue double-breasted suit and sequined black fez; he had retired his Donald Duck, Minnie Mouse, Statue of Liberty, Carmen Miranda and more recent Wolfgang Amadeus Mozart costumes.

"Getting rid of these things is a way of divesting," he explained. "I've got to get Elton out of my life and start being a little like Reg again."

The costume change, this latest divestiture, following on the heels of the auction, was aimed at making people pay more attention to his music and less to his outré outfits. To this end, Elton deleted such frothy tunes from these concerts as "Crocodile Rock" and "Benny and the Jets," the latter usually performed in the dopey falsetto that Elton had only recovered, following his throat surgery, in recent months.

Elton preferred to give forth now with the operatic melodrama of "Love Lies Bleeding (In My Hand)" and "I Guess That's Why They Call It the Blues," where he hit his stride. The blending of blues and gospel and soul into pop was what he had always done best, after all. Backed by an eight-piece band, he even traded in his customary Steinway grand for an electric piano. In yet another shift, Elton was now billing himself as a singer who plays the piano rather than a pianist who sings.

The concerts coincided with his latest album, appropriately titled *Reg Strikes Back*. It was his first studio album since re-signing with MCA for the *Live in Australia* LP. More important, it was a tip of the hat to his quiet alter ego, Reg Dwight. The album sleeve was a photographic compilation of some of the outrageous costumes the superstar had worn during his halcyon days in the seventies when he had been one of the world's biggest acts, selling over sixty million records in that decade alone.

"You get to a point after twenty years when you become a parody of yourself," Elton said. "I'd just done the whole thing to death. I still want to play concerts, but I don't want to go on stage looking ridiculous anymore. There will always be the little fun touches, but I don't want this anymore. I've got to divorce myself from that."

Once pop music had been such a freeing experience that he had even gotten rid of himself, Reginald Kenneth Dwight, to become Elton Hercules John. But the camouflage had worn thin in the face of life's realities. No matter how Elton had tried to tend the wounds of his former self, sometimes when he looked in the mirror what he still saw was the poor, unloved Reg whom he had neglected all those years ago.

Elton knew that he had to begin all over again. This time he would grow from the inside out, instead of the other way around. This meant deposing Elton, the king of kitsch, his oppressor. "I used to hate Reg quite a lot," he admitted. "Especially the name. But I think I got a little too carried away with Elton."

The LP *Reg Strikes Back* was a turning point in his life, a recovery of self, in August 1988. "I had gone through so much," Elton said. "The tabloids in England, my voice, splitting up with my wife, that I needed to dig myself out of a hole and get back to work." By now he and Renate had separated for good, prior to divorcing.

In the middle of the tabloid scandal, in fact, a deeply depressed Elton had gone back into the studio to record the album. "It's me striking back, not just musically," he explained. "It's me striking back, especially in England, against the press, and all that."

Remarkably, the return to his past was truly upbeat, a fact which surprised even Elton. By peeling back all the pretense of Elton, he was able to reach a reconciliation with the Reg in him. In so doing he could transcend self-pity (no matter how justified of late) to infuse his music with themes that were larger than himself.

In "Goodbye Marlon Brando," Elton said good riddance to "gridlock, the ozone layer (if there's any left), Dolly [Parton]'s chest, *Heaven's Gate, Rocky Five . . . Six . . . Seven . . . and Eight.*" Good riddance, he also seemed to be saying, to the detritus in his life. Similarly, "Mona Lisas and Mad Hatters II" was a social comment on New York's decay and its poetry: "Just focus on the brush strokes / And the bouquets the dancers hold."

Mixed in was the romantic and catchy "I Don't Wanna Go On Without You" and the alternately cynical and sympathetic "Poor Cow," about working-class wives and mothers. "Town of Plenty," on which Pete Townshend played guitar, had the propulsive feel of "Honky Cat" and "Crocodile Rock," but spoke of the ephemera of media fame and, wistfully, of the triumph of art.

Reviewing *Reg Strikes Back*, Ralph Novak commented in *People* magazine, "Instead of being concerned with taking Elton too seriously, it may be time to worry about *not* taking him seriously enough."

Until now Elton had never particularly concerned himself with social issues. This was, after all, the man who had played in southern Africa at Sun City, joining Rod Stewart on stage at the Superbowl there in August 1983, and then returned in October of the same year to give his own concert. Of course, depending on one's politics or spelling, Sun City, a group of noncontiguous black homelands, was either in South Africa or Bophuthatswana. Many artists tended to think it was the former and, unlike Elton, stayed away as a protest against apartheid.

Music, Elton believed, knew no political or geographical boundaries. It was just rock 'n' roll, an entertainment. Except, of course, they were artists and they took themselves seriously.

Elton and Bernie had disavowed any political, social or religious messages in their music from the very beginning. Back in the early seventies, when some critics and fans interpreted "The King Must Die" as a civil-rights anthem and claimed that the LP titled *Madman*

Across the Water referred to Richard Nixon, the pair scoffed at such notions. They were no peaceniks, like John Lennon.

In fairness, Elton had always been a generous soul, but the underpinning of his commitment was deeply personal rather than intellectual. Indeed, for him charity did begin at home, with his family and close friends as the primary beneficiaries.

From his earliest days as a superstar his fund-raising appearances at the Royal Variety Show and other places often involved helping children. Elton had a soft spot for kids, one that mirrored his own fragility as a boy, as the ungainly and unloved Reg Dwight. To date Elton had yet to worry himself about saving rain forests. In 1985 he had performed at the Live Aid concert but, of course, so had everybody else in the rock music business.

Bernie, meanwhile, had advanced beyond Elton in the political arena. He threw a Hunger Project fund-raiser around his kidney-shaped swimming pool in Beverly Hills and participated at cook-offs at the chic restaurant Le Dôme to feed the homeless.

For Elton there was, however, one issue that would galvanize him. It was AIDS. In January 1986, he had sung with Gladys Knight and Stevie Wonder on Dionne Warwick's AIDS fund-raising single "That's What Friends Are For," which hit Number One in the United States and Number Sixteen in the U.K. Elton's friends were dying around him. But it would take a young boy thousands of miles away in America's heartland to let Elton reclaim the Reg in him and make him whole.

34

Ryan White, An Extraspecial Person

In the fall of 1985 Elton picked up the *New York Times* in the waiting room of his New York voice specialist and turned the pages. There he saw a story that would change his life. It was about a fourteen-year-old boy named Ryan White. As the tears welled up in Elton's eyes, the bravery and courage of this Indiana teenager made the superstar who had everything suddenly realize how lucky he was. At that moment Elton made a vow to contact the White family.

How connected Elton would eventually feel to this boy he could not have known then. But the teenager from America's heartland would change the British superstar forever.

Ryan White was the teenager who first gave a child's face to AIDS for the country at large. Ostracized by petty-minded bigots in a small town, Ryan would eventually move an entire nation to compassion.

Ryan, a hemophiliac, contracted the deadly virus through a tainted blood transfusion. He was diagnosed with AIDS in 1984, and the following year he became a household name, when, as a fourteen-year-old boy, he successfully fought the school board in Kokomo, Indiana, for the right to attend classes.

Little was known then about how AIDS was spread, and as a result some parents and kids were fearful of going anywhere near Ryan. For months, he took his seventh-grade classes through a telephone hookup at his home, where he lived with his younger sister, Andrea, and his mother, Jeanne, a divorced factory worker.

But even after he had won his court battle against the school and returned to classes, Ryan was treated like a leper by some students. They scrawled homosexual and other slurs on his locker and taunted him in the corridors. At the local grocery store clerks threw the change at Ryan's mother to avoid touching her hands. Even at church some people shunned them. Ryan never capitulated to this cruelty: He was a real trouper.

The final indignity occurred when a bullet was fired into the Whites' home, so, in 1987, Ryan and his family moved from Kokomo to the town of Cicero, twenty miles away. He hoped that there he would be treated like any other kid.

Now, two years after the successful court battle, people were more knowledgeable about the transmission of AIDS. As a result, his proximity to other students did not set off the same alarms as before. Besides, Ryan White was an enormously likable boy and a fine student, an amiable teenager who belonged to the Booster Club at Hamilton Heights High School and liked to go to Taco Bell and Dairy Queen and read automotive magazines like any other kid.

But there was about Ryan an otherworldliness, an almost angelic quality, visible in his vibrant, kind brown eyes. He had wisdom way beyond his years. Having been subjected to the same kind of prejudices inflicted on other AIDS sufferers, largely homosexuals and intravenous drug users, he spoke out against the fears that often congealed into hatred against them. Ryan offered himself up as a messenger of goodness and decency, speaking out against the misconceptions about AIDS and prevailing on the public to find compassion for people with the disease.

Celebrities, enormously moved by the plight of Ryan and his family, began courting the boy. Hard as he resisted, this shy and reserved teenager, who only wanted to be treated like just another kid, became a celebrity himself.

On the morning of April, 30, 1986, the phone rang in the limousine ferrying Ryan White and his family from New York City to the air-port. Ryan's mother answered it. "Hello, Jeanne," said a man with a British accent. "This is Elton John."

She passed the phone to Ryan. He listened as Elton apologized for not being able to attend an AIDS benefit the previous night, at which Ryan had posed with a group of celebrities for an ad. The superstar also wanted to invite him to his concert in Texas in a few months. Ryan, overwhelmed with excitement about talking to Elton John, recovered enough to say he accepted the invitation.

The reason for the call was that the previous day Ryan had ap-peared on ABC-TV's "Good Morning America" to talk about the AIDS benefit, given by the American Foundation for Aids. When the program's host, David Hartman, asked, "Which celebrity do you want to meet most tonight?" Ryan's answer was direct and unequi-vocable: "Elton John, definitely."

Throughout Ryan's battle with AIDS, he met many celebrities, including actors Bruce Willis and Ted Danson, Olympic Gold Medal diving champion Greg Louganis, and singer Michael Jackson, who phoned Ryan once a week and bought him a red Mustang convertible. Ryan admired Elton because, in his own words, "Elton wasn't afraid to be different." It was Elton, too, who arrived in his life before the others, and he stayed until the very end.

Regretfully, Ryan had to miss Elton's Texas concert because he was in the hospital. But they would get together in the fall of 1987 in Los Angeles, when the singer had Ryan and his sister Andrea flown in a private jet to concerts in California and outfitted them with special sweatshirts, scarves and sunglasses. Elton also gave Ryan the beanie he wore on stage.

The highlight of the trip was a party Elton threw for them at Disneyland. On the hour-long trip by limousine from Los Angeles to Anaheim, Ryan and Andrea watched as Elton, in a second limousine, put on a show, standing up and sticking his head out of the sunroof to wave at them and at pedestrians.

Once inside Disneyland, Ryan needed a wheelchair to get around because he was still weak from his recent hospital stay. Elton steered the chair. After the trip, which also included a visit to Universal Studios, Elton kept in touch, by letter or phone, with the White family from wherever he was touring. It was Elton, too, who had enabled them to move to Cicero from Kokomo. He lent Jeanne enough extra money to make a down payment on a house by a lake there; the bulk of the cash had come from a movie company that had bought the rights to Ryan White's story.

But it was the small gestures, more than any trip or loan, that counted the most with Ryan. At Disneyland, for example, Elton had shared cans of Coca-Cola with Ryan, the boy some Kokomo classmates and students had feared being anywhere near. It was uncharacteristic behavior for Elton, a man who would rather buy someone a bottle of champagne than let anyone take a sip from his glass. It was also important for the boy to have people outside of his immediate family touch him, and Elton was there to provide lots of hugs and kisses.

By giving comfort to this boy, Elton was able to console himself about his own childhood. He became a father figure to the lad. By playing out this role Elton managed to recover for himself the father he had longed for his whole life.

There were many parallels in the boyhoods of Ryan and Elton, despite the generation gap. Both were children of divorce; Ryan's father, Wayne White, was much like Stanley Dwight. Though responsible about child-support payments, he was largely absent from Ryan's life after the divorce. "He didn't seem to want to know us at all," said Ryan, echoing Elton's feeling about maybe being a mistake in his father's life.

Both their stepfathers were kinder and more attentive than their natural fathers. Even after Jeanne White divorced her second husband, he was still a friend and familiar face around their home. Ryan, like Elton, also had a close relationship with his maternal grandparents. Above all, their mothers were powerful and loving presences in their lives.

During their phone conversations, Elton, recalling his days as the fat, ungainly boy back at Pinner Grammar School, counseled the skinny, hemophiliac teen with AIDS about how to overcome feelings of being an outcast. Ironically, just the circumstance of Elton being in Ryan's life created an opening for Ryan to make the friends he had dreamed about having all his life. In his senior year of high school, Ryan even had a prom date.

Elton also celebrated the bravery and dignity of Ryan White in public, inviting him, along with another boy, Jason Robertson, who had also got AIDS from a blood transfusion, to join him onstage in

July 1988 at an Athletes and Entertainers for Kids benefit in Los Angeles. Both boys were by Elton's side on the piano seat while he sang "Candle in the Wind." The song, an ode to Marilyn Monroe, had become a tribute to Ryan. Just as he befriended this brave hemophiliac boy in life, Elton would also be there to help ease him into death.

In early April 1990, Elton kept a weeklong vigil at Ryan's bedside as the boy lay dying. He had flown all day from Los Angeles to be with him, and he had brought along $600 worth of stuffed animals for other critically ill kids on Ryan's floor at the hospital. "They're too sick to care," said Elton, "but I feel so helpless in this place. I had to do something; I did it for myself, I guess."

But Elton was a great help to the White family. Drifting in and out of the boy's room, Elton took all their phone messages, cleaned up stray wrappers and discarded coffee cups. But, above all, he tried to console Ryan's mother, sister and friends, and listened to the grandparents talk about their grandson. He was a pillar of strength, a father figure to the family, someone who extended an embrace when they needed to be comforted.

Elton had also arranged for music to be piped into Ryan's hospital room and relayed a message from another star. "Ryan," said Elton, leaning over the bed, "Michael Jackson called to see how you were. You can't turn down a superstar like that. I'm Grade B compared to Michael."

But until the very end Elton was truly Number One in Ryan's book. Brushing his hand lightly over the dying teen's forehead, Elton murmured, "We need you, Ryan, and we love you." Elton broke away from the vigil only to attend the Farm Aid concert on the Saturday before the eighteen-year-old boy died.

He arrived on stage at the Hoosier Dome in Indianapolis to tumultuous applause and a standing ovation from forty-five thousand people, who also knew about Ryan's deteriorating condition and were pulling for him.

"This one's for Ryan," a choked-up Elton sang as he started to play "Candle in the Wind." Eerily, just as Elton finished another song, "That's What Friends Are For," the AIDS anthem, forty miles away in Cicero, Ryan slipped into an irreversible coma. This was the boy's last fight, and Elton, who kept in touch with the hospital the whole time, rushed into a limousine waiting to ferry him back to the boy. He returned there by nine o'clock that night.

The next day, Sunday, April 8, Ryan White died from AIDS-related respiratory failure. His pal was there, with Jeanne White, Andrea and the grandparents. Elton, with eyes red-rimmed from crying, bowed over the boy. "Good-bye, old friend," he said, his voice splintering with grief. "I love you."

On Wednesday, April 11, Elton, wearing a black sequined hat, led the congregation in singing a hymn and then accompanied himself as he sang "Skyline Pigeon," one of his earliest songs, at Ryan's funeral. The lyrics—"Turn me loose from your hands, / Let me fly to distant lands, / Fly away Skyline pigeon fly, / From all the things you left so far behind"—would ultimately be carved into Ryan's black-and-white granite gravestone in Cicero.

Elton had helped Ryan's mother arrange the funeral, and he even went along for the unpleasant task of picking out the coffin. Just before the ceremony, which was attended by fifteen hundred people, including Ryan's other buddy, Michael Jackson, Elton rehearsed the school choir of five or six kids and helped them with changes in pitch. They sang the AIDS song, "That's What Friends Are For." According to one friend of Ryan's, Brad Letsinger, it was Elton's care and concern that had encouraged kids at school to accept Ryan as one of them.

Elton was a pallbearer, along with the Los Angeles Raiders' Howie Long, talk-show host Phil Donahue and three of Ryan's friends. As he said his final farewell to Ryan, the man who had learned, finally, to touch another life through the gift of love as well as song, reflected, "These people have given me so much. They inspire me. They uplift me. They've given me more than I could ever return. Such strength and courage, such dignity and decency."

35

Back on Top Again

On June 13, 1990, Elton was not feeling well. In fact, his temperature was over one hundred and he really should have been in bed.
But that was the last place Elton wanted to be. After twenty-three
years in the music business, he had his first Number One single
("Sacrifice") in the U.K., in June 1990. There were a round of cele-
brations to commemorate this achievement.

Sleeping With the Past, his twenty-ninth album, took Elton and
Bernie right back to basics, the sixties R&B style that was their trademark, what they did best. His latest LP, *Reg Strikes Back*, had done
well enough, but following its completion Elton sat down and decided
to plan the next album more carefully. He and Bernie aimed to take
the sixties classic sound of Ray Charles, Otis Redding and Jackie
Wilson and mold it into an eighties white-soul sound.

And so in the fall of 1988, after he and Elton had decided on a
plan, Bernie flew from Los Angeles to London and started writing
lyrics. Elton meanwhile made preparations to record the album in
Denmark with producer Chris Thomas. Chris had worked on the *Reg*
LP, and Elton, who was pleased with his work, enlisted him again.

Elton decided to record in Denmark because he believed that he worked best when he went away and concentrated only on the music. Early on, from his days at the Château d'Hérouville in France, his finest work had grown out of a studio situation outside of England. There, in a self-contained environment, Elton could literally live and breathe his music.

It seemed strange that, after all the years of collaborating, it would be on *Sleeping With the Past* that Elton and Bernie would work most closely. Even back when they had shared bunk beds at Elton's mother's house, they wrote in separate quarters—Bernie in the bedroom and Elton at the piano in the living room. Now they sat down together and composed in the same room.

In all, they created twenty songs, but with great precision they selected only the ten that suited the style they wanted to achieve. One of the rejects was "Love Is a Cannibal," which ended up as the sound track to the movie *Ghostbusters*.

The album was both organic and seamless. It had taken Elton and Bernie just three songs to realize they were on to something special. Those tracks were "Whispers," a hauntingly mesmerizing and pretty ballad; the title tune, "Sleeping With the Past," an infectious, upbeat song that harked back to earlier pop but with enough spunk to enlist new fans; and the gospel-inflected "Amazes Me."

Sleeping With the Past opened with a reggae number, "Durban Deep," about the diamond mines in South Africa. Intended as a quasi-political track, it was a bit lightweight, if not simpleminded, in its repetition of "Down, down, down . . . / Going down, down, down." But the LP moved next into the powerful ballad "Healing Hands," which was destined to become a classic. It also offered the flickering neon jazz of "Blue Avenue," and a delightful bow to the Drifters in "Club at the End of the Street," done with an adorable cartoon video later on. But by far the most affecting tune was the incandescent ballad "Sacrifice." Indeed, just as Elton paid exuberant homage to the music of more than two decades before, his invigorating touch ensured that fans would be listening to him for the next twenty years as well.

Elton was jubilant about the album. "I'm so pleased," he said, "that I'm planning to do as many as five or six songs off it on the new tour, which is something I've never done before."

It was strange that Elton, who by now seemed to have been around forever, had never had a Number One solo hit in his native Britain.

Now, on June 18, 1990, it was time for a special twenty-third birthday in pop music, and Elton was determined, despite his temperature, to celebrate it to the hilt.

As BBC Radio One plugged the record, Elton celebrated at a private dinner for thirty-five colleagues and friends, including personal assistant Bob Halley, manager John Reid and singer George Michael, at London's L'Escargot restaurant in the heart of Soho. The cake, in the shape of a record, said "Congratulations." Guests lifted their glasses of pink champagne in Elton's honor.

In part, some of the congratulations belonged to BBC One disc jockey Steve Wright, whose idea it was to rerelease "Sacrifice" and donate the moneys to four AIDS charities. Elton turned up as a guest on the popular Terry Wogan talk show and declared, "Every single I shall release henceforth from any album will be toward charity. Because I think it's about time. I'm at that age when I can afford to do it and it's about time I did it."

Indeed, by now Elton had been a superstar since before many of his fans were born. He had made enough of a mark in the world to be able to make a difference. Elton lived in the homes and hearts of fans throughout the world. His music continued to pour out of the radio. It had outlived vinyl and now filled compact discs. His personal treasures, auctioned off, now occupied a place in their homes. And at London's Rock Circus, a museum of rock music, he was the centerpiece, along with Little Richard and Stevie Wonder, on a revolving platform. A figure of ubiquity, there was even a men's bathroom called "Elton John" at the Chicago Pizza Pie Factory in London.

There were still traces of the old Reg, stiff and uncomfortable with himself, on the Terry Wogan television show that week. Elton leaned forward in his seat and locked his arms around his knees. Wogan, the oleaginous host, thanked Elton for "coming on" the show. And Elton interrupted him in midsentence: "Terry," he said, with an almost imperceptible twitch, "you know I've never come on to you." The banter had an edge to it, as if Elton were still trying to gain revenge on his accusers in the tabloid press.

The singer also told how he had spent a lot of time in a children's hospital, not only with AIDS kids. Witnessing their suffering made him realize how lucky he was. He spoke emotionally about Ryan White. "I went to help Ryan's mother," Elton said. "I helped her arrange the funeral. I never had to do that before, so it was actually good for me to go through that experience. It was a sad, but tough-ening, one."

Yet while Elton celebrated his newly discovered insights and looked with pride at his professional achievements, much work still remained to be done in his private life. Over the coming months he would be forced to deal with that much-troubled area of his otherwise charmed existence.

36

One Day at a Time

The chauffeured black Bentley looked somewhat out of place as it pulled up at the old church hall in the West Hollywood section of Los Angeles. So, too, did the man wearing a baseball cap, glasses, black track suit and white tennis shoes. In fact, to the other people attending the Alcoholics Anonymous meeting, he seemed very different.

He was, after all, a superstar, a man known throughout the world for his music. But as Elton stood up and introduced himself to the group, his addiction was clearly no different from theirs. Painfully, he opened up to these strangers in the room. "I'm Elton—I am an alcoholic," he said. The words were spoken with relief.

Elton had at last faced up to his drinking problem, and at the age of forty-three, he was trying to do something about it. His addiction to alcohol, he confessed, had made him feel like a zombie for years. But it was not until his friend Ryan White died that Elton was able to admit his problem. He had taken time off from work and moved to Los Angeles, where he reportedly rented a home at $18,000 a month and drove across town to a shabby neighborhood at seven o'clock each morning to battle his alcoholism.

According to another A.A. member, Elton took the program as seriously as he did the making of any of his albums. "He is a superstar outside," the member said, "but once he's inside here he is just another anonymous alcoholic trying to overcome his problem."

After two months in the program, Elton sat on a weekday morning in the second row with a copy of the blue A.A. bible in his hand. Previously, he had made a five-minute speech, called "sharing," stressing how serious he was about the program. At this stage Elton had already been clean for sixty days, but every day was a challenge.

Clearly, he could have gone off to an expensive clinic, but instead he chose this old, unassuming locale for his treatment. No amount of money could help him now. He knew that he had to depend on his inner resources. For it seemed that while Elton appeared to have it all, he had been hiding his secret agonies under a veneer of success. Depression, stress and alcohol, along with a painful sense of isolation, had governed Elton's life. Doctors had ordered him to take an eighteen-month break from performing and recording. For the former Captain Fantastic the end of 1990 heralded a new beginning.

Though he had shed his flamboyant costumes long ago, the inner pains that had formed him in childhood still remained, and now he was finally prepared to deal with them. "I was exhausted," Elton admitted in an interview. "I'd burnt out physically and mentally. I had difficulties, but I'm working them out now."

As hard as it was for Elton to articulate his deepest feelings, his admission was not unusual from someone in his position, and he was not alone. In fact, he had even sought advice from other pop stars who had battled with their own addiction problems. Ringo Starr and his wife Barbara Bach, who had both overcome alcoholism, were only too glad to counsel him. But, above all, Elton was learning to help himself. And though eighteen months was a long time to take off from work, Elton knew it was the only way.

Never in his entire career had Elton allowed himself such an extended hiatus from work to sort out his life. But he reconciled it with the belief that healing himself could only enrich his music. He now had time for himself, and he used it well. "I do meditation stuff in the mornings now," Elton confessed. "It's new, but necessary for me to start the day off. I sit there and I pray, which I never thought I would do before. I'm much more spiritually aware than I was. I'm not a born-again Christian but I do believe in something which I wouldn't admit before."

Ordinary pleasures, without the glitter of pricey restaurants or flights across the Atlantic for a party, were becoming part of his life now. Even watching the sunset gave him as much satisfaction as any hit record. The stripping away of possessions that had begun with the auctioning of his Aladdin's Cave collection of antiques spread to other areas of his life. Elton sold his shares in the Watford Football Club and his Pig Music publishing company. At this stage, he wanted only to own his own life.

This was a man with everything who had simply lost touch. The courage of his friend Ryan White had inspired Elton to try to search out the important moments in life, and he was now going to take stock of them.

As a man with a $200 million fortune, he realized that his life would never be as simple as other people's. He also knew that he could make it more meaningful. Elton the man had given so much pleasure to so many people but had been unhappy with himself for all too long. Now he was doing something about it.

Change, he knew, would not happen overnight. But he was prepared to meet the challenge. After all, as the musical career of Elton Hercules John had proved time and time again, he was, in spite of everything, "Still Standing."

Epilogue

Even during his peak years as the pop sensation of the seventies, Elton John worried about becoming a figure of rock-music ephemera or, worse still, ending up at a relatively young age as a rock-'n'-roll has-been, reprising his greatest hits in a cocktail lounge.

But clearly that has not been the path of the Rocket Man, now into his third decade as an international superstar. With his copious gift for composing, emotive voice and electric performances, Elton John, at forty-five, continues to blaze a path of rock-music glory. At times along the way, with his mammoth tours and stage acrobatics, he has seemed to defy the law of gravity.

Indeed, Elton is, as his unofficial anthemic rocker proclaims, "still standing"—but rarely in one place. Elton keeps moving, coming up with fresh melodies that fuse generations. Parents and kids do not fight over whether to listen to Elton John; they all sing along, taking particular pleasure in Bernie Taupin's often memorable lyrics.

Elton's eclectic delight in popular music—from his teen pinup Dusty Springfield to raver Jerry Lee Lewis, from soul queen Aretha Franklin and piano man Leon Russell to the harmonizing Beach Boys—is mirrored in his own musical imagination.

His phenomenal success is the product of a considerable musical talent and a driving ambition. Its underpinning was a lonely childhood, as shy, ungainly Reginald Kenneth Dwight, in an uncompromising middle-class suburb. Out of this chrysalis came Elton Hercules John, the king of glitz, original and outrageous as he swooped down on the stage.

Elton was as much a fan as a superstar, someone who worshiped stars like Groucho Marx and Mae West, just as Elton's fans adored him. Audiences intuited and liked this quirk in Elton. And he never let them down. Success would punish as well as reward him. But even in his darkest depressions, when he might cancel a crucial business meeting at the last second, he still showed up for his fans. "Value for money" is how Elton has said he would like to be remembered.

For the moment, of course, an epitaph for Elton would be premature. The teenage fan in him just will not quit. As Elton himself admits, "I don't really want to grow up to the full extent. I'll always be a bit of a kid and I believe that's the way it is to everybody in rock 'n' roll, except maybe for the pseudointellectuals who think they want to grow up. The truth is, they don't want to grow up either."

The late Dick James once said: "I have a very short, and, I think, very explicit, summing-up of Elton—he is in fact the most introverted extrovert I've ever met. It's almost like the comedian who wants to play Shakespeare or the Shakespearean actor who wants to become a song-and-dance man."

Superstar and fan, balladeer and rocker, tender and mawkish, Elton John is, indeed, a man of many lives. And though he admits to never wanting to grow up fully, Elton Hercules John has already achieved longevity.

Afterword

As of this writing, Elton John is celebrating his twenty-fifth year as an enduring and prolific artist. A just-released album, *Two Rooms*, celebrates his and partner Bernie Taupin's gift of song. A rock-'n'-roll hall of fame, ranging over generations, from the Beach Boys and Tina Turner to George Michael and Wilson Phillips, reprises many of their hits.

Bluesology, the band in which Elton began his career, is merely a footnote in the annals of pop music history. And the band members whose names Elton borrowed are today figures of relative obscurity. Former lead singer John Baldry, who now lives in Vancouver, Canada, remains hopeful that he may revive his career. Meanwhile, back in England, Elton Dean, a saxophone player, begrudges Elton for not responding to a plea to contribute money to a local jazz society.

Ray Williams, the man who serendipitously brought Elton and Bernie together, has long since rebounded with great success as a producer of sound-track albums, including the Academy Award–winning *Last Emperor*. After a brief hiatus as a farmer, Steve Brown, the producer of Elton's first album, *Empty Sky*, continues in Elton's employ.

Manager John Reid is still a ubiquitous force in Elton's career. And today Stephen James is running his father's company, Dick James Music, but would not care to be in the same room with either Elton or Reid. He blames them for his father's death. Yet he admits that he is glad to have been a part of the early years of Elton John.

Elton John Discography

by Martha P. Trachtenberg

SINGLES

Title	U.S. Label	U.S. Release	U.K. Label	U.K. Release
With Bluesology:				
Come Back Baby			Fontana	1965
Mr. Frantic			Fontana	1966
Since I Found You, Baby			Polydor	1967
Elton John:				
I've Been Loving You			Philips	1968
The Dick Barton Theme ("The Devil's Gallop"), with the Bread and Beer Band			Decca	1969
*Lady Samantha	Congress	1970	DJM	1969
*It's Me that You Need	Congress	1970		
*Border Song	Congress	1970	DJM	1978
	Uni	1970		
From Denver to L.A. (B Side: by the Barbara Moore Singers; from the film *The Games*).	Viking	1970		
Rock and Roll Madonna				1970
*Your Song	Uni	1970	DJM	1971
*Friends	Uni	1971	DJM	1971
*Levon	Uni	1971		
*Tiny Dancer	Uni	1972		
*Rocket Man	Uni	1972	DJM	1972
*Honky Cat	Uni	1972	DJM	1972
*Crocodile Rock	MCA	1972	DJM	1972
Daniel	MCA	1973	DJM	1973
Saturday Night's Alright for Fighting	MCA	1973	DJM	1973

*Reissued in 1973 by MCA

SINGLES (*continued*)

Title	U.S. Label	U.S. Release	U.K. Label	U.K. Release
Elton John (continued):				
Goodbye Yellow Brick Road	MCA	1973	DJM	1973
Step Into Christmas	MCA	1974	DJM	1973
Candle in the Wind	MCA	1987	DJM	1974
Benny and the Jets	MCA	1974	DJM	1976
Don't Let the Sun Go Down on Me	MCA	1974	DJM	1974
The Bitch Is Back	MCA	1974	DJM	1974
Lucy in the Sky With Diamonds (features John Lennon on guitar)	MCA	1974	DJM	1974
Philadelphia Freedom	MCA	1975	DJM	1975
Pinball Wizard	Polydor	1975	DJM	1976
Someone Saved My Life Tonight	MCA	1975	DJM	1975
Island Girl	MCA	1975	DJM	1975
Grow Some Funk of Your Own	MCA	1976	DJM	1978
I Feel Like a Bullet (In the Gun of Robert Ford)	MCA	1976		
Don't Go Breaking My Heart (duet with Kiki Dee)	Rocket	1976	Rocket	1976
			Old Gold	1988
Sorry Seems to Be the Hardest Word	MCA/ Rocket	1976	Rocket	1976
Love Song (duet with Lesley Duncan)	MCA	1976		
Bite Your Lip (Get Up and Dance!)	MCA/ Rocket	1977	Rocket	1977
Crazy Water			Rocket	1977
Ego	MCA	1978	Rocket	1978
Part-Time Love	MCA	1978	Rocket	1978
Song for Guy			Rocket	1978
			Old Gold	1988
Mama Can't Buy You Love	MCA	1979		
Are You Ready for Love			Rocket	1979
Victim of Love	MCA	1979		
Johnny B. Goode			Rocket	1979
Harmony			DJM	1980
Little Jeannie	MCA	1980	Rocket	1980
Dear God			Rocket	1980
Sartorial Eloquence (Don't Ya Wanna Play This Game No More?)	MCA	1980	Rocket	1980
Les Aveux (duet with France Gall)	Released in France by Atlantic Records in 1981			
J'Veux d'la Tendresse	Released in France by Rocket in 1981			
Loving You Is Sweeter Than Ever (duet with Kiki Dee)			Ariola	1981
Nobody Wins	Geffen	1981	Rocket	1981
I Saw Her Standing There (featuring John Lennon and the Muscle Shoals Horns; recorded in 1975)			DJM	1981
Chloe	Geffen	1981		
Just Like Belgium			Rocket	1981
Empty Garden (Hey Hey Johnny)	Geffen	1982	Rocket	1982
All Quiet on the Western Front			Rocket	1982
Sweet Painted Lady			DJM	1982
Blue Eyes	Geffen	1982	Rocket	1982
Princess			Rocket	1982

SINGLES (*continued*)

Title	U.S. Label	U.S. Release	U.K. Label	U.K. Release
Elton John (continued):				
I'm Still Standing	Geffen	1983	Rocket	1983
Kiss the Bride	Geffen	1983	Rocket	1983
I Guess That's Why They Call It the Blues	Geffen	1983	Rocket	1983
Cold as Christmas			Rocket	1983
Sad Songs (Say So Much)	Geffen	1984	Rocket	1984
Whose Shoes Are These?	Geffen	1984	Rocket	1984
Passengers			Rocket	1984
In Neon	Geffen	1984		
Breaking Hearts (Ain't What it Used to Be)			Rocket	1985
That's What Friends are For (with Dionne Warwick, Stevie Wonder and Gladys Knight)	Arista	1985	Arista	1985
Wrap Her Up	Geffen	1985	Rocket	1985
Act of War (Part 1) (duet with Millie Jackson; also released as a 12″ single, Act of War Part 5)			Rocket	1985
Nikita	Geffen	1986	Rocket	1985
			Old Gold	1988
Cry To Heaven			Rocket	1986
Heartache All Over the World	Geffen	1986	Rocket	1986
Slow Rivers (duet with Cliff Richard)			Rocket	1986
Four From Four Eyes (7″ EP)			DJM	1986
Flames of Paradise (duet with Jennifer Rush)	Epic	1987	CBS	1987
Your Song (Live)			Rocket	1987
Take Me to the Pilot (with the Melbourne Symphony Orchestra)	MCA	1988		
I Don't Wanna Go On With You Like That	MCA	1988	Phonogram	1988
Funeral for a Friend (12″ single)			DJM	1988
Goodbye Marlon Brando	MCA	1988		
Town of Plenty			Phonogram	1988
A Word in Spanish	MCA	1988	Rocket	1988
Healing Hands	MCA	1989	Rocket	1989
Through the Storm (duet with Aretha Franklin)	Arista	1989	Arista	1989
Sacrifice	MCA	1989	Rocket	1989 & 90
Club at the End of the Street	MCA	1990	Rocket	1990
You Gotta Love Someone	MCA	1990	Rocket	1990
Easier to Walk Away			Rocket	1990
Don't Let the Sun Go Down on Me			Rocket	1991

ALBUMS

Title	U.S. Label	U.S. Release	U.K. Label	U.K. Release
Empty Sky	MCA	1974	DJM	1969
Elton John	Uni	1970	DJM	1970
Tumbleweed Connection	Uni	1971	DJM	1971
Friends (sound track)	Paramount	1971	Paramount	1971
11-17-70 (released in England as 17-11-70)	Uni	1971	DJM	1971
Madman Across the Water	Uni	1971	DJM	1971
Honky Chateau	Uni	1972	DJM	1972
Don't Shoot Me, I'm Only the Piano Player	MCA	1973	DJM	1973
Goodbye Yellow Brick Road	MCA	1973	DJM	1973
Caribou	MCA	1974	DJM	1974
Elton John's Greatest Hits, Vol. I	MCA	1974	DJM	1974
Captain Fantastic and the Brown Dirt Cowboy	MCA	1975	DJM	1975
Captain Fantastic and the Brown Dirt Cowboy/Elton John (2 albums)	MCA	1982		
Rock of the Westies	MCA	1975	DJM	1975
Here and There	MCA	1976	DJM	1976
Blue Moves	MCA	1976	Rocket	1976
Greatest Hits, Vol. II	MCA	1977	DJM	1977
A Single Man	MCA	1978	Rocket	1978
The Thom Bell Sessions	MCA	1979		
Victim of Love	MCA	1979	Rocket	1979
Live Collection (2-LP)	Released in Europe by Pickwick in 1979			
21 at 33	MCA	1980	Rocket	1980
Lady Samantha			DJM	1980
The Very Best of Elton John			K-Tel	1980
The Fox	Geffen	1981	Rocket	1981
Featuring John Lennon and the Muscle Shoals Horns (Recorded 1974)			DJM	1981
Jump Up!	Geffen	1982	Rocket	1982
Too Low for Zero	Geffen	1983	Rocket	1983
Breaking Hearts	Geffen	1984	Rocket	1984
Ice on Fire	Geffen	1985	Rocket	1985
Crocodile Rock	Released in Europe by Karussell in 1985			
Leather Jackets	Geffen	1986	Rocket	1986
Live in Australia	MCA	1987	Rocket	1987
Greatest Hits, Vol. III	Geffen	1987		
Reg Strikes Back	MCA	1988	Rocket	1988
Sleeping With the Past	MCA	1989	Rocket	1989
To Be Continued	MCA	1990	Rocket	1991

CHARITY/BENEFIT ALBUMS

Title	Label	Release
The Prince's Trust 10th Anniversary Birthday Party	A&M	1987
The Prince's Trust Concert, 1987	A&M	1987
Rock for Amnesty	Mercury	1987
Nobody's Child—Romanian Angel Appeal	Warner Bros.	1990
Knebworth: The Album	Polydor	1990
For Our Children	Walt Disney Records	1991

ROCK ANTHOLOGIES

Title	Label	Release
Billboard Top Rock 'n' Roll Hits, 1973	Rhino	1973
Billboard Top Rock 'n' Roll Hits, 1974	Rhino	1974
Billboard Top Hits, 1975	Rhino	1975
Billboard Top Hits, 1976 (duet with Kiki Dee)	Rhino	1976
Hits on CD	Phonogram	1984
Hits on CD, Vol. 2	Mercury	1985
Hits on CD, Vol. 3	Phonogram	1985
Hits on CD, Vol. 6	Mercury	1987
Hits on CD, Vol. 8	Mercury	1987
Rock 'n' Roll Years (1968–1971)	BBC	1987
Rock Classics	K-Tel	1987
Twenty-one Years of Alternative Radio One	BBC	1988
Classic Rock, Vol. I	MCA	1988
Classic Rock, Vol. II	MCA	1988
Hits Album 10	CBS/WEA/ BMG	1989
Rock, Rhythm & Blues	Warner Bros.	1989
B.P.I. Brits Awards '91	Telstar	1991

SOUND TRACKS

Title	Label	Release
Friends	Paramount	1971
Tommy	Polydor	1975
Ghostbusters II	MCA	1989
Days of Thunder	DGC	1990
Rocky V	Bust It	1990

Bibliography

Bronson, Fred. *The Billboard Book of Number One Hits*, revised and enlarged edition. New York: Billboard Publications, 1988.

Charlesworth, Chris. *Elton John*. London: Bobcat Books, 1986.

Coan, Edmund. *Watford Official Handbook, Diary 1989–90*. London: Watford Printers, Ltd., 1989.

Coleman, Ray. *Brian Epstein: The Man Who Made the Beatles*. London: Penguin Books, 1990.

Lazell, Barry, ed., with Dafyd Rees and Luke Crampton. *Rock Movers and Shakers*. New York: Billboard Publications, 1989.

Norman, Philip. *Elton*. London: Hutchinson, 1991.

Somach, Denny and Kathleen. *Ticket to Ride*. New York: William Morrow, 1989.

Taupin, Bernie. *A Cradle of Haloes: Sketches of a Childhood*. London: Aurum Press, 1988.

Toberman, Barry. *Elton John*. London: George Weidenfeld & Nicolson, 1988.

White, Adam. *The Billboard Book of Gold and Platinum Records*. New York: Billboard Publications, 1990.

White, Ryan, and Anne Marie Cunningham. *Ryan White: My Own Story*. New York: Dial Books, 1991.

Sources

Prologue PUBLICATIONS: Henry Edward, review, *New York Times*, August 8, 1976, Michael Pousner, "It's Elton's Show—And He Runs It," *New York Daily News*, August 5, 1976. Larry Rohter, "Elton John: Why Fans Are Hooked on His Act," *Washington Post*, June 29, 1976. Larry Rohter, "Elton John: The Music Machine," *Washington Post*, July 1, 1976.

Chapter 1 INTERVIEWS: Winnie Cluer, Elizabeth Cooper, Roy Dwight, George and Anne Hill, Joan Lewis, Helen Piena, Mick Randall, and admissions staff of Royal Academy of Music.

PUBLICATIONS: "The Fascination of Pinner," *Harrow Magazine*, Spring 1988. "The Graduates," *Classic CD*, June 1990. Neil Lyndon, "The Generation of Elton John, Rock-'n'-Roll King, Seventies Style," *Honey*, March 1985 (with introduction by Gay Search). Mary Riddell, "Yes, We Remember Shy Little Reg," *London Daily Mirror*, June 20, 1986. Eugenie Ross-Leming and David Standish, "Elton John," Interview, *Playboy*, January 1976. "Steven Spielberg and a Parade of Famed Foul-ups Prove Goonies Are Good Enough," *People*, July 1, 1985.

Chapter 2 INTERVIEWS: Long John Baldry, Margaret Baldry, Jack Barrie, Roger Cook, John Craig, Elton Dean, Roy Dwight, Cyril Gee, Roger Greenaway, Jimmy Horowitz, Mike McGrath.

PUBLICATIONS: Jane Gaskell, "Listen to a Superstar's Mother Talking Frankly About Her Son," *London Daily Mail*, May 20, 1972. "Meet the British," *Entertainment Weekly*, September 9, 1990.

Chapter 3 INTERVIEWS: Lesley Duncan, Stephen James, Caleb Quaye, Ray Williams.

PUBLICATIONS: Advertisement in *New Music Express* (London), June 17, 1967. "Cult Heroes," *Just Seventeen*, July 26, 1984.

Chapter 4 INTERVIEWS: Long John Baldry, Elton Dean.

PUBLICATIONS: Pauline McLeod, "Elton," *London Daily Mail*, November 6, 1978.

Chapter 5 INTERVIEWS: Long John Baldry, Paul Buckmaster, Lionel Conway, Roger Cook, Roger Greenaway, Stephen James, Dee Murray, Nigel Olsson, Russ Regan, Ray Williams, Larry Uttal.

PUBLICATIONS: Wensley Clarkson, "He Was a Lousy Lover, Says Star's Old Flame," *London Sunday Mirror*, February 19, 1984. Tony Palmer, "The New Elton John Won't Have to Be a Clown," *New York Times*, May 12, 1974. Don Short, "Elton Escapades," *London Sunday Mail*, June 22, 1975.

Chapter 6 INTERVIEWS: Robert Hilburn, Stephen James, Nigel Olsson, Russ Regan, Steve Todoroff, Doug Weston, Ray Williams, Norman Winter.

PUBLICATIONS: David Felton, "Elton John One Year Out," *Rolling Stone*, June 10, 1971. Robert Hilburn, "Elton John, New Rock Talent," *Los Angeles Times*, August 27, 1970. Steve Todoroff, *Leon Russell: An Illustrated History*. Forthcoming.

Chapter 7 INTERVIEWS: Bill Graham, Dave Herman, Stephen James, Phil Ramone, Ray Williams.

PUBLICATIONS: William Bender, "Handstands and Fluent Fusion," *Time*, December 14, 1970. Margaret English, "Elton John," *Look*, July 27, 1971. Albert Goldman, "Copycat in Wild Threads," *Life*, February 5, 1971. Robert Greenfield, "Elton John Steams 'Em Up," *Rolling Stone*, November 12, 1970. Philip Norman, "Rocket Man Back in Orbit," *London Sunday Times*, May 20, 1989.

Chapter 8 INTERVIEWS: Lionel Conway, Lesley Duncan, Cyril Gee, Richie Havens, Stephen James, Dee Murray.

PUBLICATIONS: Mike Jahn, "Solo or With Group, Elton John Thrills Carnegie Audiences," *New York Times*, June 12, 1971. Edward Jones, "Welder's Son Who Built a Pop Empire," *London Sunday Times*, May 8, 1977.

Chapter 9 INTERVIEWS: Jimmy Horowitz, Stephen James, Patti LaBelle, Ethel Seaford.

PUBLICATIONS: Roderick Gilchrist, "King John—Or How Reg From Pinner Played His Way to a Croc of Gold," *London Daily Mail*, June 29, 1973. Patricia O'Haire, "Madman Plays Carnegie Hall," *New York Daily News*, November 22, 1972. Kenneth Ponsford, "Stag," *Honour Before Honours*, Pinner Grammar Recollections, 1937–1982. Don Short, "My Fan, the Princess," *London Sunday Mirror*, June 29, 1978. Deborah Thomas, "Sending Himself Up . . . The Rocket Man," *London Daily Mail*, December 12, 1972.

Chapter 10 INTERVIEWS: Long John Baldry, Guy Farrow, Stephen James, Nigel Olsson, Neil Sedaka, Ron Wong.

PUBLICATIONS: Neil Lyndon, "The Generation of Elton John, Rock-'n'-Roll King," *Honey*, March 1975. John J. O'Connor, "Goodbye to Norma Jean . . ." *New York Times*, May 17, 1974. Jaan Uhelszki and Lester Bangs, "The Elton John Interview," *Creem*, May 1975.

OTHER: *Goodbye to Norma Jean and Other Things*, a documentary video written, produced, directed and narrated by Bryan Forbes.

Chapter 11 INTERVIEWS: Judith Baragwanath, David Wheeler.

PUBLICATIONS: *Auckland* (New Zealand) *Star*, February 28, 1974. *Auckland* (New Zealand) *Herald*, March 2, 1974, "Judge Grants Bail to John's Manager Pending Appeal." *Auckland* (New Zealand) *Star*, March 5, 1974, "Star, Manager Go Into Hiding."

Chapter 12 PUBLICATIONS: Steven Gaines, "The Flip Side of Elton John," *New York Daily News*, June 23, 1974.

Chapter 13 PUBLICATION: David DeVoss, "Elton John, Rock's Captain Fantastic," *Time*, July 7, 1975.

Chapter 14 INTERVIEWS: Ed Caraeff, Stephen James, Dee Murray, Nigel Olsson, Neil Sedaka.

PUBLICATIONS: David DeVoss, "Elton John, Rock's Captain Fantastic," *Time*, July 7, 1975. Henry Edwards, "Just Two Superstars From Middle Rock," *New York Times*, August 3, 1975. "Elton John," *Women's Wear Daily*, June 4, 1975. Mark Goodman, "Trimmed Down Megamillionaire Elton John Says He Also Wants to Tone Down His Image," *People*, August 8, 1975. Greil Marcus, "Elton John Super-fan," *Village Voice*, June 16, 1975. Byron Rogers, "Captain Fantastic He Is," *London Daily Telegraph*, April 30, 1976. Eugenie Ross-Leming and David Standish, "Elton John," Interview, *Playboy*, January 1976. Geoffrey Wansell, "Elton John, a Long Way From a Pound a Night, Plus Tips, in Northwood," *Times* (London), June 21, 1975.

Chapter 15 PUBLICATION: John Hamshire, "Elton . . . Escort to a Princess," *London Daily Express*, January 23, 1976.

Chapter 16 INTERVIEWS: Scott Muni, John Rockwell, Neil Sedaka.

PUBLICATIONS: Alisdair Buchan, "Elton!" *London Daily Mirror*, November 5, 1979. Time Ewbank, "Sitting Pretty, the Man Who Puts the Words in Elton John's Mouth," *London Daily Mail*, April 8, 1976. Cliff Jahr, "Elton's Frank Talk: The Lonely Love Life of a Superstar," *Rolling Stone*, October 7, 1976. Cliff Jahr, "Hurricane Elton Is 'Fee-urious' in New York," *Rolling Stone*, September 23, 1976.

Chapter 17 INTERVIEW: Roy Dwight.

PUBLICATIONS: Sally Brompton, "Elton and Me . . . Problems of a Superstar's

Father," *London Daily Mail*, May 20, 1976. Bill Hagerty, "King John Sleeps Here," *London Daily Mail*, January 21, 1976.

Chapter 18 INTERVIEW: Roy Dwight.
    PUBLICATIONS: Johnny Black, "I'm a Very *Normal* Sort of Person," *Women's World* (London), December 1989. Geoff Brown, *Time Out*, 1984 Football Association Cup Final Program. "Elton Man Lands in Jail," *News of the World* (London), September 30, 1979. Brian Glanville, "Chairman Elton," *London Sunday Times*, April 16, 1978. Barbara Griggs, "Restyled Superstar," *London Daily Mail*, December 15, 1977. Brian Madley, "Lazy Bones! Pop-Star Elton John Sounds Off . . . With a Brand-new Theme," *London Daily Mail*, March 16, 1975. Clive Ranger, " 'JR,' Who Went to Jail for Elton," *Mail on Sunday* (London), May 31, 1981. James Whitaker, "Sorry to Elton for Drug Boob," *London Daily Express*, May 4, 1977.

Chapter 19 PUBLICATIONS: "Elton Flies Into a Temper," *London Daily Express*, June 27, 1977. Philip Norman, "Elton's Other Half," *London Sunday Times*, May 1988.

Chapter 20 INTERVIEW: Andrew Hill.
    PUBLICATION: David Wigg, "Exit Elton," *London Daily Express*, November 4, 1977.

Chapter 21 INTERVIEWS: Andrew Hill, Tom Robinson.
    PUBLICATIONS: Steve Bailey, "I Felt I Was Dying," *Mail on Sunday* (London), December 10, 1978. Alex Foster, "I Knew Him Better Than His Mother," *Mail on Sunday* (London), November 23, 1980. Robert Hilburn, "Elton John—Just Me and the Piano," *Los Angeles Times*, October 17, 1978. Thomson Prentice, "Can TV's Mr. Jingle Rock Elton John Back to the Top of the Hit Parade?" *London Daily Mail*, September 5, 1978.

Chapter 22 PUBLICATIONS: Michael Binyon, "Elton John: In Russia With Love," *Washington Post*, May 29, 1979. Paul Donovan, "Elton John Superczar Rocks Them Back in the U.S.S.R.," *London Daily Mail*, May 29, 1979. Nikki Finke, "Leningrad, U.S.S.R.," Associated Press, May 21, 1979. Robert Hilburn, "Elton John Tour: Rock's Revolution in Russia," *Los Angeles Times*, May 27, 1979. David Wigg, "About My Young Elton," *London Daily Express*, May 29, 1979.
    OTHER: CBS/Fox, "To Russia . . . With Elton," a video documentary of the Russia Tour.

Chapter 23 PUBLICATIONS: "Elton's Mum Calls It a Day," *London Daily Express*, January 18, 1980. Robert Hilburn, "John, Taupin: Separate but Equal?" *Los Angeles Times*, June 1, 1980. Peter McLaughlin and Mark Liff, "225,000 Rock With Elton to Roll in $," *New York Daily News*, September 14, 1980. Lynn Van Matre, "Elton Jumps Back on the Concert Scene—But Not on the Piano," *Chicago Tribune*, May 20, 1980.

Chapter 24 PUBLICATIONS: "Empire Builder $120," United Press International, September 28, 1980. Paul Grein, "Elton John Jumps the Gun," *Los Angeles Times*, May 23, 1982. Lisa Robinson, "Fox Elton Leads Private Life," *New York Post*, June 25, 1981. Allan J. Mayer, Susan Agrest, Jacob Young, et al., "Death of a Beatle," *Newsweek*, December 20, 1980.

Chapter 25 PUBLICATIONS: Iain Blair, "The Rocket Man Is Back," *Boston Herald*, November 1, 1984. "Elton John and the Boys He Leaves Behind," *London Daily Express*, February 13, 1984. "Going to the Chapel," *People*, February 27, 1984. Andrew Goldes, "Guarding His Fortune," *Mail on Sunday* (London), February 12, 1984. Simon Kinnersley, "Good Luck, Reg!" *Sunday* (London), March 18, 1984. Craig Modderno, "Elton's Last Tour Says so Much," *USA Today*, August 23, 1984. " 'Nervous' Elton Weds His Sweetie," *New York Daily News*, February 16, 1984. Moira Petty, "Rock On! Here Comes the Bridegroom," *London Daily Mail*, February 11, 1984. Richard Shears, "The Groom Wears White," *London Daily Mail*, February 14, 1984. Richard Shears, " 'I Wanna Kiss the Bride,' Says the Song," *London Daily Mail*, February 15, 1984. Richard Shears, "A Proposal Over the Poppadums," *Mail on Sunday* (London), February 12, 1984. Liz Smith, "Elton John Showers Bride With Diamonds," *New York Daily News*, February 17, 1984. Colin White, "I Want to Have a Son," *Mail on Sunday* (London), February 12, 1984. "Why I Love Elton," *London Sunday Express*, February 12, 1984.

Chapter 26 INTERVIEW: Paul Francis.
PUBLICATIONS: Paul Francis, "My Stormy Gay Affair With Wild Elton John," *Globe*, January 8, 1991. Paul Francis, "Elton Boasted: 'I Slept With Shirley MacLaine,' " *Globe*, January 15, 1991. Paul Francis, "Elton Wed Renate Four Days After I Hit Him for Palimony," *Globe*, January 22, 1991.

Chapter 27 INTERVIEWS: Long John Baldry, Elton Dean, Cyril Gee, Stephen James, Ray Williams.
PUBLICATIONS: Philip Norman, "Elton's Other Half," *London Sunday Times*, May 1988. "Songs," Reuters, November 29, 1985.

Chapter 28 PUBLICATIONS: Fred A. Bernstein and Laura Sanderson Healy, "Elton John Is Still a Glass Act, but With New Hits, Hair, and Friends—Andrew and Fergie," *People*, September 8, 1986. "Elton John, Charming and Flamboyant, Delights Fans," *New York Post*, September 17, 1986. Frank Rizzo, "Elton John Comes Back in a Flash," *Hartford Courant*, August 31, 1986. Wayne Robins, "Elton John's Energy Still Carries the Show," *New York Newsday*, September 12, 1986.

Chapter 29 PUBLICATIONS: John Collins, David Pere and Alan Braham Smith, "Elton John's Wife Abandons Him—Just Before His Surgery for Possible Cancer," *National Enquirer*, January 27, 1987. "Elton Plans Surgery," Associated Press, January 2, 1987. "Recovering: Elton John . . ." *Time*, January 10, 1987.
OTHER: "Elton John Live in Australia," Showtime video press release, June 11, 1987.

Chapter 30 INTERVIEWS: Bill Carnie, Tommy Nutter, Tom Robinson.

PUBLICATIONS: Steve Absalom, "That One-Million-Pound Look," *London Daily Mail*, December 13, 1988. "Accuser Faces Sack," *London Daily Star*, February 28, 1987. "The Agony of Elton," *London Daily Mirror*, April 17, 1987. John Askill, "Elton John Quizzed by Vice Squad," *London Sun*, January 15, 1988. "Elton Court Move," *London Sun*, April 10, 1987. "Elton John Acts Over New Sex Revelations," *London Daily Mail*, April 17, 1987. "Elton John Sues 'Sun' Over 'Sex and Drugs' Story," *London Daily Telegraph*, February 26, 1987. Alan Hardie, " 'Bondage? It's a Beach in Sydney'—Says Elton," *London Sun*, March 3, 1991. Craig MacKenzie, "You're a Liar, Elton!" *London Sun*, February 27, 1987. Craig MacKenzie and Neil Wallis, "Elton's Drug Capers," *London Sun*, February 26, 1987. Steve Prokesch, "Twenty Papers in Britain Agree to an Ethics Code," *New York Times*, November 29, 1989. "Separated: Elton John . . ." *Time*, April 6, 1987. "Shock Disclosures Just Twenty-four Hours After He Says: 'I Still Love Renate,' " *London Daily Star*, April 16, 1987. " 'Sun' Pays Rock Star Record Sum," *London Sun*, December 12, 1988. David Wigg, "Elton—They Can Call Me a Fat Untalented Poof . . . But They Mustn't Tell Lies,' " *London Daily Express*, October 14, 1988. "Yard Move on Elton," *London Daily Mail*, February 27, 1987.

Chapter 31 INTERVIEW: Hilary Kay.

PUBLICATIONS: Patricia Blake, "Beyond the Wildest Expectations!" *Time*, September 18, 1988. Sarah Jane Checkland, "Singer's Doc Marten's Go Home," *Times* (London), September 7, 1988. Claire Clifton, "Elton John's Treasure Trove Rocks British Art World," *Wall Street Journal*, September 6, 1988. "Elton John Auction Nets $8.2 Million," *New York Times*, September 10, 1988. "Elton John to Sell Artworks," *New York Times*, January 26, 1988. Lewis Grossberger, "The New Elton John: A Brief Dossier," *Washington Post*, November 4, 1979. "Pop Goes a Fortune!" *London Daily Express*, September 7, 1988. Rita Reif, "Auctions," *New York Times*, July 15, 1988. "Sales Pitch: Who the Owner Was," *New York Times*, September 11, 1988. "Surrounded by the Souvenirs of a Florid Career, Elton John Divests to Find Living Room," *People*, September 12, 1988. Terry Trucco, "Pop Ephemera Auction: Elton John's Collection," *New York Times*, September 7, 1988.

OTHER: Sotheby Elton John Catalogs: Vol. 1, *Stage Costumes and Memorabilia*; Vol. 2, *Jewellery*; Vol. 3, *Art Nouveau and Art Deco*; Vol. 4, *Diverse Collections*.

Chapter 32 PUBLICATIONS: Baz Bamigboye, "Sad for Elton, but We All Knew It Wouldn't Last," *London Daily Mail*, November 18, 1988. Nina Myskow, "Elton: Why I Felt Guilty," *Mail on Sunday* (London), November 20, 1988. Sharon Ring, "Elton Tells Wife 'I Want a Divorce,' " *News of the World* (London), September 4, 1988.

Chapter 33 PUBLICATIONS: "Elton John's New Album Is a Throwback to Simpler Times," *Denver Post*, June 12, 1988. Paul Grein, "Reg Strikes Back" (review), *Los Angeles Times*, July 3, 1988. Robert Hilburn, "Goodbye to Elton John's Yellow Brick Road," *Los Angeles Times*, June 5, 1988. Geoffrey Himes, "Reg Strikes Back" (review), *Washington Post*, August 3, 1988. Rob Tannebaum, "Bring Back the Old Elton," *New York Post*, October 19, 1988.

OTHER: MCA Records press release for *Reg Strikes Back* album.

Chapter 34 INTERVIEW: Brad Letsinger.

PUBLICATIONS: Chuck Conconi, "Personalities," *Washington Post*, May 30, 1990. Dirk Johnson, "Ryan White Dies of AIDS at Eighteen; His Struggle Helped Pierce Myths," *New York Times*, April 9, 1990. "1,500 Mourn Ryan White," *New York Newsday*, April 12, 1990. Bill Shaw, "Candle in the Wind," *People*, April 1990.

Chapter 35 INTERVIEWS: Jonathan Ruffle, Steve Wright.

PUBLICATIONS: Iain Blair, "Glitter and the Best: Elton John Doesn't Miss the Glitz on His New Tour," *Chicago Tribune*, August 20, 1989. Carmine Buquicchio, "Elton John: Sleeping With the Past," *Good Times*, December 26, 1989. Lisa Gomez, "Number 29 for Elton John," *QC Quad*, September 18, 1989. "Masters of the Hook" (review), *Washington Post*, October 18, 1989. John Milward, "For Elton John and Fans, It's Déjà Vu All Over Again," *New York Newsday*, October 5, 1990. Gary Puleo, "Many of the Best Albums of '89 Examine Significant Issues," *Los Angeles TImes Herald*, December 22, 1989. "The Rest of My Life Starts Here," *You* magazine, *Mail on Sunday* (London), September 16, 1990. Michael Santer, "Elton John Touches Down at the Garden," *New York Post*, October 5, 1989. David Wild, "A Winning Bet," *Rolling Stone*, June 28, 1990.

OTHER: MCA Records press release for *Sleeping With the Past* album.

Chapter 36 PUBLICATIONS: "Elton: My Escape From a Pit of Self-Hate," *London Daily Mail*, April 15, 1991. Elton John, "My Battle Against Drink," *London Daily Mail*, October 13, 1990. Terry O'Hanton, "Elton's Secret Agony," *London Sunday Mirror*, January 27, 1991.

Epilogue PUBLICATION: Roger Perry, "Chairman Elton," *London Sunday Times*, September 9, 1978.

Index

DATE DUE

PRINTED IN U.S.A.